21

PURELY POSITIVE TRAINING

COMPANION TO COMPETITION

ALSO BY THE AUTHOR

SCHUTZHUND
OBEDIENCE
Training in Drive
with Gottfried Dildei

The Positive Puppy Preview

PURELY
POSITIVE
TRAINING

COMPANION TO COMPETITION

by
SHEILA BOOTH

PODIUM
PUBLICATIONS

*For my Mum
and my Dad,
who gave to me
and share with me
my most precious gift –
a love of animals.*

Special Thanks

to Patty Ruzzo,
for endless inspiration and encouragement,

and Ron Harris,
for keeping the faith in purely positive training.

Thanks also to those special friends who
provided valuable input and technical support:
Capt. Dick Bernier, Fran Bernier,
Edna Booth, Deborah Harris, Fran LeBarron,
Melani Nardone and Sandi Wasch.

CONTENTS

Section III: The Behaviors

" Ask the animals
and they will teach you. "
    – The Book of Job

" Until he extends
the circle of his compassion
to all living things,
man will not himself find peace. "
    – Albert Schweitzer

FOREWORD

I loved Sheila's first book, *Schutzhund Obedience: Training in Drive*, and I was one of many who prompted her endlessly to write a sequel.

This new book makes my heart sing. The message – the fun is in the process and the process is FUN – rings clear and true throughout. All I need to proceed with this hands-off, compulsion-free, positive-power approach to training is myself, my dog, his favorite toy, a pocket full of cookies and smiles, and eyes and a mind taught to look for what the dog is doing *right*.

One may begin applying these purely positive principles immediately, with any breed of dog, at any age or level of expertise, and no matter what the previous reinforcement history, great things will begin to happen almost at once. The most satisfying result is being teamed up with an ears-forward, eyes-bright joyous canine partner. As John Rarey, a nineteenth century horse tamer said,
"Kindness is Power."

It is my pleasure to enthusiastically endorse this book, this author, and this way of training dogs. Read it for the sake of your dog, because
EVERY DOG DESERVES THIS BOOK!
– Patty Ruzzo

INTRODUCTION

This book, like this purely positive training method, is a work-in-progress, though now it has a cover and a title. It is a story still being told. So, like all good stories, it has a "once-upon-a-time" beginning and some characters you need to meet to understand the plot.

"Once-upon-a-time" for me was the first time I ever saw someone training a dog in obedience. It certainly wasn't very motivational. Looking back, it wasn't even very good. But it took less than a minute for me to be hooked. I knew what I wanted to do. Dog training has remained my passion for 25 years now.

During that time, I sought answers – often without managing to ask the right questions of the right entity. Along the way, I learned. Sometimes I even succeeded, but the whole process was missing something. Somehow it just didn't feel right.

Then I saw Patty Ruzzo. Truly, when it's right – you know it. Patty was already a winning trainer in obedience competition when she chose to dedicate herself to training without any sort of correction. She brought her trust and respect for her dog to training, and added that all-important ingredient – love.

Those of us gravitating toward positive training were already using food, despite those other folks who told us that it was "bribery," and that the dogs wouldn't work when we didn't have the food. How were we ever led to believe all that stuff?

We had also learned to use toys and games as rewards so our dogs loved training. But we still bought into the premise that eventually you had to use corrections or the dog would never be reliable "in the ring." We compromised.

But Patty refused to compromise. She threw away her prong collar and began training without a leash. She substituted "cookie-power" and brain-power for compulsion. She decided if she had to hurt her dog to do it, then it wasn't worth it. With that decision, she opened the door for the stampeding herd of folks behind her who want to use their brains instead of their brawn to train their beloved dogs.

Then Patty suggested a seminar by Ted Turner, a behaviorist and trainer at Ohio Sea World. By the end of that weekend, I felt like I'd been training in the dark for 20 years. Somebody had just turned on the light!

Not only did we learn the difference between behavior and learning, we were introduced to the huge body of scientific evidence explaining why and how positive reinforcement works. Not only does it work, it's the only way that works without doing damage to your precious relationship with your dog.

But will this type of training "hold up in the ring?" The dolphins and killer whales perform reliably, several shows a day, during the entire season. They do this without ever wearing a prong collar or feeling an electric shock. And they play to audiences much larger and louder than are found ringside at our shows!

Well, sure, then maybe you can train this way for competition. But your neighbor will still have to use corrections to train that unruly brat dog he just got from the shelter. Right?

Wrong. Leslie Nelson found a way to use these purely positive principles in pet obedience classes. Through the correct use of positive reinforcement, owners learn how to build a strong relationship with their dogs, and teach them good manners and basic obedience at the same time.

So now you understand why you might read "Patty says," or "according to Ted," or "Leslie recommends." They are the pioneers who paved my way down this new road. Today, I'm proud to be a standard bearer for the quiet revolution in positive training.

Putting all this together has been pure pleasure for me. I have more excitement, enthusiasm and energy for training now than I've had in 25 years. Funny, the dogs seem to feel the same way! And I'm a lot closer to waking up each day and being found worthy of my wonderful dogs.

Speaking of my dogs, since they are the main characters in this story, you might as well meet them right now.

The dog who graces this cover, Espe, was the first to open my eyes. I brought her from Germany when she was four years old and titled to SchH. II. She came into my life to show me just how much damage compulsive training could do, even to the most singularly sensational dog.

Espe arrived with visible baggage, and I vowed she would never be hurt that way again. I opted to find out what motivational methods might produce, and devoted myself to seeing how joyful I could make her training.

I made a lot of mistakes floundering down the path by myself, but I learned some valuable lessons along the way. Two years later, Espe scored 298 points (100-98-100) in SchH. III at a regional championship, one of the highest scores ever earned in that sport.

Espe was my super dog, the standard by which all others will forever be measured, but Charra became the one to teach me the most about positive training. In her 13 years, she succeeded beyond my wildest dreams, and showed me so much along the way. Although I bred Charra (Espe was her mother), she was sold to an experienced trainer as a very promising puppy. She was returned to me at about 14 months old, after an international trainer and judge had deemed her stick shy and pronounced her unsuitable for Schutzhund work.

When I picked her up at the busy New York airport, Charra was unflappable in the crowd, totally food driven and wanted to jump into the spraying fountain. But once at home, she could not approach people (especially men), and would turn her back and look away if any protection work was going on nearby. She had never won at this game.

After looking up her puppy evaluation, I found she was stable and social and driven at seven weeks old. I remembered her cavorting confidently with one of the cargo crew, and even tugging on his pant leg, the day I shipped her out. We decided to keep her and try to rehabilitate her, without any expectations.

Dear Charra had very little body sensitivity, but she had far more than her share of emotional sensitivity. She played on your conscience. And being true to her wonderful German Shepherd nature, she was quite happy to do anything you asked of her. So positive, motivational training became our chosen way.

How far did Charra go? For the rest of her life, she approached everyone, everywhere, with total confidence. She was a true social butterfly. She earned her SchH. III with V-ratings (Excellent – over 96 points) in every category (tracking, obedience and protection). She also earned a perfect score of 100 points in tracking.

At eight years old, Charra retired from Schutzhund competition and began Agility (jumping 30 inches). She earned her USDAA Agility Dog title with three first places. When she was 10, she won an Advanced Class, being the only dog to qualify on that course jumping 30 inches. At 11 years young, she earned her Elite Agility Certificate (the highest NADAC title).

But far beyond all her credentials, wherever she went, she was the perfect German Shepherd ambassador. You can probably tell I was always pretty proud of her, and she was the most loving companion anyone could ever want.

So this is a story with a happy ending – to encourage you to go as far as you can with your dog. The more you believe in them, the further they'll take you. Along the way, Char taught me more than could ever be shared in one book.

My new challenge is Vino, a talented Belgian Malinois. There is a saying that, "When the student is ready, the teacher will appear." This one appeared with an agenda all his own, and enough drive and character for three dogs. All I can say is, "Lordy, I hope I'm ready for this teacher

PREFACE

Our connection with our dogs is unique. Only a dog can occupy that special place in our hearts or that constant place in our lives.

Our relationship with our dogs is precious. Training should serve to strengthen that bond and enhance the relationship.

Our dogs are special. Some folks spend more time with their dogs than they do with other people. I know I do.

Our dogs can even become surrogate children. Some owners say they prefer them to kids. After all, dogs never start saying "No!" They don't ask "Why?" They never get drunk, do drugs, stay out past curfew or call home from jail. And they never grow up and move too far away! In truth, if only they lived longer, they'd be perfect.

Our dogs offer us so much to love and enjoy, not to mention making us laugh. They are individuals who give themselves to us with such complete joy and devotion that it makes our responsibility awesome. Anyone who still questions whether animals think or feel has obviously never spent a day with a dog.

Our dogs are thinking, feeling creatures. We need acknowledge nothing more to give them their due. They learn as they grow. They make decisions. They have emotional responses. They have many qualities we admire in people. They are always true to their nature and always totally honest. In short, they are simply marvelous.

Our dogs deserve the best we can give them. In our efforts to train them, we must always respect their individuality and nurture their spirit. Only when we recognize the magnificence of that spirit can we begin to appreciate their worth. We must affirm that worth.

Our steps toward competition training must never compromise their spirit – not for a ribbon, not for a trophy, not even for a title. No other hobby or sport fosters such a connection with an animal partner. We can train a horse in a similar partnership, but the horse does not live in the house, sleep in the bedroom or go to the kids' ball games with us.

Our partnership with our dogs is unique. We must always try to keep up our end of the bargain. We must try each day to be worthy of our dogs and celebrate the wonder of our canine connection.

This third edition
is a special tribute
to Countryhaus Charra,
who helped teach me
what positive training
is really all about.

Charra,
you will live forever
in the hearts of those who loved you.

SECTION I:

The Principles

1   The Positive Way

" The special ones
steal our hearts
and give us theirs."
– Unknown

Why are we all so excited about finding these purely positive ways to train our dogs? The answer is that we just weren't comfortable doing it any other way.

Our connection to our wonderful dogs is a strong one. We appreciate the opportunity to share their essence. We celebrate their spirit. Sharing a relationship with such a sensitive, loving, responsive creature is a blessing.

Training our dogs is not only a responsibility, it is a privilege. The communication that positive training fosters is uniquely rewarding. That true exchange is a gift. In those moments of intense eye contact, when we are on the same wave length and achieve true unity, that canine connection can be truly transcending.

A while ago, I was talking with a dear friend. He is an outstanding veterinarian, a sports medicine specialist who trains his own dog for competition. His young dog had just earned a top title and is one of the happiest working dogs ever to hit the trial field.

The owner was talking about his aspirations for this dog – to aim for national competition the next year. "But if I have to hurt my dog to do that, then I'll get a new sport," he said sincerely. "We'll go fishin'! He can sit in the front of the boat, or in the back of the boat, but we'll be Gone Fishin'!" So many of us have come to that conclusion lately.

The quiet revolution in positive training just keeps getting louder – with horses as well as dogs. Maybe it started with that "kinder, gentler nation" stuff. Perhaps it is just an idea whose time has come. But more and more people want to train their marvelous dogs without hurting them and without intimidating them.

Joy in Training

A dog shows pure joy in doing something he really loves. The same joy that a dog brings to life, he can bring to training. All we have to do is figure out what the dog wants from us and how much it means to him.

The first step is to get away from our own goals and agenda and begin to look at what the dog shows us. We must make the effort to understand what the dog brings to the partnership and make him a vital part of the team.

Once we identify what the dog wants and needs from us, we can offer those rewards for the behavior we want. Discover what your dog wants, and you find the key to unlock his willingness and desire.

Keep developing this positive attitude, and it turns on a light in your dog. He starts to want to work for you and with you. As we listen to the dog, we start to realize what he is trying to communicate – what his wants and needs are. We begin to tune in to the dog's agenda and get away from our own.

The father of the German Shepherd Dog, Capt. Max von Stephanitz, knew this more than 70 years ago when he wrote, "Whoever can find the answer to the question, *How shall I say this to my dog?* has won the game and can develop from his animal whatever he likes."

This kind of dog training is fun. It's creative. It's different every day. It fosters a special relationship with your dog – an understanding of your dog – that is a reward all its own. And best of all, it's fair. The dog is always right. Think about this. How could the dog ever be wrong?

No Wrong Dogs

Dogs always do what dogs do perfectly. They chew and bark and dig and scratch and lick and jump and play and demonstrate so many other innate behaviors in perfect form, with absolutely no guidance from us.

He's a dog. He's just doing what comes naturally. Yes, we need to teach him "our way," for the sake of our life and society. But punishing him for just being who he is need not be part of that process. After all, he hasn't done anything wrong. He's just being a dog.

No dog was born in the whelping box knowing how to heel, or to deliver a dumbbell in a perfect front sit, or to slow down for a contact zone in agility, or even to come when called. So everything we call "training" comes from us. If the dog doesn't do it properly, whose fault is it? Ask yourself again.

Any flaw in the dog's performance is always in the teaching. The dog is always true to his doggie nature. I've yet to meet one who schemes to do something wrong in training so he can get punished.

If the dog isn't getting a behavior right in training, then obviously we've missed something. What we think we're teaching is not what the dog is learning. We should learn to look to ourselves. It's our problem. It's not fair to make it the dog's.

Probably the biggest advantage of positive training is that it keeps your dog trying. He keeps trying to get it right. And he keeps on trusting you.

Your dog isn't afraid to be wrong, because he knows you'll help him get it right. This is training through direction, not correction. He knows you'll keep up your end of the bargain, and be fair with him.

From von Stephanitz again: "When the dog makes a mistake, or does not understand an exercise, or fails in obedience . . . let the trainer therefore examine himself and let him ask, *Where am I at fault?* "

Who knows? Some days you might even give your dog a break and give him the benefit of the doubt. He might get a reward just for being so cute, or for being so creative, or for not leaving when he's confused, or for making you laugh. Seems to me it's the least we can do for our wonderful dogs.

Positive vs. Permissive

Positive training does not mean permissive. The dog does not get to do whatever he wants to do. The dog must demonstrate acceptable behavior in order to get his reward.

Positive training relies on positive reinforcement to elicit desired behavior. The dog must think. The dog must learn. The dog must make the right decision. He must choose to offer the correct behavior in order to earn privileges, or food, or acceptance – just like he would have to conform to the social rules of a natural pack in the wild.

Positive training, properly applied, produces dogs who know what is expected of them and who want to be right (so they can earn their valuable rewards). It produces dogs who are under control, and who know how to control themselves.

Positive training produces dogs who are happy and eager to learn. It produces willing dogs who are full of joy in their work.

Along the way, it also creates fair pack leaders. The dog learns to obey out of respect and trust, not fear. Dog and trainer truly become a team.

Basic Principles

Positive training relies on a couple of really basic principles. They're simple, but they're so powerful.

Positive reinforcement training isn't a fad. It's a scientifically proven method to modify behavior effectively and permanently.

Not only does it work, it's also humane. Bob Bailey, talking about the use of positive reinforcement to treat autistic and retarded children, points out, "Its widespread use reflects not only its efficacy as a training tool, but the basic humane attitude toward life that characterizes behavioral psychology, namely – accentuate the positive."

All organisms tend to take the path of least resistance to the highest rewards. This is true of dogs, cats, horses, amoebas and yes, even humans too.

Once you identify what your dog really wants, you've taken a giant step in the right direction. Usually, what your dog wants is attention, affection and approval. Incidentally, it's usually what we humans seek too.

One of the first questions behaviorist Ted Turner asks in his seminar is, "Anyone here getting too much attention? How about too much affection, or too much approval? Raise your hand if you're getting too much attention, or too much affection, or too much approval in your life!"

The questions bring out a valid point. Most of us would not hesitate to do those things that would earn us constant attention, affection and approval from those we love. Begin to offer these to your dog, for behaviors you want, and training becomes fun and fruitful.

Positive training serves to bring out the best in the dog. As winning trainer Patty Ruzzo says, "We don't want to put the obedience into the dog, we want to bring it out of the dog."

Think Positive

To train your dog the positive way, you have to learn to think positive. You have to start with a positive attitude toward your dog.

Begin to look to your dog for the answers. Tune in to your dog. Respect his input and you'll be surprised how much he has to tell you. In purely positive training, your dog is the one to ask.

You'll be amazed what this type of training does for your relationship. For those of us who consider our canine connection an important part of our lives, the rewards of purely positive training are well worth it all.

FOCUS ON THE POSITIVE !

2   The Relationship

*"The training method should evolve from the relationship,
not the relationship from the training method."*
— Brigitte Coulon

Before starting any training, "First, establish a relationship," says Ted Turner. This may sound like a very simple thing to do, but sometimes it is the most challenging.

A relationship can be many things, but the most important element of any relationship is trust. We want our relationship with our dogs to reflect confidence, harmony and teamwork.

Training can build up your relationship, or it can break it down. Positive training creates trust and confirms your role as a fair pack leader. Punishment damages trust and blocks learning.

Many people set out to train their dogs for the purpose of establishing their relationship. Since relationship develops mainly through reinforcement history, punishment can quickly erode that necessary element of trust. This is especially true if the dog does not understand exactly why he is being punished, or how to avoid it.

Our connection with our dogs is so different from any other relationship that it deserves some special attention. In most cases, the dog arrives ready to bond. Bonding can happen quickly, but building a solid relationship takes time. First, you must forge a strong relationship. Then you can enhance it, and eventually, over time, cement it.

Our dogs want to have confidence in us. We want to have confidence in them. They depend on us. They tend to have a natural trust in us.

Training should build this mutual confidence and do nothing to erode it. We need to offer direction and support. We need to teach clearly, and then let them learn.

Positive training fosters willing communication, a cooperative attitude and an enthusiastic love of learning. Communication and cooperation are the building blocks of a good relationship.

To develop trust, training must always respect the nature and spirit of each dog. They are individuals and must be treasured as such.

Special Connection

The relationship with a dog is unique and special. It is different from what you can share with a dolphin in a pool, or even a horse in your backyard barn. The rhythms of our lives, and our personal needs, all contribute to the emotional (sometimes even spiritual) nature of our bond with the dog.

In many ways, the companionship of a dog depends on the quality of the relationship. If we want to go on to show in competition, then the relationship must be developed with even more care, keeping in mind the future expectations and requirements.

When developing this type of teamwork, the proper relationship is just as important as proper training. Sometimes it becomes even more important, as we'll get to in the last chapter.

The level of companionship, commitment, cooperation and consideration in each relationship is a totally individual issue. We could not begin to determine guidelines for everyone's relationship. Nor would we want to. After all, it's variety that makes this world so interesting.

Each relationship is made up of the little things. How much is given, and how much is taken – on each side – prescribes the delicate balance within that relationship. Only when the little things are in balance do the big things fall into place.

Relationships also change over time. Think about the human relationships you have now versus what they were a few years ago. Experiences affect relationships.

This is true with our dogs too. Charra, my awesome 12-year-old German Shepherd, brought me home when I got lost in the woods a couple of years ago. That single incident changed our relationship – for the better, for sure – but it changed our attitude toward each other.

Char immediately assumed new privileges, like getting on the sofa and the bed without asking for permission. She began taking more responsibility and making decisions on her own, without looking to me. I just smiled.

In the woods, she kept a much closer eye on me, especially on the way home. It's insulting to have her think me so incompetent, but I love this solicitous devotion and reinforce her new attitude at every opportunity. After all, she earned it. So be prepared for your relationship with your dog to change and grow as your reinforcement history develops together.

No book can begin to cover all the differences and nuances of relationship. Volumes have been written on improving our personal relationships. Everyone's relationship with their dog is different – just as every human and every dog are unique individuals. So the delicate balance in your relationship will be just a little different from anyone else's.

However, there are certain guidelines to ensure that your relationship is built on trust and respect. Someone has to be the leader, and since you pay the mortgage and buy the dog food (and the training books), it should probably be you.

Expectations

What do you want from your dog for your lifestyle? Everyone has his own personal reasons for having a dog. Remember, the dog is usually the only family member you get to choose! Your reason for getting a dog often determines much about your relationship.

Think a little bit about why you have your dog and what you want from that relationship. Each action and reaction, every interaction, shapes your relationship. It's the give-and-take of daily life.

If all an owner wants from a dog is to cuddle on the couch and watch videos and share popcorn, fine. But he shouldn't be surprised if the dog wets on the carpet, chews up the sofa cushions, growls at the kids or runs away when called. When nobody establishes house rules, the dog usually gets pretty good at making up his own.

Being a fair pack leader doesn't mean you have to be a tyrannical dictator. You can also be a fun pack mate when you choose. But it must be when *you* choose.

A fair pack leader must be consistent. He is reasonable and forgiving. But he is always the one who sets parameters and makes the rules. He provides guidance and support and safety.

"You need to be the master, but with him not as the slave, but rather your willing partner," says Tom Dorrance, a pioneer in positive training for horses.

In simply getting your dog to adhere to your parameters and follow your rules, you are training your dog. You can do it positively, or you can do it negatively.

Training is not something that happens for 10 minutes a day on the field, or once a week at training class. It stems from the relationship, which affects every minute of every day that you and your dog share space and interact.

Positive training does not damage your precious relationship with your dog. It enhances it. Purely positive training builds a reinforcement history that promotes trust and fairness, even while fostering respect.

If you want your dog to be able to walk off leash with you in the woods, then you need to train him to be responsible. He must be reliable, stay close and always come when called. If you want to take your dog to your kids' ball games, you must teach him to be civilized and gentle around excited children.

Special Moments

Certainly some of the most meaningful, magical moments in my relationship with my dogs are when I can share their woods-wonderful-world with them. That's why I have my dogs. (And to retrieve sticks, of course.)

One of my earliest childhood recollections is wanting to be old enough to walk the dog by myself. I was about six when I started begging for this privilege. To this day, I'm still that same kid who spent every Saturday I could, out with my dog and my best friend rambling the Canadian woods around our home. Being in the woods with my dogs is the best of times for me.

But being able to share such moments obviously requires a certain level of training for my dogs. When I'm on horseback, or just walking with them, the dogs must be reliable off-leash – whether we encounter deer, horses, skunks, trailbikes or other people with dogs. Only through learning to be responsible have my dogs earned this freedom.

Relationship and training go hand in hand. The two cannot be separated. Positive training builds trust. It makes you and your dog a team, and connects you to each other. And it leads to more enriching experiences that you can share with your wonderful canine companion.

The Trust Fund

Positive reinforcement is like making deposits in a bank account. Every time you reward positive behavior, you put money in the account. At first, the bank account needs lots of deposits to make it grow. But soon it starts to earn interest. We call it the Trust Fund.

All the deposits are put in trust. Each time we reward our dog, the fund grows. Pretty soon, the Trust Fund begins to pay off. We reap the dividends. Later on, we can live on the interest the Trust Fund generates.

Eventually, both dog and owner can reap the benefits from all those initial deposits. As the trust grows, so do the benefits. Positive training pays off in the long run by building a strong relationship, and a Trust Fund both can count on.

Start Now

One of the most wonderful aspects of positive training is that no matter what has happened before, you can start now. You can begin today to put deposits in the Trust Fund. It soon starts to bear interest.

Your dog will notice right away. Poor credit history can be quickly overcome. Your dog will respond to positive reinforcement almost immediately.

You are on your way to improving your relationship. And your dog's attitude to training just keeps getting better.

Which Dog?

If you do not have a dog already, choose one who best suits your expectations. Puppies within a litter have different personalities, just like siblings. They are not clones.

Prior research can help you select the companion who best suits your particular temperament, family and lifestyle. For direction on this, consult *The Positive Puppy Preview* tape, listed in the Recommended Resources section (Page xxvii).

The Positive Approach

Even with the perfect dog, you still have to tune in to him to be able to build a good relationship through positive training. This is often the most interesting and intriguing part of the whole process. You have to find out what your dog likes to do and what he wants. Start to see where he is coming from. Get involved with his view of life.

Find out what he wants and likes, and then give him that whenever he offers you the behavior you want. Pay attention to the good things he does, and let him know you appreciate them. Too often we are guilty of ignoring the behaviors we want, but giving all our attention and emotion to the ones we don't want.

For example, when a young dog is lying quietly, he's usually ignored. The moment he starts to chew the table leg or jumps up to bark at the window, he gets attention and emotional energy, and sometimes even gets touched. More and more, it sounds like the classic example of the toddler who crayons on the wall because he knows it will bring him attention, even if it's negative.

Let's change this scenario from a reactive one to a proactive one. Go over to your dog when he's lying quietly on the floor. Sit beside him and scratch his belly if that's what he likes, or rub his ears. Make eye contact and tell him how good he's being, and how much you like this behavior. Give him a food treat. Give him your attention and affection and approval while he's still doing what you want, *before* he does something you don't like.

Begin to watch for behaviors you want – eye contact, calmly following you around, lying down on his bed or in his crate, playing with his own toys. Speaking of toys, teach him to play the games you want, before he makes up his own (like keep-away). Teach him games that help establish your leadership and enhance relationship. We'll discuss that later.

Playing suitable games is just one of the issues covered by Leslie Nelson in her booklet *Management Magic*, on her audiotape *Positively Ready*, and in her Positive Power videos, listed in the Recommended Resources section in the back of this book. Leslie focuses on four aspects of relationship – Playing, Eating, Grooming and Sleeping – known as P.E.G.S. She explains how to channel these areas into behaviors you want, using all positive reinforcement.

An owner who needs a muzzle to cut his dog's nails, probably needs to develop a better relationship before going on to more formal training. Such a relationship deficit will show up continually in training.

First things must come first – establishing trust and winning respect. With my young Belgian, Vino, we worked on our relationship for an entire year before being ready to progress to formal training.

A Meaningful Relationship

Every day, life with your dog offers you countless ways to positively reinforce the relationship you want. Look for those opportunities and use them to your advantage.

Almost every evening, one of my dogs comes over to me when I'm on the sofa. They look at me expectantly, and I don't always know what they want.

But I don't miss the moment! I take that opportunity to tell them how good they look, or how well they did something that day, or just how wonderful they are. Maybe they don't understand all the words, but they sure respond to that flow of positive emotional energy, and they can tell I'm sincere.

I'm choosing to reward their attention to me. These exchanges may seem to have very little to do with actual training. Then again, one winner of the Iditarod (the world's toughest sled-dog race) sang lullabies to his dogs at night.

Maybe this heart-to-heart communication has more to do with success than we know. It sure does serve to enhance the relationship.

So consider your relationship first. Relationship is that marvelous intangible that develops through trust and over time. It is probably the reason you got your dog in the first place.

Always pay attention to the quality of that relationship. Resolve never to let anything compromise that most important element.

Your relationship with your dog is unique, and so precious. Be sure your daily training serves to strengthen that relationship, not damage it.

A good relationship with your dog is the key that allows you to live together in harmony. Once your life with your dog is pure pleasure for you both, there's plenty of time for more formal training.

RELISH THE RELATIONSHIP !

3

The
Golden Rule

> " Yes is
> so much more
> important than No."
> – Dominique Barbier

Purely positive training relies heavily on one rule. Follow this rule consistently and you are on your way to forging a better relationship with your dog.

At the same time, training becomes easier, more fun and much more productive. Your dog starts to offer behavior you want more and more often.

**Positively reinforce
any and all behavior
that you want to continue.**

The better you reinforce, the faster you reinforce and the more consistently you reinforce – the sooner your dog learns and the easier future training becomes.

REINFORCE THE POSITIVE !

4 The Ten Commandments

"There's facts about dogs,
and there's opinions about them.
The dogs have all the facts,
and the humans have the opinions."
— J. Allen Boone

Once we have made the commitment to forge our relationship and train our dog using positive methods, we must understand some of the concepts involved. Science has set down some very specific rules for successful learning using positive reinforcement.

But this can not be like auto mechanic school. The rules need to work for your particular dog. We must remember that the dogs have the facts, and we only have the opinions. The dog always lets us know when we are doing it right, so we must learn to listen to the dog.

"Whatever works, works!" So says master dressage trainer Dominique Barbier. If our relationship is improving, our dog is paying more attention to us, and his behavior is becoming more acceptable, then it's working!

Like all true learning, it comes slowly over time, step by step. Remember when you learned to type. (I guess today it's called keyboarding.) You practiced the same skills over and over – picking out the letters carefully and pecking at them with the appropriate finger.

Then one day, you got it. Your brain connected directly to your fingers and they flew over the keyboard, finding the

19

right letter without any conscious effort. You learned – a slow process of repetition leading to a solid skill that lasts a lifetime.

You learned to read the same way – slowly at first. Then suddenly, it was easy. You no longer had to sound out words. You read in full sentences. From then on, it just got easier and easier.

What we learn slowly, we remember longer. Just like cramming for a test, learning that happens in a short time is often lost just as quickly.

Learning is the same for dogs. "Dogs are not obedient to commands; they are obedient to the laws of learning," writes Jean Donaldson. So if we want to teach them properly, we must understand some basic principles of these laws of learning.

The better we understand these rules, the better we can teach. But you don't need to go back to school to implement positive training.

If all this theory bores you, and you just want to teach your pet dog to come when called and stay when told, then breeze through the next four chapters just to get the idea. Starting in Section II, the chapters explain step by step how to use these rules to raise your puppy and train your dog.

1. Be Proactive

Positive training requires that we be proactive instead of reactive. "Good trainers fix problems. Great trainers never get to the problems." That's how Ted Turner explains being proactive.

The first part of being proactive is to prevent unwanted behavior. Allowing the dog to rehearse unwanted behavior over and over only puts the handler back in the position of trying to fix the problem.

For example, if we know the puppy is going to jump up on someone, then we want to get in there *before* the puppy jumps. We want to do one of three things with the unwanted behavior – prevent it, ignore it, or teach an Alternative Incompatible Behavior. That's a fancy scientific term for teaching the puppy to do something else – something he can't do at the same time as jumping, like sitting.

We know the puppy is going to jump. He's already given us that fact. If we are reactive, we wait until he does what we don't want, and then try to fix it. To be proactive, teach him a positive way to greet people – before he jumps.

This is another element of positive training. We get in there and teach the positive so we don't ever have to deal with the negative. We never get to the problem. The puppy never learns the wrong behavior.

Undesirable behavior does not result in punishment, however. This would only break down the relationship and inhibit learning. Punishment makes the dog afraid to try. In positive training, the dog should try all sorts of new behaviors until he discovers which ones work to get him what he wants from us.

2. Keep Them Trying

Working hard to get what they want comes naturally to dogs. Wolves in the wild must work for what they want. Within the pack, when a young wolf discovers which behavior results in gratification, or acceptance, or satisfaction, or permission to eat, he learns this valuable lesson and remembers.

Sometimes, we must reward honest effort, even if the dog gets it wrong. This keeps him trying and accelerates learning. Behavior is not static – it is always changing. So if the dog gets frustrated or confused, sometimes we must let him know that he's doing fine and we still support him.

For example, if the dog comes when we call him, but doesn't come close enough or doesn't sit straight in front, we still want to reinforce coming quickly when called. Reward his effort. Keep the dog trying and eventually he'll get it right.

We do this with a child learning to read. When he's learning the alphabet song, we encourage him, even if he gets a letter wrong. We urge him to try again, or we sing it with him.

Once he begins reading simple sentences, we don't jerk his neck or pinch his ear when he gets a word wrong. That wouldn't help him learn, and it certainly wouldn't help him love to read. We help the child to get it right. We read it with him again. We support him.

To teach a child to love to read, we foster any attempt to read, (even comic books?!). Just as we want the child to keep reading, we want the dog to keep trying for us. And we want them to love to learn.

We aim not only to have the dog behave a certain way, but also for him to *want* to learn how to behave. And we want him to enjoy doing that behavior.

How to do this is simple. Back to The Golden Rule. We positively reinforce all behavior that we want. And we positively reinforce even the beginnings of that behavior – any step in the right direction.

3. Forgive Forgetting

Always remember that forgetting is part of learning. Forgetting is part of the process, especially when learning a new task. When learning a new computer program, do you ever forget which keystroke combination leads to a certain function? Unfortunately, the dog can't go look it up in his manual. If he forgets where it is on his disk space, he needs help.

When was the last time you went through an entire day without forgetting anything? When have you made it through one week without making a mistake? In dog training, mistakes are merely learning opportunities.

If you can manage to forgive yourself, then you should be able to forgive your dog. After all, they are only dogs, and we are only people, as Patty Ruzzo says.

Be there to help your dog. Encourage him and coach him. Train by direction, not correction. When training, be his salvation, not his persecution. Remember, you're both on the same team.

4. Follow the ABCs

Learning follows a specific pattern known as A-B-C:

Antecedent – Behavior – Consequence

Any change in this order will inhibit, or prevent, learning. "Antecedent" is just the fancy scientific term for a cue. The cue is the signal that tells the dog which behavior you want. But the word "Antecedent" works better to help us remember the critical order and importance of the ABCs.

Your dog knows all about antecedents. Pick up your car keys and see if you get the expected behavior. Yep, it happens every time. Clatter his food dish and watch his response. We want to apply the same kind of reliable cues to the behaviors we want to teach our dogs.

When you start to use positive reinforcement as the Consequence, the more your dog likes what you give him, the faster he offers that behavior, or more often or more intensely, depending on how you reinforce. The important rule here is that Consequence drives Behavior.

What happens as a Consequence determines whether the dog continues or repeats that Behavior. Providing the right Consequence can improve the frequency, intensity or duration of any Behavior.

Positive reinforcement is a powerful teacher. The more you use positive reinforcement with your dog, the easier training becomes. Once the dog grasps the concept of using his behavior to get what he wants, you can teach him to do just about anything he can master physically.

We aren't the only ones who'll be learning new concepts in this positive training. Once your dog understands the rules, he learns faster and faster, and adds new behaviors more quickly. The more he learns, the more he wants to learn, and thus the easier he is to teach! For more about this, refer to *The ABCs of Behavior Shaping,* part of the Power of Positive Training series included in the Recommended Resources section in the back of this book.

Please note that, for the sake of brevity, when we use the term "reinforce," we mean positive reinforcement. We train positively. We believe in paying our dog when he works for us. And we always make sure to pay him with what he wants.

Sometimes we also use the term "reward," instead of "reinforce." It's not scientifically correct, but it's shorter – and you'll know what we mean.

5. Use Approximations

When we use the ABCs to shape behavior, we teach through approximations. That's the scientific word for steps.

Training through approximation simply means that we start at the beginning, with the very first step. We get the dog to make the first attempt at the ultimate behavior we want. We reinforce that, and then the next step, and so on, right up the ladder of approximations.

Usually, the very first approximation is to teach "topography." There's another one of those fancy scientific terms. This one means the physical aspect of the behavior. Before, we called it "technique."

So usually the first step (up the approximation ladder) is to get the dog to do what we want physically. Often, he does this even before he understands what he's doing, and long before he recognizes the cue.

Improvement in topography is recognized as a reliable way to measure learning, according to Paul Chance's book *Learning and Behavior.* If all this scientific verbiage is right up your alley, then this is a text you might enjoy. (See Recommended Resources.)

It might even help you train your dog, but effective dog training certainly doesn't demand that you get that technical. In fact, simpler is better from your dog's point of view.

Back to improving topography. Repetition improves technique. So as your dog repeats a specific behavior, his performance gets "simpler, smoother, more efficient, less variable," says Mr. Chance. Learning proper topography becomes just as important as learning the concept, especially if you plan to go on to competition.

Think of concepts and technique in terms of your own learning. You're right-handed, and now you're going to learn to hammer a nail with your left hand. You know exactly what to do. You understand the concept.

The topography is a different matter. It takes practice to master the technique of this new behavior. Would it help you learn faster if someone jerked your neck every time you missed the nail?

Asking a young dog to sit quickly and squarely on cue might seem easy to you, but most dogs aren't even aware they have a leg at each corner until late adolescence. We can provide exercises to show them earlier, such as negotiating agility obstacles. But to the puppy, wherever the front end goes, the rear just seems to follow right along. They don't give it much thought.

So the young dog might understand the concept of sit way before he can perform it as quickly and squarely and tightly as you'd like. Learning the topography here might take a little longer. We always need to work with the dog at his level to be a fair teacher – to recognize his abilities without making excuses.

Sometimes going from zero to one is the biggest step.

Once the dog has grasped the concept of which behavior is wanted, and he is developing technique, then we start to climb the ladder of approximations. To do this, we raise criteria and raise rewards.

That means we ask him to perform the behavior a little faster, or more intensely, or more completely. When he does, we give him something he really likes. Does this sound a little like getting a promotion for success at work and a pay raise along with it? Bingo.

In the case of hammering the nail, we might ask for more power, or for a more direct hit, or for two direct hits in a row before providing reinforcement. But we'd be sure to give you lots of what you wanted when you finally mastered the new step.

If we run into any stumbling blocks along the training path, we back up a step or two and get the foundation right before moving on. Think of learning as climbing a ladder. You need to get your foot firmly on one rung before you climb up to the next. Better yet, think of building concrete steps – the foundation steps must be built on something really solid or the entire structure is going to collapse.

To help your dog climb the approximation ladder, you provide direction, not correction. Build on success and keep the dog trying. All the while you enhance your relationship and build trust.

Patty Ruzzo is fond of saying, "If you're in a hole, stop digging." So that's exactly what we do. We go back and get the previous step right, or we get out of there for now. Next time, we make sure to set the dog up for success.

Remember that it is always our fault if the dog is making a mistake in something we trained – or think we trained. There are No Wrong Dogs!

We want our dogs to enjoy being with us, and to love training. So we work hard to keep training fun and make it the dog's choice – all the way up the ladder.

6. Shift Context Early

Shifting context is another complicated sounding phrase. But this is by far one of the simplest and most powerful training techniques you will ever use. It simply means to change parts of the picture, like the location.

About now you're saying, "That's it – enough long words and abstract concepts." But hang in there. It gets clearer when we apply these rules to dog training. Even if this sounds a little complicated now, you'll find yourself coming back to these rules for whatever new behavior you want to train.

In the beginning, we reinforce the dog frequently – for attention, for effort, and for the desired behavior. As soon as the dog starts to understand what we want, we begin to change three things.

First, we put a little more emphasis on the dog understanding the cue for this specific behavior. We make the cue clearer as we wean away from the little helps – the lures or prompts that helped elicit the behavior initially.

Second, we shift context. Something as simple as changing location helps the dog to clarify the cue and generalize his learning. Third, we begin to vary the schedule of reinforcement.

All that might sound a little complicated right now, but it comes easily and quickly once you start training. It's much harder to grasp the abstract than it is to work with your wonderful dog.

We just put all the behaviors we want to teach into the Positive Training Paradigm (Chapter 16). Then we tune in to the dog and keep it simple – training step by step.

7. Premack It

Now just bear with us a minute here. This is the last of the fancy scientific jargon. Actually, it's someone's name, but it's such a powerful principle that it really is worth knowing.

The Premack Principle stands for access to desired behavior. Well, not exactly. The actual scientific definition is that high probability behavior reinforces low probability behavior. For our purposes, though, it simply means that the dog learns to perform a certain behavior, one that you want him to do, to gain access to what he wants to do.

A critical concept we want our dogs to learn is that all of heaven comes through us. For example, your dog wants to go outside in the yard. You have already taught him to sit. You put your hand on the doorknob and give him the cue. As soon as he sits, you open the door. You've just used the Premack Principle. Your dog got to do what *he* wanted as soon as he did what *you* wanted.

Start using this effectively and you will be absolutely amazed how quickly the dogs get it, and what a powerful tool it is for training. It also gets to be lots of fun thinking up new ways to apply the Premack Principle.

In the next chapter, we'll even tell you how one international trainer Premacked sex (for his dog, not for himself – although it probably wouldn't be the first time this principle was used between humans). So stay tuned – it gets interesting.

8. Let Them Learn

One unique concept of positive training is that instead of being committed to teaching the dog, it works better to let them learn. There is a subtle, but staggering, difference.

The old style of militant training required the handler to take charge and make the dog do it *now*. Be the boss. Order the dog to do it and then make him. Handlers were so busy teaching, they never gave the poor dog the time he needed to learn.

We take the opposite approach. We listen to the dog. Once he grasps the concept that he can get what he wants through exhibiting the desired behavior, we know he's going to try – and keep on trying.

For those who have trained dogs before, it's easy to adopt this new attitude. Begin to see training as a cue for a behavior, not a direct command to be immediately obeyed.

This helps lighten up the attitude. It puts dog training in proper perspective. Now it's merely non-performance of a behavior, not a direct challenge to authority.

It is our responsibility to help the dog and direct him the right way so he can learn. In truth, nobody can really teach anybody anything. All we can do is help them learn.

We are the coach, not the commander. We set the dog up for success, and then we wait. Waiting is surely one of the most difficult parts of this positive training program.

We encourage creativity. We just channel it into more effort and more desire to get it right (so the dog can get more of he wants). We delight in new twists – that means he's thinking and trying. It will only be a matter of time until he figures out what we want. We laugh at new developments.

We're not training a military drill team here. We're teaching a dog – a curious, intelligent critter – our best friend, who's trying his best to get it right.

9. Do No Damage

This rule is one of my favorites. It's why I like positive training so much. If I make a mistake (Imagine That!), there is no damage done. Through all the training, the relationship just keeps getting better.

If I miss the moment (Oops!), or if I'm not clear about which behavior I ask for, or if I skip a vital approximation, or if I get my ABCs out of order, or fumble a cue, or reinforce at the wrong time, or if I get distracted (Heaven Forbid!), the worst that can happen is that it takes the poor dog a little longer to learn the desired behavior.

The fantastic part is that there is no damage to our relationship or our training. We shrug it off, or laugh about it, and go on. The dog forgives me, as I forgive him. Perhaps I give him an extra reward just for hanging in there with me.

As someone once said, "To err is human – to forgive is canine." The dog is not stressed or worried. I haven't hurt him. I'm not mad at him. He still wants to keep learning. We're still a team.

10. Keep It Fun

Training your dog should be fun. You invited this wonderful creature into your life for many reasons, hopefully not to frighten or hurt him.

Dogs offer us their complete loyalty, and we need to acknowledge and respect that gift. Training through these positive methods serves to improve communication, intensify the bond and enhance our relationship.

> Be exciting. Be enthusiastic.
> Be fair. But above all, be FUN.

Simply by following these Ten Commandments, your dog will begin to offer the behavior that gets him what he wants more and more.

This type of training develops a positive relationship quickly. It assures a solid positive reinforcement history – money in the bank, a Trust Fund you can count on.

Everything your dog wants now comes through you. Your dog is building a belief system. He has faith that all of heaven comes through you, and it comes frequently. You are fair and you are fun. So your dog begins to put all his focus and attention on you. Anyone have a problem with this?

Usually, when owners begin positive training, the biggest problem is that their dogs won't leave them alone. The dogs seek them out and offer a variety of behaviors – soliciting reinforcement.

Science calls this "spontaneous rehearsal" and we find it terribly amusing. We'd sure rather deal with this result than with any avoidance, or fear, or stress left over from training. When the dog begins spontaneous rehearsal, he's showing us he's starting to get the concept of the ABCs – that he can manipulate the Consequence through his Behavior.

Oops, sorry, we said no more fancy scientific lingo. But this spontaneous rehearsal stuff is pretty neat. Your dog is trying to please you by doing something you've taught him, without even being asked.

Who knows? Maybe you can figure out how to use this method to get the kids to do the dishes without being asked. And just think of all these fancy new scientific words and phrases you've learned to impress your friends when the conversation gets around to behavior and learning – something to try out at the next party.

BE FAIR AND BE FUN !

The Ten Commandments
of Positive Training

1. Be Proactive.

2. Keep Them Trying.

3. Forgive Forgetting.

4. Follow the ABCs.

5. Use Approximations.

6. Shift Context Early.

7. Premack It.

8. Let Them Learn.

9. Do No Damage.

10. KEEP IT FUN!

5 The Reinforcers

"You have to think,
and learn to think like a (dog)."
– Tom Dorrance

So just what is this positive reinforcement stuff? If it makes the dog obey so well and work so happily, where do we get it and how do we use it?

Whenever the talk turns to positive reinforcement, almost everyone immediately thinks of food. This is that food training method, they say. Sure, we use food. We believe in paying our dogs for a job well done. Don't you expect to get paid for the work you do?

And we pay our dogs in wages we're sure they want. That makes food a powerful reinforcer for most dogs. When you work, you want to get paid in American dollars – something that means something to you. Would you be willing to work for Mexican pesos, or for shares in real estate on Mars?

Payment must be important to you personally. It's the same for your dog, except that for payment to be important to him, it needs to be immediate. Promise of future reward means nothing to a dog.

Really, it's quite simple. Anything that your dog wants and likes, that you can provide, can be a positive reinforcer for training.

So yes, food is one of our primary reinforcers. But oh, there are so many more.

33

THE PRIMARY REINFORCERS

Science designates primary reinforcers as those that are common to all members of the species. So what do all dogs want and need?

Air / Food / Water / Sleep
Safety / Sex / Social Interaction

Some of these primary reinforcers lend themselves to training better than others. Food may be a very effective reinforcer, but it is by no means the only road to Rome.

Water

How can water be used as a reinforcer? Actually, we've used it quite effectively in one of our agility exercises.

My young Belgian, Vino, is a compulsive drinker (of water, we mean). He likes to take long, frequent drinks during his agility training (probably to help digest all the really good food he gets). One of the most difficult exercises for him is trotting slowly through a series of cavaletti. (Doing anything slowly makes no sense to Vino.)

So when he's thirsty, we place the closed water jug at the end of the cavaletti (raised poles on the ground, through which he is supposed to trot, not run). Only if he slows to a trot when we say "Easy," and negotiates the cavaletti properly, do we take the top off the water jug. Voila! He knows the routine so well now that the thirstier he is, the slower and more careful he is the first time through, to be sure to get his reward.

At home, it's easy to have your dog sit or wait or make eye contact, or do whatever you ask, before putting down the water bowl. Our dogs also love ice cubes. You guessed it! When the freezer opens and the dogs appear for their ice cubes, we get the right behavior on cue just about every time.

Now you're starting to see how positive training goes on all day long, building the reinforcement history for your relationship in life, not just at class or in a training session.

Air

Using air as a reinforcer? This one is a little limited. It's hard to make access to air a positive experience when you have to withhold it before you can give it back.

Yes, it's been used, as anyone knows who has seen the barbaric choke collar method of getting the dog to grasp a dumbbell. When the dog opens his mouth for air, the trainer sticks the dumbbell in and slackens the choker. It's not exactly positive, but reinforcement nonetheless.

We've chosen to allow our dogs free access to air – without working for it, and without fear of us taking it away. We just can't see how withholding air could possibly improve our relationship.

Exercise

Certainly access to exercise can be used easily through the Premack Principle. Your dog wants to run free in the field. As soon as he sits on cue and gives you eye contact, you release him to do what he wants.

Being somewhat macho, Vino really likes to lift his leg in new places. On a road trip, he's especially eager at those highway rest areas, where so many other dogs have marked. Last year, I just wasn't getting the response to "Wait" that I wanted for agility. His interpretation was to wait for as long as he deemed reasonable (about three nanoseconds), decide I was being too slow, and go on and do another obstacle.

So I shifted context, took it out of formal training and put it into life. I raised criteria by requiring eye contact, as well as standing still. Then I raised reward by Premacking it to something truly important to Vino.

The next time we stopped at a rest area, I put Vino on leash and let Charra go sniff around and relieve herself. Vino was incensed. I just told him "Wait" – and I waited. (You'll find that the waiting – our waiting – can be the hardest part of this positive training. But, like Benjamin Franklin said, "He that can have patience, can have what he wants.")

Vino was fixated on Char's freedom. Finally, he happened to glance up at me. I affirmed his behavior with "Yes! Wait," and immediately released him. Within three repetitions, Vino was waiting solidly and giving me intense eye contact for several seconds to be released.

By the end of that road trip, he was offering the behavior even before he got out of the van, and before I asked for it. Powerful stuff, this Premacking something your dog really wants.

Sleeping

There's no reason you can't use this for sleeping too. Every night, before giving the dog access to his bed, or his crate, (or *your* bed for sure, if he's allowed there), just ask for a behavior.

You not only get in some valuable training, but your dog starts to acknowledge you more and more as a fair pack leader, without intimidation or overt domination. Very simply, when he does what you ask, he gets to do what he wants.

Social Interaction

Social attraction is powerful for most dogs. Asking for a behavior, especially with eye contact, before allowing your dog access to other dogs makes sense. It puts your dog clearly in your hands in social settings.

Taking control of the dog's social behavior makes you a responsible dog owner. It is also a great safety valve if there are other dogs present who might not welcome your dog's advances.

If your dog is a real social butterfly with people, you can use this for access to people too. First, be proactive. Prevent the unwanted behavior, (running to other dogs or people), by having your dog on leash and close to you. Initially, be sure to have some really good food to get your dog to pay attention to you instead of to the other people or dogs.

Be fair and start at the beginning. Reinforce attention to you long before you get close to the other people and dogs. Be more fun and interesting than the other people or dogs. Remember that the step from zero to one, just getting your dog to look at you at all, sometimes takes the longest. From then on, it gets better and better, faster and faster.

At our first agility class, Vino and I spent almost as much time getting from the van to the building as we did in the class. He was so excited to see the other dogs and people there. But I was waiting for him to acknowledge my presence and show interest in the pieces of prime rib and liver I had.

By the third week, he clearly understood which behavior moved us in the correct direction – toward all the people and dogs – and offered attention to me as soon as he got out of the van. Building a solid first step is always worth the time and effort in the long run.

Sex

Most dogs these days are spayed or neutered, so that eliminates sex as a reinforcer. But it can be used.

Many years ago, a top German handler had a dog who was winning consistently at international Schutzhund trials. Consequently, he was in demand as a stud dog, which meant a female in season at a championship might distract him from his best performance. But the trainer made sure it would only enhance it.

Whenever a female arrived for breeding, the trainer introduced his male to the new visitor. Then he had her placed on the side of the training field. The faster and better the dog concentrated on his obedience work, the sooner he was released to consort with the visitor.

This is powerful Premacking. But I can pretty much guarantee if you mentioned the Premack Principle to this trainer, he wouldn't know what you were talking about, even with a good translator. He only knew what worked!

Safety

We'll leave you to ponder how safety might be used as a reinforcer. Suffice it to say that with a less than confident dog, it is a powerful reward. Incidentally, one of your most important jobs as pack leader is to provide safety. That's why the trust issue is so important between you and your dog.

Keep in mind that while you cannot alter the dog's innate temperament, you can almost always modify behavior. Temperament comes with the dog. But behavior is always in flux, and so can be changed along the way.

Positive training can never be a cookbook method. It requires the trainer to use his brain. It means tuning in to your dog, finding out what he wants, and then using that to get the behavior you want from your dog. The issue of safety is a good one to start thinking about.

The Food

As a top Hollywood animal trainer said on a recent television special, "Well, I guess the secret's out now – it's all done with food." The seals at the aquarium show are tossed a fish after each trick. The circus dogs have been catching their treats on cue for years. The dolphins in some shows even get to choose which kind of fish they want as a reward. Nobody cries foul! Nobody says it isn't real training.

Perhaps if our dogs were bigger, and more willing to hurt us, food wouldn't be considered bribery. Perhaps if we were training Siberian tigers, we would be more willing to use food. Nobody should want to hurt their dog just because they can.

The Mahouts in India have been training elephants throughout recorded history. They prefer to train captive-born youngsters, but when they have to train a delinquent teenager taken from the wild, you can guess their first step.

They use food to establish their authority. They teach the elephant that he can have food only from their hand, and only when he moves his trunk aside and doesn't touch the food with his trunk first – an acutely unnatural act for an elephant. They win trust through food. The elephant must allow the Mahout to put the food directly into his mouth.

Food is the key to establishing their relationship. Access to food is the first step. No other training begins until this is understood. Trust and respect are built through food.

In the celebrated movie *Dances With Wolves,* how does the Army officer win the trust of the wild wolf? Right – with food.

In the popular Jack London book and movie *White Fang,* how does the young man win the wolf-dog's trust? Right – with food.

Why do you think the first wolves were ever drawn to a human camp? How do you think the first wolves ever got domesticated? It's a pretty good guess that food was involved.

How did so many people ever get so resistant to using food to train their dogs? It's used all over the world, by the world's best trainers. Why? Because it works!

Food is obviously one of the most powerful manipulators of behavior. In the wild, much of a canine's energy and thought is related to finding food.

It makes sense that food is an effective and simple tool to manipulate behavior for training purposes. Why not use it to get what we want from our dogs?

But using food effectively means so much more than manipulating behavior with it. For a dog, it is natural for the food to come from the pack leader. It is natural for dogs to work for their food. It is natural for food to be a social event within the pack.

It seems to be a natural social medium for us too. When was the last time you invited a friend over *not* to have coffee, or made a date *not* to have lunch?

It's also natural for the best pack leader to provide the best food. In our training group, several dogs have already identified me as the best hunter-gatherer there. These dogs naturally seek me out simply because they know I always have the best food.

That's because Vino's food drive is easily overcome by his desire to be social. It's necessary for me to have the very best treats to convince him of my significance in his life.

Providing the best food establishes my status and emphasizes my importance. If you want to be a better pack leader, the solution is simple – get better food. Remember, the reward must have value to the dog. Consequence drives Behavior.

How did those folks ever convince anyone that jerking the dog around by the neck is training, but that using food is cheating? The logic completely escapes us.

For competition, it would make more sense if practice matches permitted, even encouraged, any kind of food or praise or petting or playing, but outlawed any type of collar correction. But for now, it remains ironically and annoyingly backward.

The same reasoning works with people too. If you want their best performance, not to mention their loyalty and respect, take them out for a special lunch, or praise them in public, when their work is exceptional. As management master Ken Blanchard puts it, "People perform best when they're caught doing something right."

So learn to take your dog to dinner, so to speak, for a job well done. Choose not to damage your relationship with punishment or intimidation.

Using food for training is simple. But using it correctly is not always easy.

The disadvantages and limitations of using food for training are caused solely by the incorrect use of food. We can use it effectively without getting addicted to it. We don't need to depend on it totally, and we don't need to use it forever.

We have so many reinforcers to use with our dogs. However, food is by far the simplest and most powerful way to start making those all-important initial deposits in the Trust Fund. You can collect interest later, but not without first paying your dues. And keep in mind that punishment always depletes the bank account.

The food must be used as a tool. The dog must first understand the *concept* of earning the food through correct behavior. The food must very quickly become the reward, not the cue.

We want learning, not just behavior. Understanding this concept completely is the key to successful training. The dog comes to expect food as a Consequence, not as an Antecedent.

One example that amazed and saddened me was a lovely, sensitive dog who had already earned a Utility Dog title in obedience, the highest degree awarded. The dog was working in agility, but was lying down slowly on the table. A visiting trainer tried to get the dog to down faster by using food.

Now keep in mind that the dog already knew to lie down on command, and also knew to lie down on the table. But the trainer wanted the dog to lie down on its own for a food reward. The dog knew the food was in the trainer's hand, but when he didn't get the food by jumping and pawing and trying to grab it, the dog just quit.

The dog was mentally blocked because of previous negative training. The dog had no concept of trying to offer an obedience behavior to earn the food. The dog simply quit trying because he couldn't get to the food. He was afraid to try anything else. Finally, the owner had to order the dog to lie down. Then he obeyed – slowly.

We want our dogs to learn the opposite concept – keep on trying. Do something else – anything. When you get the behavior right, you get the reward. This keeps our dogs motivated to learn and driven to think. It keeps them trying.

One of my favorite positive food stories is of a sweet young setter in agility class. Jennie was somewhat distracted and uninterested in performing the obstacles. She preferred to sniff around, and was wandering away from the handler at the start of her turn.

The instructor, Jackie, told the owner to get out his food. He produced a dry dog biscuit. The dog yawned and looked away. But Jackie had the answer. She asked if anyone had any better food. I offered the owner some liver that my Dad (Vino's "grandpa") had cooked that night (complete with bacon and onions for my Dad's own dinner too).

Jennie took one sniff, jumped up in the air, twirled around, did a little dance, and then flew over the dogwalk in pursuit of her handler. She jumped the hurdle and flung herself onto the table (her least favorite obstacle) and into a down position, wagging her tail so hard she almost fell off.

The entire time her eyes were bulging, glued to the liver in her owner's hand. We all roared with laughter and Jennie earned her piece of liver, known forever after as "Grandpa's Magic Liver." What fun!

There are a number of other advantages to using food for any type of training. Eating reduces stress. Have you ever been in a tense social situation, or ready to do a public presentation, and wanted a cigarette, or a drink, or a candy to suck on, or a piece of gum to chew, or something to eat? Or, as one client put it so succinctly, "How about all the above?"

The mere act of chewing helps calm us down and reduce stress. Chewing produces saliva to combat that horrible dry-mouth feeling. Swallowing frees up tense muscles and helps us relax. It gives us something to focus on.

It works the same way with dogs. If you watch dogs long enough, you see a variety of oral behaviors associated with stress and avoidance, such as licking themselves or eating grass.

Feeding a dog in a stressful situation not only helps calm down a tense dog, it helps distract a worried dog. It gives a nervous dog something else to focus on. It gives the handler something positive to offer the dog and makes the handler the center of attention again.

Using food has the added benefit of diffusing a difficult situation and making a positive association with the food. Next time, the dog tends to be less worried because he knows this is a place or situation where he gets fed.

Food is also a great barometer. Good professional groomers learn to use food – not only to help the dog make a positive association with a sometimes scary place, but also to tell how the dog is feeling. Refusing to eat good food immediately indicates a rise in stress, heading toward a level they don't want the dog to reach.

Food refusal tells them it's time to switch gears and do something else with the dog. Take him for a walk, or give him a break. Make the dog more comfortable now, before he gets dangerously stressed. So food becomes a useful line of communication between dog and human that can work both ways.

By the way, our dogs dislike having their nails cut about as much as most dogs, but we can't keep them off the grooming table when they see it. Why? You guessed it. It's a place of high food reward. They tend to see it as their own personal picnic table. And we always reinforce them to encourage that belief.

To use food effectively in training, we need to start with the basics. First, the dog must be hungry.

In the wild, dogs and wolves tend to eat sporadically, large amounts once every few days. They endure the hunger pangs in the days between. They are acutely food driven, mainly because they know what real hunger is, and they never know when they will get to eat again.

Most dogs today eat too much – and too often. Obesity is probably the number one health concern for modern dogs. Owners tend to get upset if the dog doesn't finish every morsel of every meal. Then they exacerbate the problem by tempting their pets with tasty treats from the table.

Ignore the recommended feeding amounts listed on the dog food bag. It's a good marketing strategy. These companies are in the business of selling you dog food. Your concern is keeping your dog as fit and healthy as possible.

If you want to use food as a reinforcer, get it out of the bowl and into the training program. Every quarter cup of kibble in the bowl throws away about 10 minutes of valuable training time. Get really good food, and get it out of the bowl and into your daily routine!

Let's face it – we enjoy feeding our dogs. I know I do. Now we can feed them with a purpose and get a positive result.

We all know dogs who would eat every morsel of food available and still beg for more. Charra is one of those dogs. (Like me, she's a true foodie.) But feeding her all that she wanted would only make her fat, lethargic and unhealthy. And she certainly would not have won an agility class at 10 years old had she been overfed!

Vino is the opposite. He's fussy. There are other things he'd rather do than eat – like play or socialize. He prefers real meat. He doesn't do vegetables and he won't touch fat-free. He hates anything that remotely resembles health food. He eats to live, as opposed to Char and me who live to eat.

For both dogs, for different reasons, I make sure the food I offer in training is really worth working for – nutritious and delicious. To compete with Grandpa's Magic Liver, there's Grandma's Meatloaf – another one of Vino's personal favorites. Deli roast beef or ham will do. Cheddar cheese works, but Swiss is better in summer because it doesn't get mushy as fast. Something fishy is always a fine choice, and for some reason dogs seem to flip over anything cooked in teriyaki sauce.

Patty once discovered her dogs went crazy for cheese tortellini. So we tried it. The vote was split. Charra agreed; Vino didn't. But we had to stop using it for personal reasons. Within a couple of weeks of training, I'd gained five pounds. I couldn't resist it. I ate two pieces for every one I fed the dog. Now we leave the tortellini training to others who have more self-control.

We'll get to exactly when and how to use the food in the training chapters.

THE SECONDARY REINFORCERS

Science terms "secondary" those reinforcers not common to all members of the species. The logic is that the dog must be taught that these secondary reinforcers have importance, usually by connecting them to something the dog does care about. However, many of these so-called secondary reinforcers are of primary importance to many dogs.

Toys

Most of us know at least one dog who would rather play than eat. But just like with the food, the dog must understand the concept of who provides the toy and how to get it. Toys truly can be the big guns of your training program. When we raise criteria and raise rewards, this often means bringing out the toys.

The type of toys you use, and the way you use them, are both critical to success with positive training. Some folks believe they are motivational trainers because they throw a ball for the dog at the end of the training session. This teaches the dog one thing for sure – that playing is more fun than training.

We want our dogs to show the same joy in training that they show in playing. So we incorporate the toys right into the training, whenever it's appropriate.

For toys to become a meaningful reward for the dog, the dog must want them, just like being hungry for the food. This means toys used for training are used only for that. These toys are special. These toys must be earned. These toys are worth working for.

Most people think only of Latex squeakies or other manufactured items when they think about toys. Use what the dog likes. Many young dogs can't resist the noise and crinkle of a plastic soda bottle. If the dog likes it, use it.

Some soft-mouthed breeds find a little piece of sheepskin or rabbit fur their ideal toy. For others, it's a leather glove. So find out what floats your dog's boat, and then use it. When one of our dogs chooses a stick in the woods, we use that to get a couple of behaviors on cue. We reward by throwing the stick, or playing tug.

With a dog who shows very little inclination to play with toys, get creative. Smear some peanut butter inside a Kong toy and toss it. When the dog gets it, let him lick out the food.

Place some goodies in a sealed food tube. For small dogs, you can use one of those little plastic film containers. When the dog pays attention to it, open it up and give him the food. Extend this over time to where the dog has to paw at it or pick it up, and eventually bring it back to you, to get the food.

Keeping the toys *away* from the dog is the key element in making the dog want the toy. You play with it and keep it out of his reach. Show great interest and excitement in playing with it by yourself, or with another dog or person.

When your dog shows interest, tease him with it but don't let him get it. This is the one time teasing the dog is okay – using it to build drive. The more you keep the toy away from him, the more it becomes a treasured prize. Build his desire for the toy, or food tube, or whatever you use, before letting him actually chase it.

One concept is primary with the toys – they all come from you. The dogs don't own the toys. They didn't pay for them. They don't get to keep them. They don't get to chew them up. And they sure don't get to make up the rules of the game.

To avoid the game of keep-away, a favorite among young puppies, always use two toys. This helps assure that the handler remains at the center of the game. This type of constructive play was introduced in the previous book, *Schutzhund Obedience: Training in Drive* (listed in the Recommended Resources in the back of this book).

Teaching your dog to play games by your rules may take a little extra time. But it is one of the most valuable things you can do for your dog – not only for training purposes, but to enhance his life and your relationship. Good games enable you to enjoy your time together even more. Playing together just simply makes life more fun!

Praise

Some dogs prefer praise to eating or playing. Teach them how to play properly, so you can use all the different reinforcers for training. But remember that this dog wants your approval most of all.

How many ways are there to praise your dog? Many folks get stuck in "Good Dog" as praise. How boring for your dog, and how dull.

Your dog should wag his tail wildly when you praise him. Praise should be one of your most powerful reinforcers. It will probably be the one you come to rely upon most.

Get a repertoire. Tone of voice is critical here, so make praise words sound exciting. Scientifically, the word "Yes" appears to have special reinforcement properties all its own. Although I can't say exactly how the scientists determined this, I can tell you that it is one word I save to reward outstanding performances. "Yes" generates a lot of excitement in me, and it seems to spark that same reaction in my dogs.

But you should have different kinds of praise to use as reinforcement. Phrases such as "Excellent Job!," "Wow!," "Good for You," "What a Dog!," "Thank You," "Great Job," "Good Behavior," "You Got It!," "Good Decision," "I Like That!," "Hurray!" and "Bravo!" give you a number of ways to offer reinforcement for various levels of achievement. Once you pair these reinforcers with a primary, as we'll explain in the next chapter, you're on your way to building a reliable repertory of verbal reinforcers.

From the visionary Max von Stephanitz comes this advice: "A dog, especially a young dog, can never be praised too much. Praise strengthens his confidence in his master, and in himself."

Petting

Petting falls into this same category as praise. Some dogs would rather be petted than eat or play.

Just how many ways are there to pet your dog? To calm him down, stroke him smoothly down his shoulders. To excite him, use pops on his ribs with a cupped hand. Scratch behind his ears. Rub his belly. Tickle him under the chin. Stroke his ears. Then there's the ultimate for some dogs – a good butt scratch. Get to know which kind of petting your dog likes. Some are more appropriate in certain circumstances for training purposes.

You can even let your dog choose sometimes. When I heard about the trainers letting the dolphins pick which fish they wanted as a reward, I decided to try it. So I taught dear Charra to choose how she wants to be petted. When she works well, I hold out my hand. On cue, she puts the part of her body that she wants petted or scratched against my hand. She loves it.

Back in 1925, von Stephanitz emphasized "that every lesson must conclude with a petting to keep alive in the dog the joy in his work."

So now you're starting to get the idea of just how many reinforcers there really are. In addition to food, we can offer our dogs a banquet of other positive reinforcers. And we're just beginning to discover all of them.

Eye Contact

One could argue that eye contact should be under Primary Reinforcers for dogs. But to avoid having to defend that decision, we'll leave it here.

Eye contact is an important aspect of communication for all dogs. In a wild pack, eye contact and body posture rule social interaction. Eye contact practically governs every encounter within a wild dog pack, since dogs are less violent and demonstrative than wolves in their greeting procedures and social interactions.

Eye contact may very well be the most important line of communication you have with your dog during training. Think for a moment how disconcerting it would be to carry on a conversation, or have a business meeting, with someone who never made eye contact with you. Then you begin to realize how important a tool it is for communication.

The dog's eyes reflect his thoughts and attitude – mischievous, driving, questioning, etc. Learn to read your dog's eyes. He knows how to read yours. The eyes may or may not be "the windows to the soul," but they are clear indicators of what's on your dog's mind.

There are different kinds of eye contact. Hard eye contact is driving and can be aggressive. Soft eye contact is inviting and reassuring and often accompanied by a smile on our part. A dog's questioning eye contact, with a cocked head and raised eyebrows, conveys a different message. Trust me, dogs already know all about the subtle meanings of eye contact.

Obviously, to begin training we need attention from the dog. And what is attention? Eye contact. When we reward our dog's attention by returning eye contact, we are on our way to establishing that direct line of communication that we need for training. Facial expression is very important to dogs too. So don't forget to smile!

Energy

Dogs are masters at reading emotional energy. They sense it before we do, and we can't fool them. Have you ever tried to act happy around a dog when you're really angry or depressed or worried? Ever notice how the dog knows?

The energy you express is extremely important to your dog. He cares. So when you are really pleased with him – show it. He'll know it.

When your dog stares at you expectantly, tell him what a good job he did that day on something, or just how terrific he is. He might not understand all the words, but that pure positive emotional energy flowing to him is something he understands completely. It will energize him.

This same energy is used easily in training. When we radiate that sincere emotional energy and tell them what a good job they are doing, the dogs sense it immediately. They recognize excited energy, and they know disappointed energy too. If something goes wrong, we need only withdraw that affirming energy, and the dogs pick up on it right away. If we've stuck to our positive training, our dogs try even harder to get the behavior right to start that flow of positive energy again.

Training is more productive and rewarding if you pay attention to the exchange of energy between you and your dog. They are as open to energy as they are to smells and sounds. They tend to seek out reinforcing energy and respond positively.

Allow your dog to return this energy and then respond accordingly. Keep the flow going. It's always a two-way exchange between you and your dog.

One word of caution though. If you are going to use emotional energy as a reinforcer, be sure you can control your own emotions. Dogs become acutely sensitive to emotional energy.

If you lose your composure at a critical time in training, it can stress a dog and affect his behavior. Anger has no place in training. As von Stephanitz puts it, "The trainer must first learn self-control before he can control the dog." Horse trainer Barbier, agrees. "If you lose your temper, you lose. Period."

Body Posture

Dogs can be as sensitive to body posture as they are to emotional energy. Again, within a dog pack, body posture is a vital communication tool.

Your body posture can easily and quickly become reinforcing to your dog. If you consistently respond to certain behaviors with your posture, especially if you combine that with other positive reinforcers, your dog knows he is right.

Dogs tune in so well to body posture that it becomes our responsibility to do our part correctly and consistently. Dogs read subtle body cues even when we are not aware of them. And dogs always choose body movement over words.

So if your words say one thing, but your body says another, he believes your body every time. Anyone who has ever tried to direct a dog around an agility course has found this out the hard way.

Just as with emotional energy, if you're going to use body posture for reinforcement (or as a cue), be sure you can control what you do and how you move, consistently and correctly. Be aware of yourself and of your dog's response.

Breathing

Breathing is the last piece of the puzzle for perfect communication with your dog. Responding to breathing patterns is part of your dog's predatory heritage. In the wild, identifying vulnerable prey is often done through their breathing. Sick, injured, stressed or dying animals breathe differently, and predators recognize it instinctively.

Dogs innately read body posture and emotional energy. They read them first and they read them perfectly. Couple these with eye contact and breathing and you have powerful connectors.

When a new dog comes into view, your dog can tell just about everything he needs to know. How? He reads it through body posture, emotional energy, eye contact and breathing. By the way, that's also how your dog knows pretty much everything about you, including exactly how you're feeling at any given second.

Dogs are so tuned in to breathing. Many folks tell me that their dog always comes over to them when they are upset and crying. Naturally. Crying changes the breathing pattern significantly. The person is gasping for air. The body posture is different. The facial expression is different, and the emotional energy sure has changed. The dog naturally comes over to find out what is wrong.

That is also why so many dogs perform well at home, but are so different on trial day. Stress changes breathing. When the owner gets nervous in the ring, breathing becomes rapid and shallow. Just when the dog needs him most, the owner seems to have undergone a total transformation.

He is hardly breathing. His body posture is different. He tugs at his jacket or twitches his fingers. His eyes are wide and staring, not connecting with anything. And the emotional energy sure is different!

The poor dog is now trying to work with a handler who, from the dog's point of view, has just checked out. It's no wonder the trial performance bears no resemblance to last week's perfect training session. To the dog, the handler is totally different.

Then someone has the nerve to blame the dog for a poor routine. It's always a wonder to me that some dogs hang in there at all!

Body movement, eye contact, breathing rhythms and emotional energy are all so important to your dog. We're convinced that someone could teach a dog the entire Novice obedience routine using only eye contact, body language and breathing as cues.

Recognizing how important these are helps us find new ways to use them as reinforcers for training. Vino loves it when I pant at him. He gets really excited. Another dog we help train responds joyously to her owner's laughter. Clapping, smiling, making silly noises, hopping, skipping – all these can become very reassuring and reinforcing to your dog, especially when coupled with positive emotional energy.

Even if you never want to show your dog in competition, pay close attention to your body posture, your breathing, how and when you make eye contact, and your emotional energy in response to your dog's behavior. It makes training simpler for your dog to understand and it enhances communication.

So how many reinforcers have we named by now anyway? Still stuck on food? Try jumping up and down or rolling around on the ground with him. Try making a kissing sound or popping your lips. Try whistling or humming.

Sing him a silly song. Invite him to jump up on you. Try all sorts of things. See if your dog likes them. Remember, it's only positive reinforcement if your dog likes it.

Breed Specific Drives

Some retrievers prefer to have a bird in their mouth than food in their stomachs. Some pointers would rather hunt than eat. Some sheepdogs would drop from exhaustion before they would stop herding of their own volition. And some of the guarding breeds would rather do protection work than anything else.

All these types of overwhelming desires can obviously be used very effectively as positive reinforcement for training through the Premack Principle. When the dog understands that access to these behaviors is granted by you, in return for what you want him to do, he becomes willing and eager to comply.

If your dog likes it, figure out how to use it as a reinforcer.

VARY THE REINFORCERS !

The Reinforcers

PRIMARY

Food
Water
Sleep
Social Interaction
Sex
Exercise
Safety

SECONDARY

Toys
Praise
Petting
Eye Contact
Energy
Body Posture
Breathing
Breed Specific Drives

Premack Access to Above When Possible

6 The Applications

" Dogs learn by association."
– Turid Rugaas

Now that we know the basic principles of positive training, and we realize just how many different reinforcers there are, it's time to apply this to effective dog training.

Pairing Reinforcers

Pairing reinforcers happens when you continually use two reinforcers together so they become "paired" in the dog's mind. The simplest example is if every time you give the dog a piece of food, you say "Good Dog."

Soon, the dog associates food with praise, and then expects food whenever you praise him. In his mind, the two become linked. We know trainers who have done this so well that their dogs lick their lips and start to salivate whenever they hear praise! Nothing new. Pavlov showed us that so many years ago.

That's exactly what we are trying to teach our dogs. We want to build a belief system here. We want to build in that expectation of reward through association.

For companion: For a companion dog, pairing praise with food is the most important association you can make. That way, when you don't offer food, just a sincere "Good Dog, That's It" becomes a meaningful reinforcer for your dog. Your words have been made more powerful by pairing with food.

57

For obedience: If you aspire to competition obedience, then you want to pair a reinforcer that you can take in the ring with one you can't. This works just like praise with food, but in much more subtle ways.

For example, to get full attention at the start of an exercise, when your dog sits straight and looks into your eyes in training, pair a deep breath with producing a toy. Then a deep breath in the ring before you start will not only relax you, it makes your dog super intense. To keep attention on the slow pace, pair opening up your shoulders as you start to slow down with a food jackpot (lots of small treats in quick succession).

To encourage a dog to hurry up on the outside circle of a figure eight, pair slightly heavier breathing (ours) and looking to the right with producing a toy in the right hand. We have seen some dramatic results with this one working in the ring, especially for the group in Schutzhund.

For agility: If you want your dog to fly through the tunnel at warp speed and then look to you, pair a noise with a toy. Every time you send the dog into a tunnel in training, associate an excited sound (like "Woo-woo-woo") with throwing a favorite toy the moment he shoots out the end.

Then teach him to find you, as soon as he exits, and come to you to play. Next, have him come to you and take a directional command to get the toy, all paired with an exciting sound while he's in the tunnel.

On course in a trial, when your dog hears that sound, he'll turn on the afterburners in the tunnel and then look for you the moment he emerges. You've paired reinforcers – one you can take into the ring, with one you can't.

After the trial, you must return to throwing the toy sometimes when you make that noise. This keeps the paired association strong in the dog's mind.

We want to keep the dogs believing. That's how to keep them working hard to get it right – get them to *believe* they might be rewarded.

In Competition

By the way, for anyone still skeptical (like I was) about whether you can really succeed in competition on a purely positive program, we want to reassure you here that it can be done. It has succeeded beyond our wildest dreams.

This is not a fragile program that holds together only if everything goes perfectly. Ron Harris trained his wonderful German Shepherd, Lars, to fine scores in SchH. I (97-90-96) without ever giving the dog a correction. For that success, they traveled all the way to Germany. Many things went wrong – really wrong – both at home and in Germany. (We'll get to that story later.)

But honestly, I was amazed to watch the video of this young dog (21 months) just hang in there and keep on offering the right behaviors in hopes of getting rewarded. The dog's belief system was strong. And the relationship had been made super solid because of the purely positive training (reinforcement history).

Lest anyone tell you that positive training takes a lot longer, I also want to assure you that, in most cases, this simply isn't true. I had the privilege of coaching Ron and Lars, and in more than 15 years of preparing dogs for Schutzhund trials, I have never known a dog to go for his first title with fewer hours of training time under his belt than Lars.

The reason it seems to take longer is that, in the initial stages, we work on the dog's agenda, not ours. So the first few steps require some patient waiting. This learning to wait (for us) can be the hardest part of the program.

But once the dog grasps the concept, he works harder, longer, and with a better attitude and greater reliability than in any other training program I've ever seen. Once they believe, the dogs just keep trying harder.

If you're wondering whether it can work for formal obedience competition, just look at Patty Ruzzo's record with Luca, her Champion / Obedience Trial Champion Belgian Tervuren, who has also won at the Gaines Regional. Better yet, watch this team perform on one of her videotapes (see Recommended Resources). This partnership is pure poetry-in-motion. The brilliant performances reflect their relationship and personify the peak of purely positive training.

So many positive reinforcers can be taken into the ring. By the time you get there, your very presence and relationship with your dog, indeed even the work itself, have become intrinsically reinforcing for him. He loves to work and he loves to work with you.

Your eye contact has become a connecting beam of light that neither one of you wants to break. You smile at your dog and he wags his tail and grins back. You perform in happy harmony while the two of you show what a training relationship is all about.

Add this to the paired reinforcers that you bring into the ring, and you are on your way to certain success.

Clicker

One conditioned reinforcer that illustrates pairing is the clicker. This is a small plastic device with a piece of metal inside which, when pressed, emits a sharp click. This sound has no appeal of its own, and so it must be paired with something important to the dog.

The program is called "Click and Treat" because the sound of the clicker must be paired with food to make it meaningful to the dog. The association must be established.

At first, the click means come to me and get food. This is expanded into the dog's understanding that the click means he is performing the behavior correctly at that moment and is on the right track for reinforcement.

The clicker is an effective tool for helping the dog (and the handler) mark the precise *moment* when the dog's behavior is correct. Used properly, it helps clarify the situation for the dog. With practice, the handlers also get much better at observing the dog's behavior and reinforcing at the right moment. It helps them watch for the dog to do something right.

Any paired reinforcer is like a battery that needs charging. Every time you use the clicker, you discharge the battery, as Pamela Reid explains in *Excelerated Learning* (Recommended Resources).

So any reinforcers that you are pairing for the show ring need to be paired frequently in training so that one maintains its association with the other. You can't just pair them in the beginning and leave them alone, or the battery goes dead.

In training, the one you plan to use in the ring must be continually associated with the one you will leave behind. And between shows, return to pairing these reinforcers to recharge the battery and keep the association strong.

Timing

As in any training program, timing is extremely important. The delivery of positive reinforcement must come as close to the desired behavior as possible for your dog to learn which behavior leads to reward.

Any time you can offer reinforcement *while* the dog is performing the desired behavior puts you way ahead of the game. When you can't do that, reinforcement within a few seconds is absolutely necessary for learning to occur.

Scientists hold that anything more than three seconds away from the behavior probably does not promote learning. Aim to keep the reinforcement aligned with the behavior as closely as possible. That's the easiest way to help the dog learn the fastest.

With reinforcement, always remember that timing is everything! On the other hand, if you miss the moment and reinforce at the wrong time, there's no damage done.

Maybe it takes a little longer for your dog to learn, but the trust between you has not been broken. You haven't hurt him. That precious relationship isn't damaged. He still hangs in there with you and keeps on trying. Besides, you'll get it right next time!

Reinforcement Ends Behavior

One important rule to remember is that reinforcement ends behavior. So if you want the behavior to continue, in the beginning you have to cue that behavior again.

This means that when teaching the dog to sit, at first, when you praise and feed, he tends to get up. He got his reward and, for him, the game's over. This isn't always the case, but it happens enough that it helps to understand why.

There are simple solutions, as you'll see when we get into the actual training. Cue the behavior again right after reinforcement – just to remind him what he was doing. Or use reinforcement in continuum, giving the dog a number of tiny treats in succession.

This helps prevent post-reinforcement pause. That's the scientific term for when the animal stops offering the behavior for a short time right after reinforcement.

Just recognize that this pause might occur and get proactive. Vary how the reinforcement is offered, or add another cue during or immediately after reinforcing, or end the exercise with release, or cue another behavior right away.

This pause is really no big deal to us though. We know what's causing it and we know how to avoid it or fix it. In everyday training, usually we don't care that reinforcement ends the behavior, especially if the dog was successful.

In competition, it isn't a factor because we won't be feeding the dog in the ring. There, we'll wait for the end of the exercise to reinforce (with praise and petting and energy). By that time, the dog fully understands to continue the behavior in hopes of terminal reward.

In agility though, being aware of this rule can make a major difference. When a handler praises the dog for lying down on the table, and the dog gets up, it can be because, to the dog, the reinforcement ended the behavior. Or when a dog is doing the weave poles well and the handler praises excitedly with "Good!" right before the last pole, and the dog pops out early, usually it's for the same reason.

In training, we take special care to be sure the dog understands that praise is not release. We want to be able to praise our dogs during the exercise. Only a specific release marks the end of the behavior. We work to teach the dog this, but it helps if we never forget that reinforcement ends behavior. It's one of the laws of learning.

As we progress to less predictable reinforcement, frustration motivates the dog to try harder. (This is the same principle that makes slot machines seem fun to play.)

In time, the dog learns to continue certain behaviors even after he receives his reward. Once he has a true belief system that more reinforcement is coming, he gets more and more intense as you get more unpredictable with rewards.

Leslie Nelson says that the best trainers are "quick, generous, variable and unpredictable." Being variable and unpredictable are certainly the hardest. We'll just keep reminding you as we get into the training chapters and, like the dog, we expect you'll get better as you go along.

Bridging

In some cases, we want to let the dog know he's doing the behavior correctly, but we also want him to continue with the exercise. This is called bridging.

For example, in teaching the dog to come when called, we want to let the dog know he's right the moment he starts to moves toward us. So we use praise to reinforce that very first movement toward us. That's a bridge. The dog then continues coming toward us, and we offer terminal reward when he completes the exercise and arrives close to us.

When you want to reinforce a specific behavior at the very moment it is correct, it helps to think of it in terms of a flashbulb going off at that particular second, capturing the moment in time. I call this the "Kodak moment."

Used correctly, the clicker can be a useful tool for bridging. The sound is very quick, so it identifies a specific second, that "Kodak moment" when the behavior is just what we want. The clicker has no emotional energy of its own, like praise does, so it does not tend to distract the dog from the exercise. The clicker is also never dependent on any body language, so the dog does not have to look at you. He can continue to concentrate on the job at hand.

Let's say you are teaching the dog to go over a series of jumps without touching them. Using the clicker at the very moment the dog's back feet clear the jump without touching would be reinforcing that "Kodak moment," when he has done it just right. Then he can continue jumping. This is an effective bridge.

Or, for teaching the weave poles in agility, the dog must enter on the right side of the first pole. Just at that "Kodak moment" – when the dog's nose clears the first pole on the correct side – the clicker (or a "Yes") can be the bridge to reinforce perfect performance in that moment. Then the dog can continue through the weave poles.

When training with the clicker, many find that it works best when used for only a few specific exercises. It seems to be more meaningful to the dog when not overused.

It also helps to pair the clicker with praise as well as with food. That way, when you don't have your clicker, or you want to wean from using it, your dog easily converts to "Yes" as a bridge instead of the clicker.

Some people prefer to keep using the clicker because it dissociates the human response from the behavior. We prefer to make that human response a major part of our training, so we begin right away to associate the clicker with the word "Yes."

Another good example of bridging is when teaching a dog to retrieve. The moment the dog picks up the object and turns toward you, praise or click (or both) to let the dog know he's done just the right thing. Then he continues back to you to deliver the prize and get his terminal reward.

Bridging is specifically meant to be reinforcement that doesn't end the behavior chain. But don't be surprised if this does happen along the way. For example, the handler bridges the retrieve at the moment of pickup and the dog happily spits out the dumbbell and flies back to the handler. For the dog, reinforcement ended behavior.

The dog just doesn't understand the full behavior chain yet. With more training, and more exposure to the concept of the bridge, he'll get it. But now you know why the dog might do that. It's not disobedience – it's obedience to the laws of learning.

Stimulus Control

Here's the scientific jargon again. Putting a behavior under stimulus control simply means that the dog responds to a specific cue with the corresponding behavior.

Really, that is all training is – putting behaviors under stimulus control. To teach this properly though, paying attention to the cues we give is crucial. The cue we want the dog to follow must be the same every time.

If you use a body signal and a word, the dog tunes in to the body signal every time. That's more natural for him. Eventually you have to fade the body movement if you want the dog to respond to the word alone.

A classic example is when the handler wants the dog to sit straight at the left side to prepare for heeling. The handler tells the dog to sit and, at the same time, drops his left shoulder back and turns his head to look at the dog to be sure he sits straight. He does.

The next time the handler tells the dog to sit and doesn't turn his head or drop his shoulder. The dog almost always sits crooked, looking up at the handler expectantly for approval. The dog has not learned to line up a straight sit without the handler's head and shoulder movements as a cue. In fact, all that body help has prevented the dog from learning how to sit properly when the handler's shoulders are square.

The dog needs to understand that each behavior has a cue. In the beginning, what delights handlers most about this positive training, is that the dog begins to offer a variety of behaviors in hopes of reward. As we mentioned, the scientists call this spontaneous rehearsal.

We call it the Which-One-Will-Work-This-Time Game, since the dog offers a variety of behaviors just trying to get what he wants from the handler. As appealing as this might be, reinforcing this behavior does not help the dog to learn. In fact, it diminishes the importance of the cue in the dog's mind.

When this spontaneous rehearsal happens, (and it will if the handler is reinforcing properly), use this opportunity to give the dog a specific cue for a behavior he is learning or already knows. If the dog offers the correct response to the cue, reinforce. Should the dog offer the wrong behavior, turn away and ignore him.

When the dog solicits attention again, by all means give him another chance by giving him another cue. Be sure to put the behaviors you want on cue as early as possible in the learning curve. Without consistent cues, you'll get lots of behaviors, but no learning.

The poor dog will be cueless – not clueless!

This would be like having a computer program where the functions appear at random – pretty useless. A program is only useful when certain functions appear only as the result of specific keystrokes. It's the same with dog training. Behaviors not on cue (under stimulus control) are useless.

Be crisp and clear and consistent in your cues. Always get them in. They are a major part of the all-important ABCs.

Thresholds

Training the dog to continue a behavior for a certain period of time without reinforcement is called increasing the threshold. This is extremely important in training the stays. Just because the dog will lie down for several seconds, doesn't mean he will remain there for three minutes.

Building thresholds is one of the most neglected areas of training. Extending this time needs to be done slowly and somewhat exponentially. We'll explain this in more detail when training stays.

But right from the start we suggest that you not expect too much, too soon. Pushing dogs past their current, comfortable threshold produces confusion and is not fair training. Always set up for success.

Place Conditioning

One of the easiest ways to train a dog is to teach him to perform a certain behavior in a certain place. Place association is simple for a dog to understand.

In the kitchen, we get fed. In the park, we play. At obedience class, we behave. In the crate, we lie quietly. At grandma's house, we drool and beg for food.

Dogs have great memories for what happens in certain places. Take the dog back to a field where he chased a squirrel weeks ago and he almost always remembers exactly where that squirrel went. This is another remnant of his predatory heritage, when having such a good memory for places served him well.

We can use place conditioning (also called place association) to great advantage as an Antecedent in teaching certain types of Behavior. On the other hand, the dog comes to associate that Behavior with only that place. The place becomes part of the Antecedent, or cue.

If you want your dog to perform a behavior reliably on cue, not just in one place, then move the location as soon as the dog starts to understand even the beginnings of that behavior. Shifting context early means the dog won't get the behavior right so often so soon, but it assures that the behavior is under stimulus control and not dependent on place conditioning.

Shifting context early doesn't make you look like such a great trainer in the beginning. But in the long run, the dog learns the cue faster, the behavior is under better stimulus control and the dog's performance becomes more reliable.

Opposition Reflex

If you've ever seen a little puppy the first time on a leash, you've seen opposition reflex in action. As soon as the owner puts any tension on the leash, the puppy plants all four feet and pulls in the opposite direction with all the energy his little body can muster. Opposition reflex is a strong, natural component of a dog's physiology.

They even have specific muscle reflexes to prevent them from falling over in case what they are pulling against gives way. Humans, on the other hand, tend to fall backward when the other end of the tug-of-war rope is released.

All those trainers pushing down on the dogs' butts to get them to sit are initiating opposition reflex. Not only that, but pushing down on a young dog's rear end, when his ligaments and tendons are still developing, can cause physical damage.

When using opposition reflex in training, be sure to use this powerful reflex in your favor. Positive training is such a hands-off, voluntary cooperation program that physical opposition reflex plays very little part in it. When we do use it, however, we use it to our advantage instead of fighting against it. You'll discover how in the training chapters.

Just a quick word about emotional opposition reflex. Be aware of it. It's a reality – with dogs, just as with people. The more attention and energy and emotion handlers put into getting the dog to stop doing something, like eating horse manure, the more determined he becomes to do it.

Dogs are dogs. They have their own ideas about gourmet tastes and perfume smells – what's appealing and what's disgusting. Get proactive and prevent the unwanted behavior. Distract him, or offer him something better. Give him something else to do, or just let him check it out if it's not poisonous or harmful.

Be careful to avoid putting all your attention and energy on something that develops the same emotional opposition reflex we often see in the toddler. He's always the most determined to investigate whatever "forbidden fruit" he's been told is off limits. It's only natural.

The Applications

Pair Reinforcers.

Consider the Clicker.

Perfect Timing.

Remember Reinforcement Ends Behavior.

Bridge Effectively.

Put Behaviors Under Stimulus Control.

Lengthen Thresholds Gradually.

Understand Place Association.

Use Opposition Reflex to Advantage.

Recognize Self-Reinforcing Behaviors.

ALWAYS CONSIDER TEMPERAMENT.

7 The Words

" Words! Words! Words!
I'm so sick of words.
I get words all day through,
first from him now from you.
Is that all you blighters can do? "
— Eliza Doolittle
(or a confused dog in training)

Let's face it. What we all really want is a remote-controlled dog. Except instead of having a remote control device like for the TV, we want to use words.

The problem is that the part of a dog's brain devoted to processing words is probably about five cells big, and that may be an exaggeration. Those cells might have expanded a bit over thousands of years of domestication, but probably not by much.

Nowhere in a dog's natural life are words important. Body posture and eye contact are enormously significant. Emotional energy and breathing also play a major role in dog communication, as we've already discussed. But words?

Right from the beginning, if we want words to become important to our dogs, we must first teach them this concept. If you're thinking it would be easier to train your dog completely with hand signals, you're right. Body movement means much more to a dog than words. They naturally deal in body cues, but never with words.

Patty uses a great expression, "Put a word on it." Every behavior your dog exhibits that you want to continue, or that you eventually want to put on cue, put a word on it.

But first we must teach the dog what the word means by associating it with the corresponding behavior. Only then can we use the word as a cue.

The old rule was to say the word once and then make the dog do it. That hardly gave the poor dog any chance to learn the word. It just plain wasn't fair to the dog!

A lot of repetition is needed for the dog to learn a word cue. When teaching a child to read, think of how many times we point to the picture of the dog and say "dog," before the child gets it right consistently. And kids are at least as smart as dogs. Right?

Each word should have a specific meaning. Use the same word consistently for the same behavior. So if "Down" means to lie down, it should not also mean to stop jumping up or to get off the sofa.

We must realize that often it takes the dog longer to learn the word for a behavior than it takes for him to learn the behavior itself. The word must be repeated over and over, in conjunction with the corresponding behavior, before the dog truly understands that word as the cue for that behavior.

Getting behavior under stimulus control is all about word association. And training is all about getting behavior under stimulus control.

The First Time

Eventually, we want the dog to respond to a cue the first time. He should come when called the first time, not the second or third. But it takes a number of repetitions of the word before the dog can understand its meaning and which behavior is required.

Often, the failure in training is that the handler simply has not repeated the word enough times in association with the corresponding behavior. The dog doesn't yet understand what that word means in every situation.

A typical training scenario goes like this. The dog offers the desired behavior on cue a couple of times because all the antecedents are the same. He knows the behavior, but he hasn't fully learned the word as a cue yet.

Then one day, the dog gets punished for not obeying. Not only does confusion and resistance set in, but the dog perceives the trainer as an unfair pack leader. The poor dog doesn't have a clue why he was punished. He's still *cueless*. But he sure knows it has something to do with the handler, who keeps insisting that the dog knows what to do because he did it yesterday.

Trust breaks down. The dog stops offering behaviors because he might be wrong and get punished. He becomes inhibited and stressed. This is what we mean when we say the dog is "blocked." He can't think or react because he is too worried about being wrong.

Remember, there are No Wrong Dogs. If the dog doesn't do something right, then in some way we have failed to teach it properly. We must assume that responsibility.

So until the dog demonstrates that he understands the word, over time and in a variety of different situations, we should not assume that he does. When we shift context, we usually see the dog struggle to offer the right response. He's still thinking and trying, so how can he be wrong?

Teaching vs. Learning

Sometimes, the behavior the handler associates with a word is not the behavior the dog actually learns. What the handler thinks he is teaching is not what the dog is learning.

For example, in the retrieve exercise for formal obedience, the dog sits and waits while the handler throws a dumbbell. The handler says, "Fetch" (no body cues allowed), and the dog goes out and gets the dumbbell and presents it to the handler with a sit in front.

The handler thinks he has taught the dog to pick up the dumbbell on the word "Fetch." But with most dogs, if the handler throws the dumbbell behind him instead of in front, the dog runs out to where he expects the dumbbell to be (in front), even though the dog saw the handler throw it behind his back. Very few dogs do a correct retrieve in this scenario unless this variation has been added to their understanding of the word "Fetch."

What the dog learned is not what the handler thought he taught. He thought he taught that "Fetch" means to find the dumbbell, pick it up and bring it back. But the dog only learned to run in one direction to a certain place. When the dog shows you this, it is certainly not the dog's fault. The teaching just needs to be clearer and more complete.

Eight out of 10

Scientists acknowledge that a behavior is learned when the animal responds correctly to the cue 8 out of 10 times, in 10 sets of 10. Then they move on to the next step.

Wait a minute! That means two of the repetitions might be wrong! Exactly. Even the scientist leaves room for forgetting, or being distracted, or missing a cue, or other variables. The scientist doesn't run for the throw chain or the prong collar. And neither should we.

If your dog is offering the right behavior, on cue, 8 out of 10 times, over several training sessions, then you can move on to the next approximation, or consider that the dog has learned that cue for now. In training however, we rarely repeat an exercise 10 times in a row. Most of our dogs are way too bright and creative. They'd get too bored.

But now you know how science defines learning, in case you were interested. If your dog is getting it right 80% of the time, I guess that means you can be scientifically happy, or maybe it means you can be 80% happy.

Tone of Voice

Along with wanting the dog to respond the *first* time, we also want him to respond to normal tones of voice. Considering that the dog's hearing is so much more acute than ours, it doesn't make any sense to shout.

As with most conversation, you get more attention with a whisper than a shout. Better a soft, inviting tone than a harsh drill sergeant barking out commands.

To the dog, the *tone* of voice is much more important than the actual words. Dogs are tremendously sensitive to pitch. That's how they can distinguish the sound of your car from all others.

If the handler teaches the dog a cue in a certain tone of voice, and then changes it one day (like when he's nervous in a trial), he probably won't get the response he expects. The dog can learn the word in different tones, but the cue has to be taught that way, using various tones as a shift in context.

Your voice is most effective when used sincerely, softly and sparingly. Handlers who chatter at their dogs soon get tuned out. So no babytalk, no chatter and no yelling – ever. Save your raised voice for a real emergency.

Make your words meaningful. Keep the tone the same. Make your cues consistent. Make the conversation count.

How Many?

If dogs only have a few brain cells for words, then how many words can they really learn? The answer is unknown. As far as we've seen, there may not be any limit. We've never seen a dog "hit the wall," so to speak, and run out of disk space for words.

Many dogs respond reliably to an impressive number of words and phrases. However, the more words the dog knows, the greater the risk for confusion. All the other antecedents come in to play here.

For example, if the dog knows to "Leave" something alone that he is investigating, and he also knows "Weave" for the weave poles in agility, the possibility for confusion exists. The words sound so much alike.

But because the dog has never been told to "Leave" the weave poles, and has always been highly and enthusiastically rewarded for completing (or even attempting) them, the poles themselves become an antecedent for "Weave." The dog can tell the difference because the situations are so different.

But if my weave pole word is "Weave," then I would certainly avoid using "Leave" as a cue not to take that agility obstacle. I would choose another word that clearly sounds different to the dog.

Word vs. Signal

For a dog who needs to know lots of behaviors on cue, it is easier for the dog to learn signals than words. Such is the case with Hollywood dogs.

These wonderfully trained dogs learn lots of words. But the trainers also use hand signals and body cues to elicit different behaviors from these highly responsive dogs. Some cues are words and signals together, to make each cue clearer and more specific for the dog.

Speaking of words and signals, if a whisper requires better attention, then so does a small signal. Dogs see movement much better than shapes.

If you're teaching a signal for a cue, make the signal small, but with a clear movement. The signal can always be exaggerated in a distracting situation, but teach the dog to pay attention to a signal that is as small as possible.

Keep in mind that dolphins distinguish between signals with the position of just one or two fingers from a trainer on shore. And our dogs aren't even under water.

So although there might not be a specific limit to the word cues a dog can learn, there are ways to vary the cues and combinations so the dog can differentiate between them more easily.

Getting the Concept

Yes, you can teach an old dog new tricks. But it's easier if the dog already knew some old tricks. Let us explain.

The most important part of teaching your dog words is teaching him the concept that words mean something. Look at how long it takes a human baby to understand words. But once they start talking, and get those wonderful positive responses, the words come faster and faster. They've got the concept.

At first, words mean nothing to a dog. They respond to sound, emotional energy, tone of voice, eye contact, body language, breathing and all those other things so important in their natural world.

When we start training, our first job is to teach the concept that our words have meaning. Once the dog grasps that concept, he starts to pay attention, listening for the words he knows. Now he wants to learn. That makes new words easy to teach.

So if an old dog already knows about words, teaching new ones is easy. But teaching the concept of learning words to an older dog would be more difficult. Nothing in his life experience so far has taught him that words are meaningful.

Take the time to teach the concept. Build a solid foundation on a few words. Then future training is easier.

Phonetics

Understanding subtle differences in word sounds is challenging for a dog. He simply did not arrive with any phonetic ability whatsoever.

As with the words "Leave" and "Weave," when there is a drastic difference in the other antecedents, the dog rarely gets confused. But teaching him to distinguish between "Sit" and "Stand," in the same setting, can get tricky. We've probably seen more confusion between these two words than any others in training.

Why? Think about it. Both words start with the same letter. Both are one syllable long so they sound the same. If they are spoken in a similar tone of voice, it becomes difficult for the dog to distinguish between them. Phonetics is just not a natural part of the dog's repertoire.

The words must have an individual sound for the dog. So if you give the "Sit" cue with rising inflection in your voice, and begin it with a "Zzz" sound, it is more distinct.

If you say "Stand" beginning with a "Shhh" sound, and keep your voice low and steady, it sounds less like "Sit" to the dog. The more unique the word sounds to the dog, the easier it is for him to recognize it reliably.

Remember how sensitive the dog is to pitch and tone. Use that to your advantage when teaching word cues that the dog needs to identify in similar situations, such as in the moving sit and stand exercises in Schutzhund.

Think about how the words sound to your dog when choosing cues. Confusion between words doesn't merit punishment, just clearer teaching to help the dog understand better. For the dog to learn the differences between words takes time, repetition and clear cues.

It's unlikely that a dog would make an intentional mistake here. He knows he gets positive reinforcement for the right decision. So he chooses to stand when he knows it's the cue for sit? Why would he? So he can fail to get rewarded? I don't think so. In positive training, the dogs always give their best and try their hardest.

Word Association

The most important aspect of teaching words to your dog is that the word gets associated with the behavior it is meant to cue. Proper word association is vital to the learning process. It is absolutely necessary for putting the behavior under stimulus control.

Exactly when to add the word to a behavior is a topic of some debate among trainers. We want to start saying the word as soon as possible, so the dog can start making the right association. But be sure to say the word only when the dog is doing precisely what you want that word to mean.

So while the dog is sitting properly, keep repeating the word "Sit" to give him the opportunity to make the proper association. The more times he hears the word, the faster he can learn it. While the dog is lying down, repeat "Down" over and over, so he comes to associate that word with that behavior.

Every time he makes eye contact, put a word on that behavior (like "Watch"), and repeat it again and again while he is looking at you, thereby giving him time to make the proper word association. This sounds so easy, but it is radically different from previous training methods.

This becomes even more critical if you want to teach a behavior that you cannot manipulate, such as barking on cue. Yelling "Speak! Speak! Speak!" at the dog for hours won't help him figure it out. But if every time he barks, for any reason, he hears "Speak! Good Dog! Speak!" he just might start to make the association.

Ever see this scenario? The family dog rushes to greet the visitors and, as usual, jumps up. While he is jumping, the owner screams "Off! Off!," (or worse, "Down! Down!"). Rarely does the dog respond. He has heard this word over and over while jumping up on someone. The word has become associated with jumping up.

Finally, the dog exhausts his greeting behavior or he gets punished. His four feet are back on the floor. This desirable behavior has no word – no cue.

Now the dog is doing what is wanted, but he gets nothing – no attention and no reinforcement. Silence reigns. The dog is ignored because his behavior is no longer unacceptable – until the next time.

So be careful not to associate the word with the wrong behavior. If the young dog is offering a lopsided puppy sit, and you eventually want to compete in obedience, wait until he offers a tight, tucked sit before putting that word on it.

Word associations work best if they are made *while* the dog is displaying the behavior with which we want him to associate the word. We need to focus on the desirable behavior and put a word on that. That's being proactive.

Too often folks wait for the dog to exhibit unwanted behavior, and then give that their attention and emotional energy. And they even put a word on it!

So resolve to be clear and concise and consistent in teaching your dog word association. Once he gets the concept, and realizes your words are now meaningful in his life, you'll love what he does next. He starts listening!

Positive Words

Choose words carefully and make them positive. The dog's name should always be a positive word, never a reprimand spoken in a harsh tone. After his name, praise words are the most important ones to teach.

The word "No" is way overused with dogs. Give him something to do and put a word on that behavior. Tell him what you want him to do and reward him, instead of nagging him to stop something.

Positive training teaches the dog to respond to a quiet tone of voice. The dog comes to expect sincere praise coupled with positive emotional energy. With these dogs, a serious "Ah! Ah!," spoken in a sharp tone, becomes a mega aversive because they have never been desensitized to a harsh tone.

Dogs can learn to endure punishment and aversives, just as they learn to tolerate abuse. They become inured to it. But when dogs have never known this, just a sharp word becomes extremely meaningful to them because they're so tuned in to your voice and your tone.

At the risk of focusing on the negative here, when using your voice as an aversive, do it rarely and be sure the reprimand fits the crime. Keep it out of the competition training game entirely.

Looking away during heeling is not nearly as serious a crime as stealing food or bolting out the door or growling at another dog. For looking away, just a reminder like "Hello," in a slightly annoyed tone, should suffice to make the point. Use the harsh tones only for the serious crimes.

Save the big guns for something important in your relationship or lifestyle, for an emergency or something life-threatening. Words like "Oops" or "Whoa" can be used effectively in training if needed. They are less severe than "No" and evoke less negative emotion from the handler.

In daily life, negative words are most effective if kept to a minimum and used proactively, before the dog gets into trouble. If you're too late, "Leave It" can be a valuable cue, meaning leave that alone and come here to get rewarded.

If you want to use a word to indicate to your dog that he is not on the right track to reinforcement, use a more positive word than "Wrong." Tell him "Try Again," or "Nice Try," or "Another One." Use action words, not negatives. Positive words keep your energy positive in training.

Make every effort to focus on positive words. Put words on attention and being near you. Avoid "No, no, NO!" Tell the dog what you do want – name it and reward it.

Formal vs. Informal

Just a word here to those who want to train for competition such as formal obedience, Schutzhund or agility. Teach two sets of words. Here's why.

The wife is training the dog. She teaches the dog "Down" to mean lie down – a specific behavior leading to generous reward. Husband uses "Down" to mean go away and lie down and leave me alone. This is rarely reinforced. Naturally, the children say "Down" when he jumps up. If the dog does lie down, there is rarely reinforcement. Even if there is, the dog usually gets up when he wants anyway.

Now the wife joins a class to sharpen skills for an obedience title. The word "Down" has pretty much lost its meaning to the dog. No specific criteria have been established. Reinforcement history is lacking and the word association has been lost. "Down" no longer designates a specific behavior for which there is immediate reward and which is to be continued until released. The dog is already in a grey area with this word.

The solution is simple: put a new word on the desired behavior and then keep it strictly for formal obedience. Competition training is far more successful when the word cues are used only for those behaviors, each with specific criteria and resulting in consistent reinforcement.

Even in a single-person household, using sit and down around the house tends to lessen the meaning of these words, especially if the handler has the dog sit to shove a pill down his throat. Keep the competition words and cues specific to that training and be sure they are highly reinforced.

In the same vein, if the dog already ignores the word "Come," it makes more sense to teach a new word with appropriate criteria and rewards, than it does to try to convince the dog that "Come" has a new meaning. Keep your words specific and teach your dog that they have meaning.

Establish Criteria

Our dogs understand the word "Down." It means to lie down where they are and to remain in place until released. We use this word for the long down exercise.

"Relax" is our informal word. It means to find a place, anywhere nearby, and lie down and chill out. We don't care where they do it, or if they chew on a stick or sniff around. And they can pretty much get up when they want after a reasonable period of time.

But the German "Platz" is our competition word. That means hit the deck as fast as possible with all four legs tucked underneath (the Sphinx down). The dogs know this word gets reinforced quickly and frequently with really valuable rewards. They also know to stay alert and intense, because if they are called they need to leap up and come streaking to us as fast as possible.

All three words are different cues for lying down. But all have different criteria.

Come when called is in the same category. To our dogs, the word "Come" means they need to get over to us right now from whatever they're doing and arrive close enough to get touched or be fed. Then they can go back to being free.

But the German word "Hier" (pronounced "Heer") means bolt to me in a straight line as fast as you can run, and sit straight in front and make eye contact because you are in for some really super reinforcement. The dogs have no trouble distinguishing between the two cues for similar behavior in different circumstances.

What confuses a dog is when the same word means one thing one time and another the next. This breaks down the concept that words truly do have meaning. The dog ends up in a grey area, with no clear understanding.

Keep training black and white for the dog. Make sure competition cues are crisp, clear and consistent. For more success, keep certain words only for competition training.

On the other hand, you can teach your dog a competition cue very effectively in everyday life, provided you maintain all the criteria. Remember Vino learning to "Wait" – with eye contact – in order to have access to new places? We use this daily to allow him access to what he wants most.

So although we might not work agility every day, this is one behavior we can practice. He waits for permission to chase squirrels, to go out into the yard, to get out of the van, to get off the porch and to go for a walk in the woods.

Every time, he must offer the specific criteria for "Wait." He must stop immediately and stand absolutely still. He must make eye contact with me, and he must wait to be released.

Or what? Or he doesn't get to go do what he wants. Believe me, Vino is clear about this in life – and in agility. But I am very careful not to get sloppy and break down any of the competition criteria in everyday life.

Release

Speaking of release, the word for release is one of the most important to teach your dog. Eventually, the release becomes powerful positive reinforcement in itself. Just as the dog needs to understand the concept that words have meaning, he also needs to learn the concept of holding a position, or continuing a behavior, until the release.

Every behavior has a beginning and an end. The cue starts the behavior. The release ends it.

The release word should be short and dynamic, and become second nature to you. Pair it with high rewards and high energy to make it more meaningful.

For years we've used "Okay" as a release word. It's natural to us and, unfortunately, it's too much of a habit now to change easily. But it's not a preferred release word. We say it so much in conversation that we often use the word "Okay" unintentionally. The dog hears it and releases himself. "Free Dog" or "Let's Go" or "At Ease" are much safer and more specific word cues.

Choose your release word carefully and then use it consistently. It is a cue for freedom and play and fun and energy and reward.

Different Criteria

Although we've said that words normally do not play a part in a dog's natural life, once he grasps the concept of responding to words, the possibilities are endless. Now you can teach him to do anything, just by following the ABCs:

(Antecedent – Behavior – Consequence).

You can teach him to start on his right foot, just put a word on it and reinforce only that behavior. If you want him to start with his head up, simply follow the same plan. The possibilities are limitless.

Just be sure to establish clear criteria for response to each word. To illustrate, my dogs understand a variety of cues for similar behaviors so they can walk with me off leash.

"Heel" means a specific position at my left side with some attention. The German word "Fuss" (pronounced "Foos") is our formal cue for eye contact, full attention and a much more exact position.

"Right Here" means to walk close enough to me to be touched. This is a strict criterion, so I use a more serious tone of voice. It's acceptable if I can only touch their tails, and they don't have to look at me. But if I can't touch them any more, they are too far away from me. Walking forward ceases until they get close enough again.

"With Me" means to walk with me, but they don't need to be close enough to be touched. For this behavior, I accept anything up to about 10 feet around me. This has more relaxed criteria, so I use a softer, calmer tone of voice. They can walk in front or behind or at either side, but they still have to be aware of where I am going.

"Too Far" means Vino has just stepped over the boundary of being too far away from me. In the woods, this might be a hundred feet or so. In the driveway, it might be 25 feet. At agility class, it might be just a few feet. When he hears this cue, he stops and waits for me to get closer. He doesn't have to come back to me. (Charra's cue for this is "Stay Close." I need different words for each dog since they often travel separately in the woods.)

"Check In" means wherever you are, whatever you are doing, make solid eye contact. It means to check in because I have a message for you. This requires a quick response, so my voice is sharp and insistent.

Immediate response to this word always results in really high rewards because it is also a competition cue for agility. On a course, they are moving at high speed some distance away from me. "Check In" is an emergency cue to get their attention when I need to give them information to keep them on the right track.

By the way, to avoid using a leash around the property, the dogs also know "Porch" (stay on the porch, like when the UPS man is driving in), "Path" (walk only on the path, like when it's muddy or new grass has been planted), and "To the Van" (go and wait by the van, like when Mom forgot something and has to go back and get it). Yes, you can teach them just about anything.

Each word or phrase have different criteria. The variations can be subtle, but they must be clearly established and consistently reinforced.

You can get yourself into a little trouble teaching all these words to the animals, though. Chief, the horse, knows some words too. Unfortunately, some of them are the same words the dogs know. "Easy" means to go slowly, and a clucking sound means to hurry up.

We all have to walk a few hundred feet down the road to get to the bridle trails. The two dogs are always out in front, eager to get there and wanting to pull on their leashes. But Chief (being a lazy Quarter horse) is dragging his feet behind me because he'd rather still be back in the pasture with his pals and his hay.

Clucking to Chief to speed him up makes the dogs crazier. They take it as permission to lunge to the end of their leashes. Telling the dogs "Easy" slows the horse down even more. They each hear what they want to hear. I'm being pulled in two different directions, inciting opposition reflex in the dogs and the horse. My arms are about to come out of their sockets and it feels like I'm on the rack at the Spanish Inquisition. It made for a difficult few hundred yards.

The answer? I taught the dogs a new word to slow down and not pull. It was way too hard to think about changing Chief's vocabulary at this point. Now I just stick a carrot in my back pocket to motivate him to keep up. But it illustrates how you have to be careful when you teach the animals to respond to your words!

Our dogs are capable of distinguishing amazing nuances if we take the time to teach them properly. They respond in remarkable ways and can learn so much.

We just need to teach ourselves to be good positive reinforcement trainers – to teach the right word association and give clear cues. When we do our part, the dogs usually do theirs.

MAKE WORDS MEANINGFUL !

8

The Zen

" The creatures ...
teach us how to live in the moment. "
— Margo Lasher

Dogs are perfect Zen beings. They dwell only in the present moment. The past is over for them. The future is inconceivable.

Dogs always exist in this very moment – right now. This is all there is for them. Dogs learn. Dogs remember, but they always dwell in the now.

Our challenge is to stay in the present moment with our dogs. Only then can we truly communicate.

We talk about seeing that "Kodak moment" when we need to reinforce. Our best training can be done only when we dwell in that moment with our dogs – their moment.

The same is true of horses. Dressage trainer Barbier advises his riders, "Always be here and now."

Olympic gold medalist Lanny Bassham, author of *With Winning In Mind*, says, "Wherever you are – be all there." This especially applies when working with dogs.

Only we know the plan. We have the goals. We can picture that perfect behavior or exercise. Our dogs know only what is happening now.

We need to realize fully that, for our dogs, there is only the here and now. Only when we begin to focus on this moment, their moment, does our training reflect true communication.

Only in their moment can we begin to understand their perspective. Only then are we in total harmony. Only then can we truly tune in to the dogs.

Agility competition, like most sports, is where the Zen moment really counts. So many faults happen when the handler is either one second too soon or one second too late for the dog.

At one trial, I was concentrating on being sure Charra completed all the weave poles. She had been cutting out two poles early, because of a glitch in the way I had trained her.

As we approached the weaves, my attention was toward the end of the poles. Sure enough, she missed the first pole and entered a few poles in – reflecting my focus perfectly. It was a clear wake-up call. Stay in the moment with your dog.

When problems arise in training, if you know enough to ask the question, you probably have the answer within yourself. If you don't, ask your dog.

Your dog holds the solutions. He knows more than all the training gurus and dog experts combined. Remember, the people only have the opinions. The dogs have all the facts.

As Inspector Poirot said of Bob the Dog, "He does not have to speak in order to know."

Look to your dog. Listen to your dog.
Ask him the question. He knows the answer.

TUNE IN TO YOUR DOG !

9

The
Corrections

" Violence begins
where knowledge ends."
– Unknown

" No human being has the right to say
to (an animal), you must or I'll hurt you."
– Monty Roberts

For now, just put off any corrections. You can always
get around to them later, if you so choose.

Today, put them off for just one more training session.
Keep on showing the dog the way, rewarding the behavior
you do want. Teach him just a little longer. Be sure he really
understands what you want. Trust that he always gives you
his best.

Just as I was finishing this section, a dear friend called
late one night. He is a Police K-9 handler in Upstate New
York and his German Shepherd, Rio, enjoys a well-earned
reputation for being an exceptional working dog, especially
in scent work.

The K-9 training unit had spent that entire morning in
an exhausting, but productive, drug detection sweep of a
huge jail facility. Rio had worked long and hard, and been
very accurate and successful. That afternoon, against his
better judgement, the handler agreed to run a track as a
demonstration for some of the newer K-9 handlers who had
recently joined the group.

One of the training directors was extolling Rio's virtues as a phenomenal tracking dog and expounding on his reputation to the newcomers. From the start of the track, Rio was not focused for some reason and his tracking performance was miserable. Nobody knew why, but for the first time he was having real trouble working out the track.

The point of the phone call was to share a defining moment. The handler said that all the way home he couldn't figure out why he felt so good when his dog tracked so terribly. "Then I finally got it," he said. "It was because I didn't correct him in any way."

Police K-9 handlers are not, as a group, known for being the most motivational trainers. Most are still stuck in the old militant attitude toward dog training.

But this handler flat out refused to interfere with his dog in any way except to help him. He knew that if Rio could, he would. He followed his intuition, his inner knowing, and was fair to his dog. They drove home with their relationship intact and only the handler's ego slightly deflated.

The moral of this story is that it just plain feels good to trust your dog. If a veteran cop can manage to do it in front of his peers, so can you.

Help your dog learn. Tune in to him just a little more closely. See if you can't find a way to learn it together.

Put that correction off for one more day. Then ask yourself again, "Is the dog really entitled to this correction?" The dog has the answer.

Be your dog's salvation, not his persecution.
Be his best friend.

BE WORTHY OF YOUR DOG !

SECTION II:

The Basics

10

The Body

" We are the choices that we have made. "
– Francesca Johnson

The mind-body connection is strong in the dog. He demonstrates his health and energy through his every move. A healthy dog is a joy to watch – his love of life is infectious.

Your dog's activity reflects his attitude, and he never fakes it. He can only learn and perform within the limits of his body. Training is easier and faster when the dog is in peak health. To be mentally alert, he must be physically sound.

In health as in training, always look to your dog for the answer. Observe his energy level. Tune in to his health totally. Note his habits, such as stretching, barking and shaking himself, so you can be aware of any changes in his demeanor. Be aware of the look in his eyes.

By reading this book, you have already made a commitment to your dog to improve your relationship and learn about positive training. We invite you to go one step further – take responsibility for your dog being as healthy as possible. Begin with learning just a little bit about proper nutrition. Then go on from there if you want.

To get the best out of your dog, provide him with the best. Most dogs thrive on what is naturally good for them. All-natural foods can make a big difference to many dogs. Their bodies are smaller than ours and often are more sensitive to toxins and additives and preservatives.

97

What's most natural is usually best. Remember that they are meat-eaters. They thrive on fresh food. In the wild, they work hard for their food. They don't always eat every day, and you never see a fat wolf in the wild.

Studies confirm repeatedly, in a variety of species, that minimum nutrition works best. That means the least amount of nutritious food needed to fuel the body produces better bone and stronger tissue, and puts the least stress on the body's metabolism, resulting in a longer, healthier life.

In the past few years, there has been a revolution of sorts in nutrition – back to the natural. There has also been a major resurgence of the traditional therapies and treatments.

More and more owners, as well as veterinarians, are finding that these alternative forms of medicine are well suited to keeping dogs healthy. The preventive therapies are proving valuable for both dogs and horses, especially those who are expected to be athletes.

Holistic healing for dogs is becoming more popular as its benefits become apparent. We urge you to investigate the natural, non-invasive alternatives when treatment is needed. More importantly, we recommend that you take the time to find out more about supplementation and prevention, so less treatment is required.

The Recommended Resources section in the back of this book offers information on health and nutrition topics. It also lists holistic veterinary associations and specialties for referrals. Check them out. Consider the choices.

GO NATURAL !

11   The Agenda

" ... to permit our animals
to express themselves, and never
to inhibit that which God gave them."
– Carol Harris

One hallmark of positive training is that we work on the dog's agenda instead of ours. We always approach the dog with a sincere concern for his well-being, consideration of his attitude and utmost respect for his individuality. We want him to be a willing partner in·training.

This sometimes means not reaching a specific goal on schedule. It can even mean backing up a few steps in the program, or changing our training time. But tuning in, and learning a little from our loving partner, always makes for better training.

Who Begs Who

Often this is the scenario at home. Dog begs for food. Owner sends dog away. Later in the day, owner wants to train. Owner begs dog for attention. Dog looks away.

Change the scenario. Dog wants what you have – perfect time for 30 seconds of training. No more begging. Now it's called training.

Dog solicits attention – perfect time for training. Take a short break and work on sit or down or eye contact. Get a behavior on request. Then give the dog what he wants – a few minutes of your attention and praise and petting.

The dog is telling you it's a perfect time for him to learn. He's ready! He wants something. You already have his attention and desire. Listen to him.

When the dog tells you he's ready, use that two minutes to your advantage. Lots more can be accomplished in two minutes of the dog's "now," than in 10 minutes of the owner's designated "training time."

This doesn't mean that the dog only gets trained when he wants. You set up your own schedule, but you also tune in to the dog and take advantage of that unscheduled time when he's ready to learn. Don't miss the moment!

At first, work on the dog's agenda. Soon, he shows he wants to work – because he gets so much out of it. He loves training and he wants to work with us – anytime. Now we can work on our agenda.

The dogs can get pushy about this though. One of my fondest memories is of the day Charra forced me to do obedience. We were working toward her SchH. II, so we were training pretty regularly at this field.

We were there to do protection work that day, not obedience, but the helper was not there yet. I was not in the mood to work obedience, but Charra would have none of it.

The moment I let her out of the van, she slammed herself into heel position and started driving me with her eyes. Then she went and grabbed a hose (her favorite toy). There was no doubt about it – she wanted to work.

So we did almost an entire obedience routine (which we rarely do) and it was fabulous. She came into season the next week, so we suspended formal obedience training.

The weekend after, she earned the coveted V-rating (Excellent) in obedience, despite 95-degree heat, Char being in full season and soccer balls bouncing over from the adjoining field. I suspect that much of that success had to do with the last rehearsal – the day Char made me do obedience.

Put training into real life. Recognize that most of your time with your dog is training. Every interaction teaches him something. Keep the issues in life black and white. Make the parameters clear and consistent. Set down the rules and stick to them. Be consistent.

Seize the Moment

Training on the dog's agenda also means watching for those times when the dog is offering behavior you want. We already mentioned noticing when the young, energetic dog finally goes to lie down.

As he settles quietly, usually that is the moment he becomes invisible. But that is exactly the moment you want to reinforce. Go to him. Sit beside him. Give him your attention. Put a word on it, like "Relax." Give him your approval. Rub his belly.

Of course, with a young dog, by now you always have treats in your pocket. Feed him and stabilize the behavior you find so desirable. Reinforce his calmness.

Reinforcing this behavior when it's your dog's idea is much easier than fighting with an energetic puppy to lie down when he wants to play. Catching him doing something right is one of those win-win situations.

Slower is Faster

"There is a time to go very slowly. If you go slowly at this time, you are actually going faster," says Tom Dorrance, a pioneer in positive training methods for horses.

Build your foundation slowly and completely. When your dog's foundation is solid, all the steps above it come easier and last longer.

Teach the first few concepts completely. Give him time to learn those first few behaviors totally – anywhere and everywhere. Let the dog learn to learn.

For a child who learns the alphabet properly and understands phonetics, reading comes easily. He can sound out words and figure them out for himself. Likewise, a dog who thoroughly understands the ABCs of positive training, and masters the basic behaviors completely, will zip through more advanced training.

He understands the concepts. He's learned how to think and how to work out problems. Most love the challenge presented by advanced training.

Understand Youth

Dogs mature at different rates. What a driven Border Collie or a precocious Belgian might master at 10 months can be almost impossible for a young Rottweiler or an adolescent German Shepherd.

The young dog gives indications right away when the trainer is asking for too much too soon. Watch for signs of the young dog getting discouraged or overwhelmed. Every dog has his own capabilities at each age and these should always be considered as training moves along.

Four years old seems to be some sort of magic age. It's even inspired a little rhyme:

> *What they can do at four,*
> *They can't do before.*

For the larger breeds, especially the slow-maturing males, four is the age when they become dogs. They're puppies for about a year. As one-year-olds, they're like toddlers. Sometime around two, they become juveniles. Then for two years, they're going through a sort of protracted late adolescence. At four, they blossom.

We want to train the youngsters. That window of time between 7 and 16 weeks is priceless. But we must be willing to watch and wait. Our expectations must be reasonable.

Some exercises requiring physical dexterity might not be perfected until later. Behaviors that feature self-control, responsibility or confidence improve with age. Likewise, exercises that need focus and concentration, such as extended heeling or longer stays, must be built over time.

Many things a dog can do when he is two, he couldn't have done at one. So be reasonable in your expectations, considering his age. As the dog gets older and gains some life experience, he becomes a cool dude in comparison to the socially and emotionally naive adolescent or juvenile.

Big dogs look deceptive. Like their wolf counterparts, they reach full size at about a year, but won't be fully mature for another two or three years. Be especially sympathetic during teething (three to six months), and watch for periodic growth spurts. Keep on training, but keep it simple and successful.

The process of growing up poses plenty of challenges and complications for the young dogs. Life itself provides lots of lessons. Pushing them too early in formal training is not fair. Perfect relationship issues.

Teach them all the manners they need to know. Use these issues to teach them the concept of using their behavior to get what they want and that words have meaning.

Show them that all of heaven comes from you, as soon as they listen and respond correctly. Teach them to play the right games. Convince them that training is fun and you've made the perfect start for surefire success through positive training.

The Waiting Game

Waiting for the desired behavior can seem to take forever. In fact, it usually involves only a few seconds or a few minutes. But this goes against the old militant attitude of, "Make the dog do it *now!*" We must learn to be patient.

One helpful way to get a new attitude is to pretend you are training a Siberian tiger. You wouldn't be tempted to prod him into a sit or jerk on his neck for his attention. Bring your brain and think how you would get your dog to do this if he were an animal who really could, and would, hurt you.

At Sea World, Ted Turner talks about going to work in the morning and standing around with the other trainers, drinking coffee, waiting for the dolphins and killer whales to calm down in their pools so they can release them into the training area. Since the trainers want to reinforce only calmness, they must wait for calm behavior before opening the gates.

If one of the bosses comes by while the entire staff is standing around, drinking coffee and spectating, of course he wants to know what they are doing. They tell him, "We're training our animals." Actually, they are simply watching and waiting for the right behavior so they can reinforce it. The boss probably walks off mumbling something about lazy, overpaid workers.

I once asked Ted what to do about a dog who growled at me when I went to let him out of the kennel. His reply was simple: "Wait." I knew instantly what he meant.

I was too embarrassed to admit that I had never waited more than about 30 seconds. Then I gave in and let the dog out anyway. I just needed to wait longer – until he stopped growling. Had I made that initial investment of those extra few minutes (or even seconds), I could have extinguished the unwanted behavior quickly and easily. Instead, I had reinforced the unwanted behavior by being impatient.

So don't be afraid to wait. Patience pays off. In the beginning, you'll seem to be waiting a lot. Then all those minutes begin to pay off. Further along in training, the waiting gets to be fun – watching the dog think and work it through.

Spontaneous Rehearsal

Then you usually get a new wrinkle – the dog offers too many behaviors at once! He's so eager to get reinforced, he can't wait to do you what you want, so he gives you all of it together.

Spontaneous rehearsal always makes us laugh. It's so much fun to have such a willing (and eager) partner in training. We don't reinforce it, because these behaviors are not given on cue, but we do delight in it. We just love to watch them be creative. It means they're thinking and trying to please us.

When you think about it, we really do have those couple of extra minutes to wait for the right behavior. We're going to share our life with this companion for so many years ahead.

Make the investment early. Learn to wait. Learn to watch. Learn to enjoy training time and not hurry through it.

Moving Forward

Just as we lay the foundation at the dog's pace, so we move forward when the dog is ready. All trainers bring with them their own expectations of what the dog should do and when. Positive training sometimes requires the trainer to alter those expectations according to what the dog is showing him.

The dog might act like he has fully mastered a certain behavior and so the trainer decides to move forward. Then the next day, the dog shows confusion. He is unsure and offers the wrong behavior. This is not the time to "make the dog do it." Now is the time to back up to what the dog does know and get that right again.

There is no need to call the dog stubborn or willful, or worse yet, stupid. The dog has hit a steep incline in his learning curve, that's all. Confusion and forgetting are necessary parts of learning.

Maybe it's even the trainer, who is trying to teach something too fast. Maybe he missed a step. (Good Heavens! It couldn't really ever be *our* fault, could it?)

The mistake doesn't matter. It only matters how the trainer responds. Remember: Consequence drives Behavior. Mistakes are simply learning opportunities. Let the dog learn through lack of reinforcement. Let him identify what doesn't work. That helps him learn.

Let the dog experiment with his behavior. That's what we want. Allow mistakes. Encourage experimentation. Only by identifying what doesn't work can the dog learn what does. The young bear fishing in the river learns as much by what doesn't work to catch a fish as by what does.

Jumping in and helping the dog out isn't always the answer – that only inhibits experimentation. That makes him dependent on continual help from the handler.

Examine the agenda and the program. Forget the future goals and focus on the dog. Consider how to best help him learn. Give him a little time to see if he can work it out. Sometimes, we must learn to wait.

The Three Rs

My criteria for moving forward are the Three Rs – Response, Responsibility and Reliability. Response means the dog is responding to the cue correctly, in a variety of places.

Once you have Response, teach Responsibility. This means the dog should be responsible for maintaining the behavior until released or given something else to do.

So at first, the dog learns to respond to the cue for sit. The he learns to remain sitting until released. That's his Responsibility.

Once he is being responsible, increase Reliability. That means he responds correctly to the cue and is responsible for maintaining the behavior almost all of the time.

The scientists accept 8 out of 10 for this, but our wonderful dogs get it right more often than that. If not, we look for what we might be doing wrong. But we would never ask our dog to do the same thing 10 times in a row, unless it's a really exciting exercise, like agility. We'd both get too bored.

Consider the Three Rs as a standard to tell you when to move forward. Train all three as part of each behavior.

Getting Stuck

At some point along the way, every dog gets stuck somewhere. When he does, resist the urge to coax or cajole him into the desired behavior. Pleading and persuading are the least effective training methods we've seen to date.

Sometimes you can wait it out. If the dog is getting stuck in another behavior, like eye contact or front sit, look away or walk away. Turn your back on the dog.

The same goes for barking at you. Many dogs bark when they get frustrated. Walk away from the dog until he stops. Then give him a cue for a behavior that calms him and doesn't produce barking – one that he already knows, such as lying down. Return to the other exercise later.

If the dog continues to bark, give him a time out. Teach him that barking means Game Over. If he wants to play, he has to play by the rules. Sometimes you can even show him the reward he might have earned before you put him away in a quiet place. Start again in a few minutes in a new place, and set him up for success.

In some cases waiting is just not practical. Consider the information your dog is giving you. If you can't figure it out quickly, then put the dog away while you think it through. Set up for success the next time. Arrange to prevent the unwanted behavior. Back up a step. If you don't like what's happening, change something. Identify the weakness and be sure to work on only one thing at a time.

Let's say the dog is having trouble with the see-saw in agility. He is unsure when the board moves. This is not a time to coax and cajole. This type of reassurance is seen as reinforcement by the dog. His hesitation is earning him your attention and energy. That won't help him master his fear.

Get out of there and set up an exercise where the dog can be successful – such as a board on a brick on the ground. Or put the table under one end of the see-saw, so it only tips an inch or so. Or just *slowly* tip the board yourself.

Set the dog up to make the correct decision himself. When he is successful, use his favorite reinforcers. Keep the rewards high, but resist the urge to encourage and coax. That only makes him dependent on continual help and reinforces exactly the behavior you don't want.

One day, a dog who was already working well in agility, decided that jumping on top of the collapsed tunnel entrance was better than going into the big black hole. Trying to coax the dog off the top and into the entrance wouldn't help the dog learn. The exercise is not to jump on the top and then go in the entrance.

Process the information he's offering. Better to back up a step. Calmly take the dog off the top. Prevent the unwanted behavior that the dog has already shown you he's going to try. Have someone hold the dog at the entrance while the handler raises the fabric at the other end so the dog can see him. Attract the dog with great food or a favorite toy.

Rebuild the foundation. Set up for success. Let the dog make his own decision to get it right so you can reinforce. Then move along – right back up the ladder.

Teach Responsibility. Avoid begging or coaxing or encouraging or always helping the dog get it right after he has done it wrong. Forget pleading and persuading. They reinforce wrong behavior, become a crutch and make the dog dependent. Even worse, they inhibit learning.

Taking Time

Much to everyone's dismay, learning doesn't happen in one astonishing revelation or in quantum leaps. It happens in slow increments, over time, just like a child learning to read or you learning to type. The brain needs time to process new information.

Never underestimate the role of time in learning. In 1997, researchers at John Hopkins University confirmed that, "Time itself is a very powerful component of learning." Dr. H.H. Holcomb and others mapped brain activity to determine how long it takes people to transfer a new skill from short term memory to long term memory. The study indicated a window of about six hours for the human brain to transfer new information to permanent storage.

This window of time "is necessary to render the memory invulnerable and permanent," Holcomb concluded. During that time, learning a similar skill interfered with the brain's transfer mechanism.

Who knows how long a dog's brain takes to do this? But the study confirms the usefulness of putting the dog away for quiet time right after he begins to master a complicated new task.

So teach in small steps and then give the dog the quiet time he needs after training to process new information. Remember that what is learned slowly stays, but knowledge crammed in quickly is soon lost.

Allow your dog to learn slowly. You'll encounter less forgetting and training will proceed faster.

Backing Up

Anyone who has ever potty trained a child knows that things reach a point where they are going along smoothly and successfully at home. Then something changes the routine.

You go away, or company arrives, and the child gets excited or distracted. Training breaks down. This is a normal setback. Just go back to what worked and reinforce that. It's not a time to get mad at the child. That wouldn't help him learn. And it won't help build a trusting relationship. He knows what to do, but he forgot.

Forgetting is a normal part of learning. And a child is at least as smart as a dog, right? So learn to wait. Learn to forgive. Learn to back up. It's all necessary for learning.

Backing up is always a hard thing for trainers to do. Along with waiting, it is one of the challenges in positive training. Going along with the dog's agenda requires a major change in mindset from other conventional training.

It's a leap of faith. Take the chance and your dog will make a believer out of you.

Pushing the Agenda

For folks who have competition in mind, the agenda issue can get tricky. Once a trial is scheduled, training tends to escalate – in frequency and importance. The pressure is on. That's just about the time the exercises seem to start falling apart.

Dogs are so sensitive to emotion and intensity that they sense something has changed. They respond to the pressure transmitted by the handler. Maybe the dog starts to worry a little. Maybe that causes him to make a mistake. This leads to more handler frustration and, usually, more training.

The normal learning curve is for the dog to display initial behaviors quickly, especially while getting reinforced almost continually, and then they can get a little stuck. Some folks call these learning plateaus. Usually, it just means the behavior isn't under reliable stimulus control yet.

The dog shows frustration. He gets confused and offers another behavior. This stress can manifest actively (barking or jumping) or passively (lying down or walking away). Some dogs offer avoidance behaviors, such as eating grass, licking themselves or chasing a bug.

The dog isn't being bad. He isn't stubborn or willful – just confused. This is not the time for correction. This is the time for guidance and support – no matter how close the trial date looms.

The best way to deal with this is just to reinforce the dog for hanging in there with you. If the reinforcement history is solid (all positive), the dog recovers quickly and keeps on trying. Your relationship brings you through.

This is the time to take stock of training. Was the approximation jump too big? Was the cue clear? Was the emotional energy exchange appropriate? Was the distraction too great? Watch the dog and use the information he gives you. The trainer needs to go back a little and end this session with success.

But use the information for the next session. Re-create the scene. Rewrite the script. Set up for success next time, even if it involves lower criteria. Listen to your dog.

Keep the lines of communication open. Keep the dog free and clear to think and try. Keep all his responses uninhibited and he'll get it right soon enough. This is truly the "No Fear" method of training.

Put It In Perspective

Try to put the mistake in perspective. It's only dog training. Those weekday jobs are supposed to stress folks out, not the weekend hobbies.

Yes, I'm being a little facetious here. I do understand how you feel. If anyone had said, "It's only dog training," when I was preparing for a national, or a world team qualifier, I would have lost all composure and branded them an idiot.

But it really does help to get your goals in perspective a little right before the trial. Whatever the performance, you still take the same wonderful dog home with you after the show.

The trial is just a test of training. If you haven't damaged your relationship along the way, there is still plenty more fun and learning ahead. Your dog is your companion for the 99% of life that is outside the ring and you still have all that pleasure.

Always remember that your dog doesn't care how many titles he has before or after his name. He doesn't show off his ribbons to his friends. He's more likely to drool on that trophy than to admire it.

All the dog cares about is that he is loved and that he gets to do what he loves. So keep showing in perspective by remembering how your dog feels about it. Be sure he is having fun too!

Make the Test

One useful plan for showing is to pick a date before the entries close and run through a practice competition. Make a test and see how the dog does. It often helps simulate trial nerves (for the handler) to get someone to video the performance.

If the dog does not work up to your standards, better to put off trialing until the dog is ready. Concentrate on training your dog. There will always be another dog trial.

If your dog punches out a perfect performance, then lighten up. Your dog has passed with flying colors. Enter the show. Then go back and build the basics. Polish the parts – with lots of extra reinforcement. You've done the test. You know your dog can do it.

Get back to fun training. Rehearse your part without your dog. This type of change in your training routine will make you and your dog fresher and more ready for the trial than any last-minute panic training could make you. And when you do your part in the competition, the dog usually does his.

One fantastic side-effect of purely positive training is that when training breaks down, even if it happens in the ring, relationship tends to carry you both through as a working team. We can't tell you the number of times we've seen the dog try harder when something goes wrong at a trial.

That's what a good relationship is all about – one part of the team comes through for the other when it counts.

Who Knows?

Patty tells a great story about an Afghan who was progressing nicely in motivational retrieving. He was already going out and picking up the dumbbell quickly and cleanly and returning it to the owner.

Then one day, in the same location as usual, the dog didn't want anything to do with the dumbbell. He just looked at it, stood there and seemed worried. The dog had never had a correction, and this certainly wasn't the time to start.

So Patty just began reinforcing the dog for being there. Anytime the dog got anywhere near the dumbbell, Patty had the owner praise and feed and give the dog all the things he liked. She forgot about asking him to retrieve that session.

A week later, the dog bounded out to get the dumbbell as if nothing had ever happened. He's been retrieving reliably ever since. What happened? Who knows? We can have lots of opinions, but only the dog has the facts. He was obviously trying to tell them something.

The dog had some worry we can never know about. It surely wasn't worth hurting him or scaring him. For what? A ribbon? A trophy? An untimely response here could have ruined the dog for that exercise forever.

Even worse, it might have broken down trust in the relationship. So why take a chance? Give the dog a break. Trust that he knows why, even if you don't. Trust that if he can, he will. Believe that he's being honest with you – he always is.

Remember that when the dog doesn't understand something, it's the fault of the teaching, not the dog. The instruction has not been clear enough. Positive training is not about pushing, but about always allowing the dog to become the best he can be.

There will always be another trial. But there might not be an opportunity to rebuild any damage done to your precious relationship with your dog.

Unique and Individual

Each dog is a unique combination of temperament traits. Each one is an individual. Positive training aims to recognize and validate that uniqueness. Always consider your dog's individual nature when making a plan for training.

Everyone runs into quirks in their training program. That's because, although the expectations and the exercises are the same, each dog is one of a kind. The goal is to affirm your dog's special traits and work with them.

Celebrate your dog's strengths and emphasize them. Enhance them and develop them. Recognize his limitations, without making excuses.

Knute Rockne advised, "Build up your weaknesses until they become your strong parts." Keep on working, but with respect for your partner.

Don't give up. It took me three years to teach Charra to play tug-of-war. Her cooperative attitude was, "If you want it, you can have it." It wasn't in her nature to want to fight with her master. But now she will play tug forever – with anyone, anywhere, with anything they can hold onto.

We just kept on working at it, making it a fun game for both of us. Keep encouraging your dog. Give the game a chance. Just because it doesn't work the first time, doesn't mean it won't work in the long run.

Look to your dog. See who he is and understand his motivation. If you're training a sighthound in competitive obedience, or an alternate breed in Schutzhund, or have a Northern breed in agility, recognize who chose this career for this dog. For the most part, these dogs were designed for something different – in body, mind and spirit.

Accept the challenge, but don't blame the dog. He didn't choose this career. Given a chance, most dogs choose to do what they were bred for. Border Collies herd. So if you have a BC who chases the children endlessly, or tries this behavior with cars too, understand that his breeding is showing.

The dog is just demonstrating who he is. Separate the behavior from the dog. He's not a bad dog – his behavior just needs modifying to suit his role in our society.

The same goes for the German Shepherd who barks at the door, the terrier who digs, and the water dog you can't keep out of the pool. Dogs are always perfect at being themselves.

So when your dog adds some instinctive behavior to what you're trying to teach, rise to the challenge. Science calls this instinctive drift, and it's only natural. Just laugh and keep on training. He's just showing you, once again, who he is. Try to remember who's agenda you're on now.

Make A Plan

Before you go to train your dog, make a plan. Know what you want to do, but be flexible. Be proactive. Anticipate the action. Set an agenda, but set up for success. Look at the future goal, and then decide what to work on today.

First, look at the big picture. Establish all the criteria involved. Then break it down and identify each individual criterion to plan your approximations for training. As Ken Blanchard says, "If you don't know where you're going, any road will take you there."

If things aren't going the way you hoped, then change today's plan. There's a lot to be said for getting out of there when a problem develops. "If you're in a hole, stop digging."

Often things go wrong because the dog just doesn't understand yet. In science, operant conditioning of a behavior can take 100, even as many as 1,000, repetitions for the dog to learn a complicated task. And the laboratory dogs are only learning one task at a time. They don't have all that life stuff to cope with too.

So be patient and do your homework. Take each step slowly, but keep it interesting and exciting for your dog. Have a plan, but be flexible. Keep listening to your dog. Tune in to his agenda.

If you like to keep a written journal of progress, the most useful method is to focus each entry on what to do during the next session. This saves time and paper.

Today's session shows the results of the last session, or the last few sessions. Only in the next session will you see the progress made today. (This is especially true in tracking, for those who train in that discipline.)

So plan the next session. Process the information your dog gave you today. This session is gone – you can't get it back. Put your focus on how to set up for success next time.

Training Times

Training times should be short and fun. They should leave the dog wanting to do more. And they should be a little unpredictable. They should be a balance of fun and training. But not the same balance every time.

If they don't start well, if the dog isn't ready, then do something else. Get something simple done well. In training horses, Barbier points out that "The first five minutes will establish the mood of the whole (training) session. If it's bad, quit and try again some other day," or even a little later, in a different place.

Watch the dog for when he wants to train. Watch for his attention and activity, and reward that with training.

Keep sessions short and lively. Better to do a couple of five-minute sessions than 15 minutes that gets worse and worse. Barbier recommends, "Do a short 100% job instead of a long, nothing job."

Tune in to your dog right at the beginning of a session. Consider his attitude and energy level. Perhaps today you had planned to work on getting faster recalls. But maybe it's the first warm day of spring and your dog is feeling the heat. Or maybe he's just not acting up to snuff that day.

The dog is telling you it might be a better day to work on calmer, quieter exercises, like stays. When you gear each session to your dog's mood, instead of yours, training becomes more productive and successful.

Total Attention

Whenever and whatever you are training, be absolutely sure to give the dog your total attention. Stay in that Zen moment with him. You should not even notice anything else going on around you. To get all his attention, you must first give him all of yours.

If something happens to distract you, clearly release the dog before doing anything else. Give him an informal "Relax" cue if you want him to lie down. But don't leave him on a formal stay if you're not going to pay attention to him. Never leave him in a grey area. Be sure he knows the game is over for now, before you deal with the kids or talk to your friend.

So often, we see the dog still offering attention and behavior while the handler is busy gabbing with a friend. Tell the dog clearly when the session is over or is temporarily interrupted. Keep the lines black and white for the dog.

Traveling Training

When traveling, rest areas can be fantastic training venues. My best trial ever – my "one moment in time" – was at a major, regional Schutzhund event in Florida one February. We'd been cooped up by a New England winter since early December and, on the drive down, we were really enjoying being outside again.

Whenever Espe (my cover girl) and I would stop at a rest area, she'd get really excited. So I tried a tiny bit of training (like 30 seconds, one behavior only), and a whole lot of playing, in a variety of orders.

She was ready. Every time we stopped, she couldn't wait to get out of the car to see what we would do together this time. I spent my driving time planning the next session.

Some stops we'd just have Doggie Appreciation Time until she pushed me to work. As it got warmer and warmer, we got better and better. Over two days of rest stops, training less than one minute, we were having more and more fun.

Obviously, it worked perfectly. The next weekend Espe made her memorable score of 298 points (100-98-100). We had our best day ever – and on the right day! We had trained on her agenda all the way – short and sweet.

So summon up all your enthusiasm and confidence. Get started. Enjoy your dog. He's waiting. He knows. And he's always right.

LISTEN TO YOUR DOG !

118

12

The Leash

" Rely on your relationship,
not on your leash."
— S.B.

Anyone who ever attended a group obedience class remembers the instructor yelling, "Loose leash! Loose leash!" all night. They repeated it over and over, like it was the holy mantra for all effective dog training.

Well, guess what? It turns out they were right – maybe not for the right reasons, but they were right nonetheless.

Those instructors wanted a loose leash to enable the owner to make a more effective correction. That was the basis of the "trick and jerk" method.

We want the leash loose because the leash signifies control. As soon as the dog pulls on the leash, he takes over control. He doesn't have to worry about where the owner is, he knows. He has no need to look at the owner or check in.

The dog on a tight leash becomes the leader. The owner becomes the follower. Tension on the leash signifies pack support to the dog in whatever he is doing. The owner becomes just another pack member, playing back-up to the dog in his pursuit of the moment. The dog on a tight leash has abdicated his responsibility. He is not responding to the owner – the dog has become the leader.

Even worse, a tight leash means that when the leash comes off, the dog will be gone. If you ever want off-leash control of your dog, then he must feel like a feather on the end of the leash, even if he is a hundred-pound Rottweiler!

Consider how foals are trained to halter and lead rope at an early age. Even the young, fractious Thoroughbreds at the racetrack are all reliably halter trained. Why? The answer is obvious. A horse dragging a person around on the end of a rope would be very dangerous indeed.

The horses learn very early not to pull on the lead rope. Whoever is on the end of the rope is in charge. Imagine that your dog will grow into a 1,500-pound horse, and leash training gets done much more quickly and seriously.

Be the Savior

As in all positive training, I want to be the good guy to my dog. I want to be his salvation, not his persecution.

Previously, teaching the puppy about the leash has been called "leash breaking." In positive training, we have no desire to be involved with "breaking" the puppy of anything, especially something he hasn't even learned yet!

We've all seen the little puppy on the leash – bucking and fighting and pulling back, screaming and biting in panic as he's being dragged around, while the owner pleads with the puppy to come with him. This first attempt at training begins with a fight and rarely does anything to improve the puppy's view of the new owner as a safe and fair pack leader.

Happy to Hitch

We change the scenario. As early as seven weeks old, we teach the puppy to hitch. After the pup gets used to wearing a collar around his neck, attach a short light line. This line is about two feet long, with no knots in it and no handle on the end. The pup could get a leg caught in the handle loop and injure himself.

Let the pup drag the line around for a day or so – always under supervision of course. Don't touch the line unless it gets caught on something, then untangle it.

Once he is used to this, go to a quiet place with no distractions, preferably the back yard. Make sure the pup's flat buckle collar is tight enough so it cannot slip over his cute little head. Tie the puppy to something solid, like a post or a tree, on a leash about three feet long.

Attach the line either up high or right at ground level, so the pup can't get too tangled. Then sit nearby (about 20 feet away), watch and wait.

Of course the puppy resists. But we don't want to be part of that. We do nothing while he fights with the leash and the post. Keep in mind that often he's also fighting to get *to* us now, instead of *away* from us.

As soon as he stops, we go over and "save" him. We reinforce his calmness and his acceptance. We praise him and pet him, unhitch the leash and let him follow us around (dragging the leash) while giving him lots of little treats of really good food. We still don't touch the leash.

Voila! We are his savior. He's so happy to be with us and to get away from that mean old post. We let the leash do the bad part, and we just step in and do the good part. To the dog, we are the good guy and we have all the good stuff.

Tie the puppy up (or "hitch," as it's called in Border Collie lingo) once or twice a day in different places (indoors and out). He soon accepts the restraint of the leash calmly – without biting or fighting or screaming or otherwise resisting.

Holding On

Once the puppy exhibits calm acceptance, reinforce that calmness and acceptance with everything he wants – especially companionship. Feed and pet him and praise him there, and then unhitch him.

This time, hold the end of the leash. By now the pup is so conditioned to hang in there, he's happy to walk right along with his savior, often looking up and smiling.

Is this the imprint we want for walking on a leash? You betcha! Just keep on feeding and praising and petting him and telling him what a great job he's doing.

Should the pup lunge to the end of the leash for some reason, just stand still. He's learned that fighting the leash gets him nowhere. And if we've really made an imprint of being the good guy, he quickly turns his attention to the savior with all that good food.

From this day forward, we resolve never to pull on the leash as a correction. The leash serves only one purpose – to prevent unwanted behavior. It is used as a safety feature, not a training tool.

Learning to hitch is an extremely valuable lesson for a dog to learn. To remain calmly and quietly, wherever the owner attaches the leash, is an important exercise in self-control for any dog. It is a useful skill in many circumstances.

Older Dogs

The first thing most dogs and puppies do when first hitched (because they are so smart!) is to try to chew through the line. If they succeed, they will try to escape this way forever. Their belief is set.

So be sure that the pup cannot chew through the line you use to tie him up. When teaching an older dog, use a plastic-coated cable that will resist his efforts to chew it.

Be sure the dog cannot slip out of his collar and always tie him to something sturdy, like a tree – obviously not to a chair or something that he can move. Always supervise the dog when he is hitched, so you are there to untangle him and prevent him from hurting himself.

When starting leash training, it helps to remember how working elephants are taught. The young elephants first have their leg tied to a tree with a sturdy chain. When they get older, they can be tied anywhere with just a silken thread.

Their belief system has been set. Set your dog's belief system in no pressure on the leash, right from the start, and it is done for life.

Teaching the dog to hitch is not only a useful skill, it also gives you early insight into the dog's temperament. How vocal he is, how hard he fights, how soon he gives in, the different ways he tries to get free, and how he greets you when you rescue him are all valuable clues to his personality.

Exceptions

Now that we've made the rule of loose leash forever, let's mention the exceptions. One important exception is when you need to give the puppy confidence in a certain situation. Remember that a tight leash indicates pack support. We'll discuss this more in Chapter 14: The Puppies.

Another time a tight leash is useful is when letting the dog pull to build rear end muscle development. If you want to do that, put a word on it, like "Mush!" or "Go On!" This can be quite useful for getting your dog to pull you up the hills when cross-country skiing. Some folks tell us that's cheating, but we just ignore them.

A tight leash is also the right tool to incite opposition reflex and provide pack support. That's how it's used in protection work. The handler holds the dog back to offer support and to build drive so the dog wants to go forward toward the bad guy. The tight leash is used here as a specific tool for a special purpose.

One more exception is for German Shepherds showing in conformation to the German standard. They must go out in front and pull hard, on a tight leash, at the walk and the flying trot. This behavior is usually taught from a bicycle to improve the dog's condition and stamina, so he's pulling the handler along on the bike. Besides, the good dogs can trot faster and longer than most people can run.

Just so you're sure these dogs know about loose leashes too, they must all be Schutzhund titled (tracking, obedience and protection) to be able to show in an adult conformation class, or to receive breeding papers, according to the German standard. Incidentally, every one must also have a certified hip X-ray, pass an endurance test and a temperament test (including being gun-sure and accepting of passive strangers). German Shepherds are a quality-controlled breed in Germany. (Just a little aside to expand your dog knowledge.)

Responsibility

From the beginning, we want the leash to mean responsibility. The dog should know where the owner is and not put any pressure on the leash. Our goal is for him to feel like a feather, following us around wherever we lead.

A loose leash is the beginning of control. It is the beginning of the dog recognizing who's in charge. A loose leash is the start – and the key – to off-leash training.

Wolf packs aren't held together by leashes. Young wolf pups allowed to follow along on their first outing have one priority – staying as close to the pack as possible.

We can foster this same desire in our dogs if we simply learn to rely on our relationship instead of our leash.

EXPECT SUCCESS !

13 The Beginnings

Starting out the way you want to continue is the easiest way to train. Great beginnings lead to happy endings. "Good trainers fix problems. Great trainers never get to the problems." So begin as you mean to end.

Being proactive assures that the dog learns the correct behavior right from the start. But before formal schooling begins, the dog needs to understand a couple of concepts.

These "great beginnings" stay with the dog forever. Taking the time to develop the right habits from the start pays off throughout training.

If you have an older dog, trained in a different method, no need to despair – just start right now. Begin at the beginning. The good news is that once you change this dog's basic attitude, once he grasps the concept of positive training, future learning gets easier.

The Food Attitude

Canines evolved as natural gluttons. This is a biological necessity. In the wild, they never know when they will get to eat again. They never get fat because they work hard for what they eat.

Obviously, for food to be a reinforcer, the dog must be hungry. But this can be more difficult than it sounds.

Most dogs today are overweight. It's easy to check. Run your fingertips gently along the middle of the dog's ribcage. You should be able to feel the ribs easily, without pressing. If not, the dog is technically overweight.

If you can feel the dog's ribs, check his hipbones. Place your flat, open hand on his croup – the part of his back just a few inches in front of his tail. You should feel the hip bones as slight bumps rising toward the ceiling. They should be present, but not protruding, or the dog may be too thin. Learn to check your dog's weight weekly and adjust his food ration accordingly.

There should also be a marked dent in the dog's body, just behind the last rib. Canines were never meant to look like Kielbasa sausages with a leg at each corner.

A dog's body should show definition. He should have a waist (just like we should)! As we noted before, when it comes to food – less is better. That's what the nutritional studies conclude.

Those Extra Pounds

Carrying extra weight is unhealthy for a dog. It's killing them with kindness. An overweight dog is getting more food than he needs. Get the food out of the bowl and into the training program.

For a pet dog to be a little overweight is not really such a disaster (although he'll live a longer and healthier life if he's not), provided he is still hungry enough to be motivated by food for training. But if you aspire to do any sort of jumping with the dog, such as formal obedience or agility or Schutzhund trials, then any excess weight can compromise the dog's health and soundness.

This is especially true of larger breeds under two years old. The tendons and ligaments of young dogs are still very elastic and some growth plates may not be fully closed yet.

Any excess weight at this age can put a serious strain on the juvenile's structure and lead to soundness and health problems later in life. Jumping in competition demands that the dog be an athlete.

You don't see any fat athletes, especially those who run and jump. Before your dog attempts any athletic endeavor, be sure he is in good condition for that activity.

Now we admit that teaching a dog how to eat sounds like a real joke. But you'd be surprised how many folks arrive for training with dogs who don't know how to take food properly. For many, this must be taught.

The Chow Hound

If the dog is a real chow hound, he probably nips at your fingers trying to get at the food in your hand. This dog must learn how to take food properly. Training isn't fun if our hands are sore and bleeding. But more important, taking food properly is a control issue. The pack leader controls the food, and the dog simply is not allowed to bite you.

For a long time, we let dogs get away with this. We loved their crazy food drive and we just put up with the pain. Then one day a diminutive woman arrived with a huge young German Shepherd. His giant head was on its way to matching that of a St. Bernard.

While doing a front sit in training, the dog leapt up and took her earring out of her ear with his incisor teeth. This was a post earring through her pierced ear, and it happened so fast that I had trouble believing that he really did it – the first time. The woman explained that the dog had done this since he was a puppy, so she had stopped wearing earrings.

Then, on another front sit, he did it again and took out the other one. I was astounded by how quickly and deftly this huge dog had accomplished this feat – and without a mark on either ear.

A few minutes later, as they were working on food-motivated heeling, he tried a little too hard for the food and pinched her finger, making it bleed. I had a revelation on the spot! If this huge dog could remove an earring with his mouth, he could certainly tell the difference between a piece of food and her finger.

That was the end of excuses for any dog hurting the handler to get the food. Dogs are completely capable of controlling their mouths – what they bite and how hard. They must be taught to take food gently and correctly.

Besides, pushing and biting at the hand are not the behaviors we want to reinforce. The dog must understand that he has to offer some sort of required behavior before we deliver the reward.

How To Eat

For the chow hound, start with kibble. It doesn't make any sense to use roast beef to get them to calm down about taking food. Begin teaching this *after* the dog has eaten and is not so hungry. As you will see, most of our "kitchen training" is done before dinner, when the dog is ready to eat. But this skill of taking food gently is best taught when the chow hound is not so hungry.

Sit in a chair with the kibble out of the dog's reach. Take one piece at a time and hold it between your thumb and forefinger. The dog must learn to take it gently between his incisors (the small teeth in the front of his mouth), and only when you present it and give him permission to take it. He is not to put his whole mouth, or even his canine teeth, on your hand, and he is not to hurt you.

The reason the owner sits in a chair for this is so that it doesn't resemble any sort of training. It gets you closer to the dog's mouth, and tends to be more relaxing for everyone involved.

Present the food right to the dog's mouth. Avoid letting him snap or lunge for the food. He must wait until you allow him to eat it. Put a word on it, like "Take It" or "Gently" or "Easy" when you release the kibble between his front teeth. Praise when he takes it properly.

If he tries to bite your hand or grab the food, close your fingers tightly. Jerk your hand away and get offended. Cry "Ow! Ouch! That Hurt!" in a deeply pained voice (which is usually easy). Put the treat back in the container. Be sure he doesn't get reinforced for this inappropriate behavior.

Let him read the change in emotional energy, while not getting reinforced. If you have rarely used serious negative energy and words with your dog in the past, they have the desired effect immediately. No need to feel guilty – he deserved it. Biting is a serious offense. Wait a minute or so, until both you and the dog are calm, then try again.

If the dog is really insistent on biting, offer him your fingers with no food the next time, or offer him something inedible. Get him to think and check out what is in your hand instead of just biting at it. Vary these techniques, until he calms down and starts using his brain instead of his teeth.

Be sure not to tease the dog. This just makes him crazier to get the food. When he is gentle, give it to him right away. Put it right into his mouth between his front teeth, praising and repeating your chosen word, like "Easy. Good."

Once he is taking the kibble properly in your after-dinner sessions, go to before dinner. When he is doing kibble properly before dinner, switch back to after dinner but use more tempting food, like a slice of hot dog or leftovers.

Get the proper behavior for moderately tempting food before trying favorites like roast beef or cheese. Often with this dog, you can train with pieces of broccoli or peas or popcorn, or other less fattening and less appealing goodies, since these food-driven dogs can easily become overweight.

Table scraps make fine training food – no need for waste. Provided it's not sweet or spicy (and isn't full of preservatives or pesticides or other poisons), just cut it up after dinner and put it in little plastic bags in the freezer. A few seconds in the microwave and you're ready to train.

Right from the beginning, the dog learns two vital concepts – that you control what he wants and that only the correct behavior results in his attaining that reward. Once he understands these principles, positive training has begun.

The Picky Eater

Now to the other side of the coin, the dog who really doesn't care much about food. Fortunately, these are much more rare than the wolf-like food drive of most dogs.

Owners of food-obsessed dogs tend to feed them too much so they don't feel guilty when the dog is always hungry. Owners of picky dogs do the same thing for the same reason – to avoid feeling guilty. Picky dogs make owners feel that somehow the food they are offering is not suitable.

So the owners offer the dog more and more tempting food until they find one the dog can't resist – the way Vino loves Grandpa's Magic Liver. But you can be sure Vino only gets that delicacy in training. Why waste it in his food bowl? Vino does his best eating during training. He's learned that's where he gets the best stuff. He's discovered where his fortunes lie – and he works hard for them.

Back to the food bowl. Usually, the smart dog holds out longer and longer until the food he's offered suits his taste that day. This dog is not only getting more and more fussy, but now *he* is controlling the food!

This relationship is off to a questionable start about who's in control here. Instead of having a food-obsessed dog, often the result is a food-obsessed owner determined to find something tasty enough to tempt the dog.

For those owners with picky eaters, take heart. There are two important facts you must accept. First, no healthy dog ever starved itself to death. (Cats, maybe. Dogs, never!) Second, dogs who are picky when they are young almost always become much better eaters as they get older, provided they are not spoiled by choice.

Some young dogs don't eat well because they are simply being given too much food for their needs. I know this is hard to believe, but many owners come to me and say their dog is a fussy eater. They say food training won't work because their dog has no food drive. Now I know for a fact that if a dog has no food drive, he's dead. Amazingly, upon checking his ribs, I find that the dog is overweight. No wonder the dog can afford to be picky – he's being overfed.

Some juveniles don't eat readily because they are just too busy doing other things. They'd rather play than eat, or they're too distracted, or they're too sensitive, or they're too worried. Most of these reasons sort themselves out as the dog matures, provided the owners maintain the proper feeding program.

The Food Program

For any picky eater, whatever the reason, get the good food out of the food bowl and into the daily relationship. Make the food matter. Make it nutritious and delicious. Use roast beef or cooked liver or cheese or hot dogs (all natural, please) or teriyaki chicken.

Cut the food into pieces to suit your dog. Obviously, German Shepherd cubes are bigger than Sheltie pieces. Use the smallest size pieces that are reasonable for your dog. Then you get more training time for every pound of food!

Each piece should be bite-sized. This means the dog should not have to chew the food before he swallows it – that only interrupts his concentration.

Use soft food that the dog swallows right down so he looks for the next piece right away, not biscuits or other crunchy food that requires chewing.

Before normal feeding time, sit in a chair with a small container of this special food. Make a big fuss about opening the container and giving your attention to the food. Eat a piece of it yourself if you can.

Get the dog's attention and sort of tease him with a piece of the food. Let him smell it and lick it, but not get it. Hold the food tightly between your thumb and forefinger and raise it a little higher as you make the dog stretch to reach it.

When he's really interested and trying hard, tell him "Get It" and let him take it between his front incisors. Praise and pet him and tell him what a good job he's done.

This might seem silly, to praise the dog just for eating. But with this type of dog, it is especially important that you pair praise with food right from the beginning. Remember pairing reinforcers?

Do not ask the dog to sit or offer any behavior for this food for now, just get him interested and let him eat it when you put a word on it. Move your hand around until the dog follows the piece of food wherever it goes until you tell him to "Get It."

Make this a fast game, with lots of praise and positive energy whenever he eats a piece of food. If the dog eats 10 to 20 pieces of food this way the first session, stop.

Immediately feed the dog *half* his normal food in the normal place he eats. He has two minutes, by the clock, in which to eat his food or you pick it up and store it in the fridge for tomorrow.

No treats or between-meal snacks for this dog. Be sure you explain to the family how important it is for them to cooperate in these first few days of training – no biscuits or other snacks from anyone else.

The Dog's Choice

Remember, you are not starving this dog. We don't believe in starving dogs. We're not making him miss a meal. You offer him good food. It's okay for him to choose not to eat. It's his decision.

Dogs like making decisions. It empowers them and gives them confidence. Let him decide – no encouragement or enticement, no coaxing or cajoling, no pleading or persuading, no more emotion around the food bowl. He eats, or the food is gone until the next meal.

You control the food – no treats, no biscuits, no table scraps from anyone until the next session. Start that session right before dinner, with the really good treats again, in exactly the same place as the first session. A little place conditioning helps cue the dog about what is going to happen.

If the dog is not interested in the special food you present before his meal, fine. Give him a few opportunities to eat what you offer, with you still sitting in the chair. If he doesn't want it, no problem. Put his food dish away and wait for the next meal time. Again, no treats or biscuits or scraps.

You are not starving him. You offered him delicious food and he chose not to eat. Allow him that choice.

This food program is a productive learning experience for the dog. We have never known one who resisted food for more than 48 hours. He learns that what is offered is what's available and that you control the food. He learns that you are really happy with him when he does eat. There is no more negative emotion at feeding time.

The good food comes out of the food bowl and into the relationship and the training program. In this program, we keep the really good food for training and make sure that the food in the bowl is less appetizing than what we offer personally.

Eventually, we'll offer the good food only in exchange for behavior. And remember to cut the food down to half portions until the dog gets really excited about the special treats you're offering.

No skipping meals unless the dog chooses not to eat. No starving the dog. It's up to him. Just keep cutting the portions in half until he's eating everything you put in his bowl within two minutes. When the dog cuts back on eating, you just cut back on feeding. This is being proactive.

In the reactive scenario, owners tend to get frustrated and upset when the dog doesn't eat all his dinner. Feeding becomes a time of negative emotion, so the dog eats even less. But with this food program, feeding the good treats becomes a positive time for you both.

Stop reading the dog food bag as to how much the dog should eat. They only want to sell you more food. We know several hard-working German Shepherds who are such "easy keepers" that they eat barely one cup of food per day in their bowls. And we guarantee they get more exercise and have more energy than most dogs.

Yes, we make sure the food in training is both nutritious and delicious. But we let their bodies decide the proper amount of food, not the dog food company. The body is the perfect calorie-counter.

Following a proper food program for a picky eater usually brings results very quickly. Food becomes a time of joyous sharing between you and your dog. Feeding time becomes bonding time.

Pack status is confirmed and reinforced through food. It's simple and it makes sense. Both you and your dog begin to look forward to feeding time and the "kitchen training" that always precedes it. This is one of those great beginnings that makes positive training more productive because food has now become a meaningful reinforcer.

Kitchen Training

Kitchen training is the zero to one step in positive training. Kitchen training got its name because that's where it happens for us. That doesn't mean it has to happen in your kitchen, especially if the kitchen is the busiest room in your house.

Kitchen training means a few minutes, or even seconds, of training right before feeding time. Prepare your dog's food, with him watching, and put it on the counter. If the kitchen is too busy, then go to the garage or the basement.

Kitchen training is a special time between you and your dog. It happens in a place free from distractions. The quieter the place, the better.

The ritual is always the same in the beginning. The dog is ready to eat. All the **A**ntecedents are there. When the dog offers the desired **B**ehavior, the **C**onsequences are terrific. He gets what he wants – better food than goes in his bowl. We're already teaching the dog the ABCs.

The dog is present, attentive and ready. These first small steps teach the dog that the food comes from the pack leader and that certain behavior is required to get it – gentleness and calmness for the chow hound, interest and focus for the fussy eater.

This is first basic step up the ladder of positive training. Does it seem too simple or too easy? Trust me, this is the beginning of a strong foundation upon which to build all the other behaviors.

Take the time, those few minutes each feeding, to lay this good foundation. We'll use kitchen training to teach the start of several other behaviors once we get going.

If you feed your dog twice a day, you can get in twice as much kitchen training, provided you have the time. But don't pressure yourself.

If mornings are just too busy for you, or if you're not a morning person, then use the evening meal for training. Cut down the portion of the morning meal to be sure your dog is more than ready for kitchen training in the evening, or vice-versa.

Kitchen training takes so little time and is so valuable. If every shelter dog got five minutes (or less) of "kitchen training" at feeding time, their behavior would probably improve and so would their chance of success in a new home.

The Cookie Jar

Want to feed your dog treats and dog biscuits? Great! Just start to make the "cookies" count. (And be sure to factor them in as part of your dog's daily ration.)

Place a couple of different cookie jars in various parts of the house. If your dog happens to follow you into that room, ask the dog to sit (provided he knows that already).

If he responds correctly, praise and release and give him a cookie out of the canister. If he doesn't, tell him that's too bad, reach in the cookie jar but get nothing out. Walk away and let him try again next time, at least one hour later.

As training proceeds, you'll have lots of different behaviors to ask for so he can earn his cookie. You'll also find the dog pays much closer attention to you around the house. Eventually, you can be unpredictable! Don't always go to the closest canister. Praise, release and go get a cookie from the jar in the other room. Take the dog with you at first.

Later, when working on stays, you can ask the dog to stay while you go and get the cookie – first to the cookie jar in that room and then to one in another room. The dog gets up? Who cares? Just show him the cookie he could have had and put it back in the jar it came from – no second chances. He'll get the game pretty soon, provided you're not climbing the ladder too fast and skipping steps.

Resistances

We just have to put in a note here about resistances – the people's, not the dogs'. We've heard so many excuses about why not to use food for training.

My favorite story is about a woman who came to the first obedience class with her young Border Collie. The instructor showed how to use the food for attention and how to get the dog to follow along while walking.

The second week, the dog was fixated on the owner, following her around intently wherever she went. The teacher was pleased with the performance and quietly suggested to the owner that she now give the dog a piece of food.

The lady looked perplexed. "You mean you actually want me to feed him some of this?" she asked, looking at the chunk of cheese in her hand. The wonderful dog had been heeling all week, making great eye contact, hoping for just a taste of the cheese.

Now this was a Border Collie. He was probably just as happy to work as he would have been to eat. But we do think it's only fair that you actually give the dog a bite of the food once in a while when he does what you ask.

The story clearly illustrates the resistance some folk still have to feeding their dog in training. For those who begin to accept using food, their first question is usually, "When do we stop using the food?" We call this the Law of Diminishing Rewards.

Many trainers tell us that they use food a lot in the beginning. Then, when the dog knows what to do, they don't use it much anymore.

Suppose you went for a job interview where they said they'd pay you $500 per day to learn a certain task and they'd expect you to learn it in two weeks. After that, they'd pay you $50 a day to do the same task. Would you stay for much more of the interview?

Once the dogs know their job well, and they perform reliably and get better and better, why would we want to stop paying them? We think it's only fair to give them even more of what they want.

It's the Consequence that drives the Behavior. Keeping the rewards high insures that our dogs are happy to keep working – just as you are happier when you know there's a fat paycheck waiting at the end of the week.

The other common question is, "Do we really have to carry food and toys around all the time?" The answer is no, you don't have to. Once you've made enough deposits in the bank, and praise becomes meaningful to your dog, a sincere "Good Dog," along with petting or some other reinforcer, can be effective.

You always have your voice or your hands. But food is such a simple and powerful primary reinforcer, that it just makes sense to use it – and keep on using it.

For us, it's really no big deal. It's easy to get in the habit of carrying cookies. We love the ears up and eyes bright attention and attitude it fosters. We don't have to feed or play all the time, but we like paying our dogs for a job well done. And we'd much rather carry cookies than a choke chain or a prong collar.

We hope that, after getting into this program, you'll find that you enjoy feeding your dog and playing with him as much as we do. After all, they do so much to deserve it.

Play Time

Along with teaching the dog to take food properly, positive training becomes much more productive when the dog learns to play the right games. When we talk about play, we do not mean play with other dogs or the dog amusing himself. We mean playing with toys with us – playing games in a constructive manner.

The goal is to teach the dog to play by our rules. We choose the toys and we choose the game. We always make ourselves the center of the game. When we control the game, we have a powerful reinforcer as a tool for training.

Games have a lot to do with relationship. One of the first games that a puppy plays with a toy is keep-away. This is the one where the puppy parades past another puppy with an object in its mouth, tail high and eyes bright, and then dashes off to keep the object away from the other puppy, who inevitably gives chase.

This is a game of control. It is the first game in the puppy's repertory and it is the last game we ever want to play with him. We can't catch the puppy. We can never win this game, but we can use our brain to outsmart the puppy.

The answer is simple – always make sure to have *two* toys. From the beginning, we make sure we structure this game according to our rules.

Two Toys

When using toys, play with two identical items – two balls, two sticks, two squeak toys, two plastic bottles, two pieces of hose. This type of game was introduced in the *Schutzhund Obedience* book (see Recommended Resources) and called "two-hoses" because we use two foot-long lengths of soft rubber hose to teach it.

As mentioned in Chapter 5: The Reinforcers, the essence of raising desire for the toy is to keep the toy *away* from the dog. This is just like in keep-way, except that now you're doing the keeping away. Get the picture of how this changes who controls the game?

When the dog really wants the toy, you oblige him and throw it, not too far away the first time. As soon as he picks it up, you start focusing on the second toy, tossing it up and down and having a fine time with it.

Soon, the dog wants the toy you have. The moment he drops the one he has, you throw the other one. You end up standing in the middle while the dog rushes back and forth retrieving the first toy and then the second toy, never getting the chance to play keep-away because you always have another one. It's great for conditioning.

If the dog does get a notion to play keep-away, just walk away playing with the other toy. The game soon loses its appeal when the dog is the only one playing.

Vino, being a creative Belgian, had to find a new way to play this game. While he dearly loves the two-hose game, his terminal reward now is for me to let him get the second hose while he still has the first one in his mouth. He's in heaven when he has all the toys and has bent our rules. Now we just laugh and call him the "two-toy-boy."

We definitely didn't permit this twist in the game for the first two years – while we were still sorting out our relationship and leadership issues. But these days, well, sometimes ya just gotta let a Belgian be a Belgian.

Building Drive

If the dog isn't overly interested in toys, pick up *all* the toys except one bone for chewing. Make access to the toys part of a fun time with you. Like the picky eater, these dogs tend to make the owner feel guilty – searching for the perfect toy, usually in vain.

The dog gets spoiled by choice, while the owner keeps trying to find something the dog really likes. Just as with food, the toys are something you control, something that develops the right relationship, something the dog wants. Just like feeding, don't satiate the dog. Keep the toys for special times and for training.

To build play drive, tease the dog with the toy, but be fair. Always give him a chance to get it, but he must try hard.

Run away from the dog and make him chase you to get the toy. Run around a tree or other barrier to try to keep him away from you and the toy.

Let him watch you play with the toy – alone or with a friend or with another dog. Ignore the dog's interest. Avoid trying to push the toy in the dog's face. He will only learn to want it by *not* being able to get it.

Put the toy on a rope so you can always keep control of it. Keep it moving and keep it close to you. Don't throw the toys too far away from you. Always keep yourself at the center of the game.

The *Schutzhund Obedience* book goes into greater detail about how to build drive for the hoses and other toys, and how to play the game for ideal conditioning. But if you just teach the dog informal games with two toys – you always having the other one so you are at the center – you establish control in the relationship even while you are having fun together.

For obedience competition, also teach your dog to deliver a toy to your hand on cue. Teach this early. You can still play the two-hose game, but he must also learn to deliver to your hand to make future retrieve training easier.

You don't want him to do a spectacular retrieve and then spit the dumbbell at your feet to continue the game. Look ahead. Be proactive so you never get to the problem.

Even with a toy-crazy dog, who plays anywhere and everywhere with everything, save some special games and toys for training. These games become even more meaningful to this dog when used as rewards for advanced obedience.

Tug-of-War

Tug games usually get a bad rap in dog training circles. Certainly they can lead to trouble if played the wrong way – by the dog's rules.

The owner must set the rules. Usually, it's not the tug-of-war part that creates the problem, it's who starts the game and how it ends. Remember that you own the toys. You buy the dog food. You pay the mortgage. And you own *all* the toys. Therefore, tug starts only when you say and it ends when you say.

Certainly tug-of-war is not a game to play between any dog and owner who have leadership issues to work out. It is never a game to play by the dog's rules, where the dog drags the owner around until the owner gives in and the dog wins the toy and proceeds on to keep-away.

Tug games must start with a cue and end with a cue. Teach "Ready-Set-Get It!," Make the dog wait before he can begin. The game starts when you say, not when the dog is pushing the toy at you to make you play with him.

The dog must also learn to "Out" or "Let Go" or "Give" on cue. Build this positively using a food reward, or the reward of getting the toy back, or playing with another toy.

If the dog refuses to give up the toy, calmly reach under his chin and take hold of his collar. Keep your other hand on the toy, but release any tension on it. Pull the dog's collar *toward* you. This takes the opposition reflex out of the game and that takes the fun out of it for the dog.

There's no hurry, just wait. When the dog gets bored with this and releases the toy, put the word on it, praise and feed. Then he can play again. The dog quickly learns how to start the good part of the game again. Once the rules of the game are clearly established, tug can be a rewarding game that also reinforces leadership and control.

But never, ever, allow children to play tug-of-war games with the dog. Children are rarely capable of enforcing the rules consistently and clearly. Such games with a child can confuse the dog about who is in control.

The two-hose game, or hide-and-seek (where the dog finds the child), are much more suitable games for dogs to play with children. For other suitable games, consult Leslie Nelson's *Management Magic* (Recommended Resources).

Learning to take food properly, and learning to play the right games – by the right rules – are two of the most important beginning steps in the positive training plan. Start your dog off on the right paw in these two critical areas.

The dog learns that all of heaven comes through you. Take the time to teach your dog or puppy these basics. They will pay off throughout your positive training program.

BEGIN AT THE BEGINNING !

14

The Puppies

" I multiply the times that my pup feels joy."
— Daniel Debonduwe

Puppies are sponges. They absorb whatever comes their way. They arrive ready to learn and learn they do – either the right way or the wrong way.

Everything done right with a puppy is a major deposit in the Trust Fund. Every desired behavior you encourage and reinforce is a solid investment in the future, like buying a baby a Savings Bond to help with college.

Make your major investments early. Make those deposits in the bank in that first year, the first few months and weeks, and especially in those first few days your puppy comes home. Then you can draw on your Trust Fund forever.

If you take in an older dog, start the same way. Begin the way you intend to continue. Make those initial deposits in the first few days, weeks and months of the relationship.

Begin at the beginning. Build a foundation you can rely on. Invest now in the future.

Who Is That Puppy?

Puppies are ready to learn when they are seven weeks old. Most learn behaviors even earlier than this, as we'll explain later. By seven weeks, in all breeds, the puppy's brain is developed enough to start serious learning. Their bodies might be catching up for months, or even years, but their brains are already in full swing.

Taking the time, at this early age, to see what each puppy shows, and placing each puppy accordingly, is the best step a breeder can take – for the puppy and for the owner. Following a kind and careful puppy evaluation, such as *The Positive Puppy Preview* (see Recommended Resources), offers insights into the personality and temperament of each puppy.

Done properly, such an evaluation indicates strengths upon which to build and reveals weaknesses which can be counteracted through proper exposure. Many fears can be overcome with the right kind of early compensation.

For example, an insightful puppy evaluation can identify a fear of heights. With such a puppy, place the hungry pup on any high, solid surface (such as a picnic table or stone wall) and positively reinforce the desired behavior. Be sure to prevent him from peering over the edge or from falling off and scaring himself more.

Place a few pieces of really good food in front of the pup and wait. Thanks to his marvelous, inquisitive, adaptable puppy nature, he soon starts to relax and show interest in the food. When he does, praise and pet him. As soon as he relaxes, lift him down to the ground. If he relaxes enough the first time to eat the food, all the better.

Fear Behavior

Avoid giving any attention to the puppy when he is exhibiting any sort of fear or apprehension. What we think is reassurance, the pup perceives as reinforcement – he registers it as approval for his fear behavior. The behavior continues because, in the pup's mind, it produces rewards.

Far too many owners "Poor Baby" their puppies until an initial minor fear response escalates into chronic neurotic behavior. The same holds true for fear of thunderstorms or gunfire. When the owners try to reassure their dog, he thinks they like this behavior, so it continues and escalates.

The dog is getting rewarded – praise and petting and attention – for fear behavior. Nobody can reassure a puppy or a dog out of their fear. Best to ignore such behavior. This is not cruel – just realistic behavior modification.

Back to the pup on the table. When the fear behavior is ignored, and the desired behavior is reinforced a few times with a hungry young puppy, the fear of heights usually disappears forever. Many of these puppies actually seek out higher places as they grow up because they remember them as places of such high reward in their earliest experiences.

Curing Carsickness

If the pup gets carsick, work on zero to one. Put the puppy in the car frequently while the car is *not* moving. Break the association that the car moves and makes the puppy feel sick. Spend a little time with the pup in the car each day, not reassuring his fear, but reinforcing calmness, relaxation and interest in food.

Keep the car stationary until the puppy can eat in the car without getting sick. Then start with very short rides, preferably on an empty stomach, to really fun places – like the park or a neighbor's yard. Most pups get over being carsick very quickly when the wrong association is broken and the correct behavior is reinforced.

Footing Fears

Likewise, puppies who show apprehension about slippery floors or strange footings can overcome this quickly. Let the pup play on a tile floor with a calm sibling or another (smaller) pup who doesn't care about slippery footings.

Instead of feeding the pup in a bowl, scatter small pieces of really good food around a hardwood floor and let the pup roam around and vacuum them up. Do the same on a large piece of plastic or a wooden plank on the floor.

Soon the pup is willing, even eager, to negotiate strange surfaces because of exposure and confidence-building through positive reinforcement. The disguise job quickly becomes complete.

Stairs fall into the same category. Avoid reassuring or coaxing at any time the dog is showing apprehension. Only reinforce the dog's efforts to move forward and get to the tasty treats on the next stair.

However, breeders must recognize these compensations for what they are – disguise jobs. The puppy still has the same genetic hole in his temperament. Such information should be seriously considered when selecting breeding stock. The puppy is genetically what he is when evaluated at eight weeks old, not what some great owner or trainer makes him.

Breeders should always be realistic about evaluating their own puppies and breed only for the improvement of their line – not just physically, but especially in temperament. Objective puppy evaluation is the only sure way to do this.

Who Goes Where?

For competition agility, choose a puppy who doesn't care about footings and shows no fear of heights. Although these two traits can be easily disguised if done early, should something go wrong during training, the naturally confident dog recovers much better than the disguise job.

For competitive obedience, choose a puppy who is a natural retriever, shows great confidence in himself, and whose high food and prey drives overcome stress quickly. Training and showing is easier and more fun for this dog than for one whose drives diminish under stress.

For Schutzhund, the most likely candidate is usually the bold, confident people-loving puppy with high prey drive, who is a natural retriever. An experienced trainer might look for one who shows some fight drive, even this early in life.

For a companion, pet owners who want a couch potato to play ball with the kids once in a while should avoid the high-drive, bold puppy. They want to search out the laid back, relaxed people-puppy who prefers to be dependent and submissive. This is the one who'll be happiest lying at their feet begging for popcorn.

Far too many excellent dogs wind up in shelters every year, or are put to death, because they were matched with the wrong owner. One nice thing about writing a book is that you do get to stand on the soapbox once in a while. But back to raising and training those precious pups.

The Right Start

Puppies are our greatest gift and our greatest resource. They're the future for all us dog lovers. They melt our hearts and they inevitably grow up to be dogs. Our responsibility is to help them become the best dogs they can be.

Puppies need to be exposed and encouraged. They need to be stimulated and supported. They need to be understood, and they need to be guided. Most of all, puppies need to be protected. Think how different we have made their lives from the natural way they would be raised in the wild.

We want our puppies to live in our world, so we need to show them that world. But we need to introduce that world without fear or trauma. We want them to feel welcome in our world, so let's welcome them to it gently.

First, accept that puppies can be annoying. Suspend any judgement of their behavior. Dog behavior is never "good" or "bad" – it's just dog behavior. They have no moral guidelines. Learn to see behavior for what it is – either "acceptable" and to be encouraged, or "unacceptable" and thus to be discouraged or extinguished. Lose the moral judgement and emotional baggage – they just get in the way of seeing the wonderful puppy for who he is.

Exposure With Protection

Perhaps you eventually want your new puppy to enjoy going to the kids' baseball games. Fine, take the puppy to a game. But protect the puppy from the overwhelming noise and action and attention of all those over-stimulated kids who want to pet and poke the puppy all at once. For some puppies, this would be about as pleasant as having aliens investigate your body in their spaceship.

Let the puppy sit with you and watch, from a quiet place at the side of the field. Bring your best treats. Of course, you won't take him there until he understands the leash (see The Leash) and takes food properly (see The Beginnings). We're being proactive here, right?

Watch the puppy. He soon shows when he's curious and interested in moving closer. Then you can let him do so with confidence and with support from you. If this isn't on his first visit, who cares? We're on the pup's agenda now (see The Agenda). Overwhelming him at this early stage won't help him enjoy ball games any more later in life.

Puppies are curious beings. If they aren't frightened off, they almost always want to investigate. Allow the puppy to approach the children, instead of vice-versa, preferably one at a time at first.

Hand the child a piece of food and let him feed the pup instead of poking him. Avoid letting children pick the puppy up. Few children know how to do it properly to make the pup feel secure. Let the puppy keep his feet on the ground for now. Give the puppy just a little bit of time in the beginning and it pays off tenfold in the end.

One very serious word of caution. Fireworks displays and busy state fairs are two places that should always be off limits to young puppies. Sure, a few puppies can handle anything, anywhere. But those puppies are few and far between. It's not worth taking a chance.

And it's certainly not worth the risk to take your darling new puppy somewhere that might completely traumatize and overwhelm him, not to mention the health risk that such places pose. It was at a state fair in northern New England many years ago that parvo (canine parvovirus) escalated its insidious spread. Far too many puppies died a horrible death from exposure at the fair or from others who had gone to the fair.

Seeing The World

If you eventually want your dog to go into town with you, then by all means take your puppy into town. But don't drag him out onto the busiest sidewalk you can find. Keep him away from the supermarket entrance for now.

The first time, park somewhere busy. But let the pup sit on your lap in the car and watch the world go by. On the second visit, take him out of the car to a quiet place and allow him to explore the area around him – on leash, of course.

Give him time to absorb the sights and sounds of new places from a reasonable distance. Let him approach things one by one, and only when he shows *he's* ready. Things we take for granted can seem overwhelming to a puppy. Let him take his time.

Be careful never, ever, to reassure any fearful behavior. Ignore it. You're not being cruel. Reassuring fear responses insures their continuation. The pup thinks this is the right behavior to get attention. He thinks you like it!

Instead, ignore the response you don't want and wait. When the pup shows any forward movement or curiosity, that is the moment to pet and praise and support. If you want the pup to move toward something, toss a couple of pieces of really good food on the ground in front of him to encourage him to move in the right direction.

Lure him toward any new object with food in your hand, as you feed it to him, of course. Don't try to tease him or fool him. Be a fair pack leader and positively reinforce desired behavior – moving toward something instead of away.

Welcome the puppy into your world, but do it slowly. Expose the puppy to everything he is eventually going to see and do, but do it carefully. Go one step at a time to be sure the pup is not overwhelmed or traumatized or frightened.

Future Careers

For competitive obedience: By all means, take your puppy to a trial, but start by letting him hang out at the edge, safe in his crate. This way, he can see what is going on, but you avoid any negative experience.

When and if the pup seems ready to investigate, take him closer with an older, confident dog whom he already trusts. Puppies mimic behavior of pack leaders, so be sure this older dog exhibits exactly the behavior you eventually want from your puppy.

For Schutzhund: Sure, take the puppy to your club field, but let him hang out and watch from far enough away where he feels safe. Wait until he shows that he wants to venture closer, and then put him away.

There's plenty of time for him to get to know what's happening here. Better to put him away while he's still curious. Then he'll be even more interested next time.

Wherever you take your puppy, always remember to protect him from big dogs and over-eager people, especially children. Don't put him in that position until you are sure he wants to be there and is old enough to handle the situation confidently.

For agility: The same rules apply when taking your new pup to the agility field. Let him watch, but avoid letting him get crazy over the exciting things going on.

Otherwise, you're making an imprint for him being crazy in the future. Reinforce calmness and attention to you. If you do walk him around the field, keep him close to the ground.

Avoid letting him get on anything higher than a plank flat on the ground until you're sure he can handle it. Letting him get stuck in the collapsed tunnel or slip off the dogwalk or scare himself on the see-saw at this tender age, just because he wanted to go there, is not being the proactive protector we want to be for young pups.

Would you let a toddler loose in the world to see what trouble he could find? That's why they invented playpens. Keep that same attitude with your puppy.

Tight Leash

As mentioned in Chapter 12: The Leash, occasionally a tight leash can give a puppy confidence. If you unwittingly get into a situation where the puppy is unsure, put a little tension on the leash to give him some pack support.

No need to choke him or pull him around – that little tension on the leash lets him know you're behind him all the way. A puppy raised positively has never known the leash as anything negative from you – he's never had a correction with it – so the leash can become a support tool in this instance.

If the situation is too overwhelming, pick the puppy up and get out of there. Stay calm, but leave. Note the pup's reaction to the circumstances and be more proactive next time. Let the puppy watch from farther away and move closer at his own speed.

But if the puppy is just showing a little hesitation in approaching something strange, give him some support with the leash. You might find he's more willing to move forward when he knows you are right behind him.

Inciting opposition reflex here, by holding him back, also makes him want to go forward more. Be careful not to support the puppy with the leash if he's showing fear to a person or another dog.

Should he begin alarm barking at either, immediately put slack in the leash (see The Manners). We don't want to support this type of behavior, ever.

Early Parameters

Puppies can learn parameters right away. In the wild pack, they are taught where their boundaries are the first day they emerge from the den, should they stray too far.

Puppies should learn to love the crate. Introduce it by tossing in a handful of small treats and letting the pup vacuum them up.

Leave the door open at first and let the pup go in and out. Put a small marrow bone in the crate and let the pup chew on it in there. Teach him right from the start that there are always really good things in the crate.

Housetraining is obviously going to be the first major step. (Just please, let's not call it "house*breaking*.") So much has been written about crate training and housetraining that we won't take up the space here.

Pick a good book that uses a positive method. Suffice it to say that with a good schedule and proper supervision, housetraining can be completed for life in the first week the puppy comes home, and often within the first few days.

Being proactive means getting to the crate *before* the puppy wakes up screaming and you are forced to reward that behavior by taking him outside. For those first few critical days, every couple of hours during the day and night, (that's right, set your alarm!), wake the puppy up and take him outside before he starts to make a fuss. Get in there before you get to a problem!

In all the early training, we strongly advocate the Rolled Up Newspaper Method. This came from the Internet, with no credit or attribution. We'd be happy to give credit to whoever invented this marvelous method.

A rolled-up newspaper can be an effective training tool when used properly. For instance, use the rolled-up newspaper if your dog chews something or has a housetraining accident. Take the rolled-up newspaper and hit yourself over the head as you repeat this phrase:
"I FORGOT TO WATCH MY DOG!
I FORGOT TO WATCH MY DOG!"
If your dog laughs at you when you do this, praise him.

Do all the things with your puppy that you eventually are going to want to do. Handle his legs and feet. Inspect his paws. Touch his nails individually so you can cut them later. Look in his ears. Brush his coat – everywhere. Hold his tail. Massage his back. Look in his mouth.

While you do all these things, reinforce calmness with petting and praising and food treats. These things are much easier to get done with a little puppy than with a resistant adolescent.

Home Alone

Unfortunately, puppies need to learn to be alone. Understand that this is not a natural situation for a puppy.

In the wild, a pup would never be alone by choice. But very few domestic dogs have the luxury of living a life without ever being left alone.

Even if you are home all day with your dog, or he is with another dog, you must prepare the puppy for being alone in case he is ever sick. If staying at the vet when he's sick becomes the first time the dog is left alone, recovery is much more difficult because of that stress factor.

Puppies cry when left alone. It's a survival instinct. In the wild, being alone means death. So unfortunately, you're probably going to have to let your puppy cry for a little while until he learns he can survive it. Make sure the pup is tired when you put him in his crate.

Toss in a handful of kibbles (the smallest you can find) when you leave to take the pup's mind off separation anxiety. The first time you close the crate door for any length of time, give him a small marrow bone to chew. Make a positive association.

Never let the puppy out while he is protesting or that behavior will continue forever. If you reinforce barking and carrying on in the crate with what the pup wants – getting out to be with you – his belief system is set.

It's also a good idea for the puppy to spend at least one night away from home before he is six months old. This means having him stay with your most trusted "dog-loving" friend for one sleep-over and at least one meal – to be sure he'll eat when away from home. Surviving this night away from home, and coming to depend on someone else, are vital to prepare your pup for what he might encounter later in life.

Again, this makes any future change in routine easier for the dog because he survived it when he was young. It's preparation for staying at the vet's in case he gets ill, staying at the kennel or reducing the stress should you ever move to a new house. Get this single night and day out of the way early, when he's still an adaptable puppy, and he's better prepared for any future changes in routine.

Positive Pursuits

Be sure you spend as much time in positive pursuits with your puppy as you do in setting parameters. Watch for what your puppy loves and share it with him. Puppies are pure positive energy.

Getting involved with your pup's perceptions and investigations is a true delight. If he's stalking a bug, watch it with him. If he's rolling in the grass, tickle his tummy. If he's paddling in the water, wade in there with him.

Let your puppy show you a new perspective on the world, where everything is approached with wonder and joy. Giving you new eyes is his greatest gift to you. Sharing these moments with him can be your greatest gift to him.

Start Training Early

Teach the puppy games that you want him to play for all his life. Encourage him to bring things to you. Always be delighted when he brings anything to you, even the remains of a dead mouse or your kid's chewed up sock. It's always better than him running away with it.

Teach him to come find you and other family members. Hide-and-seek is a fun game for puppies, and it sure beats the alternative – him running away from you.

Begin reinforcing desired behaviors right away – like eye contact. Put a word on it and feed and praise. Reinforce any attention to you, especially following or coming to you from any distance.

Eye contact is wonderful behavior. I encourage it in puppies and reinforce it every time. I just love it when they give me that intense attention. Personally, I happen to like my dogs looking at me with ears up and eyes bright. I guess if I preferred the other view I'd be a sled dog musher, where the view is always the same.

Even very young puppies can learn important behaviors. Those first few learned behaviors become deeply ingrained in the puppy. We call them "default" behaviors because the pups tend to offer them the most, and they almost always offer them later in training, whenever they get confused or frustrated.

Never Too Young

Eight weeks old is not too young to start. In fact, puppies can learn even before that. One truly conscientious breeder begins training while the pups are getting weaned.

When the pups are five or six weeks old, and feeding time is becoming an exciting ritual, she brings each puppy into the kitchen individually. But before feeding him, she uses a special treat to teach the pup to sit squarely and give eye contact. Within a couple of days, these puppies are sitting and giving solid eye contact to anyone who comes within range in hopes of a tasty treat or individual attention.

The only drawback to such early training is that these puppies can be difficult to evaluate. Put them in a new room with a stranger and they all run to the person, sit squarely and make eye contact, hoping for a reward. It's hard to tell which ones are dominant or pushy or sensitive or submissive when they all offer this same default behavior!

The evaluator has to be creative to get them to reveal their true nature. But who wouldn't want an obedience prospect, or even a pet, who defaults to this behavior?

These pups have already learned a vital concept – offering behavior for reward. They are on their way to sure success in positive training.

When pups grasp the process this early, learning is easier for them their whole lives through. Yes, you can teach an old dog new tricks, but it's much simpler with a dog who has already learned to learn, and especially with one who began as a little puppy.

Puppies are so responsive. They are so uninhibited. They show you everything, and they never lie. They are so delightful and so malleable. They are blank slates waiting for you to write what you want on them. They hold so much promise.

Puppy Classes

Kindergarten puppy training has become a popular concept. Thank goodness the old rule of waiting six months to start training has been thrown out and is almost obsolete.

Puppy classes can be a great place to start. To be sure it is safe, investigate the class yourself before you take your dear little puppy. First, find out about the instructor. Then observe a class yourself, before you expose your precious pup.

Be sure the class uses food treats and toys. Avoid any class that advocates pushing puppies into a sit or down position and making them stay there.

Always be extremely cautious about letting anyone you don't trust completely ever handle your impressionable puppy. Protecting him is your primary job as pack leader.

Puppy classes are for constructive, positive beginnings and for correct socialization, especially if your puppy is an only dog. But socialization here should be constructive.

When the puppies train for half the class and then are all turned loose for puppy free-for-all in the last half, the puppies learn that playing with other dogs is more fun than training. We want our puppies to think that training with us is the most fun of all and the best place they can be.

Socialization should be allowed for a brief time, only a minute or two, between two compatible puppies. Then the owners should intercede and get the pup's attention back on them, with the Name Game (explained in the next chapter) and a tasty food treat of course.

Access to playing comes through you. Freedom is a part of heaven that you control. The puppy should learn right from the beginning to come when called, even while playing with another puppy.

Social interactions should be somewhat controlled. In free-for-alls and group socialization, the bullies get pushier and the gentler pups get even more submissive and worried.

Bullies should be socialized with bigger, stronger dogs, preferably skilled adults who put them in their place safely and surely. Unsure puppies should interact with other gentle puppies until they gain confidence and get bolder in their encounters with other pups.

Each puppy must learn his place in the world. But there is no reason he can't learn it slowly, step by step, and in a positive manner. The pup should find the world a friendly place and be given the time to build his confidence along the way.

Enhance what is natural for your puppy. Get involved in the good times. Puppies are passionate in their zest for life. Share that joy and your relationship starts out on a solid foundation.

ENJOY YOUR PUPPY !

15

The Manners

" Properly trained,
a man can be dog's best friend."
– Corey Ford

Puppies are precious, and many truly are precocious. But they arrive with no privileges.

Privileges must be earned. And these privileges are earned by? You guessed it – offering the correct behavior. What is acceptable behavior for our society must be taught to the dog.

In a dog pack, there is discipline and duty. Among dogs, it is not only preferred, but absolutely mandatory that member dogs join in greeting procedures. It's a biological necessity. Dogs carry out this greeting ritual by licking the other dogs' lips and sniffing the genitals – not exactly what we had in mind for our dogs to be socially acceptable.

Greeting Procedure

So let's take greeting procedure first, since now we know why dogs are so driven to jump up on people (to get to their face) or to sniff in embarrassing places. We've already taken the first step – acknowledging that the dog *is* going to jump up. It's his nature. Besides, he has already shown us that he will.

First, be proactive. Establish specific criteria for greeting procedure right from the start. Begin with the way you allow the puppy to greet you.

Only allow the puppy to greet you the way you want him to greet others. Later, once he has mastered acceptable behavior, you may grant him the privilege of jumping up on you if you want, but only when you give permission.

Supervise how he greets others right from the start. Set up the situation with a friend willing to help. Set up for success the first time.

Use a leash to prevent the unwanted behavior of the dog rushing over to the person and jumping up. Have several pieces of really good food in your hand. Let the dog eat them one at a time as you approach the other person. Keep the dog's head level so he doesn't start to jump.

Once the dog arrives at the other person, he also feeds the dog to keep his head level. Between bites of food, praise and pet the dog (yes, both of you) as you tell him "Off," or whatever word you have chosen for this behavior. Associate the word with the behavior you want – all four feet on the ground. (Vino's cue for this is "Four On The Floor!")

Continue to use the word "Off," with praising and petting, when his behavior is acceptable, in between feeding. Using the word while the dog is taking the food doesn't hurt, but it doesn't do much good either. The dog is concentrating on eating the food, not on his position. Tell him "Off" during those moments when you are withholding the food by closing your hand. Keep your hand low to keep his head low.

Should the dog try to jump, both of you turn your back on him – no need to scream "Off" or knee him in the chest or jerk him down or knock him over or pinch his feet. He can't deserve a correction because we haven't taught him anything yet. He's just doing what dogs do naturally.

As soon as his feet hit the ground again, reinforce and remind him what the word is for that behavior. Give him back your attention and touching and positive energy *while* his feet are on the floor.

The Right Reinforcement

Be sure that you are petting the dog in a way that pleases him while he is not jumping. Some like their ears scratched, others like different types of petting. We want the dog to learn that he gets what he likes by being on the ground. Make the reinforcement meaningful.

What you offer needs to be especially reinforcing for the dog here because you are trying to extinguish a behavior that is important and natural to him. Consequence drives Behavior. So when he exhibits the desired behavior, all feet on the floor, give him what he wants – petting and praise and food and positive emotional energy, and maybe even to lick the person's face after all.

For a dog who's determined to get to the person's face, ask the person to bend down to the dog's level while the dog still has his front feet on the floor. This can be is a powerful reinforcer for acceptable behavior – getting to lick their face.

End the licking by reminding the dog to "Leave It" or "Enough" or "That'll Do" and have the person stand up again. Return to using praise and petting and more food for "Off." Continue this until the dog exhausts his desire to greet the person and calms down.

For the dog who sniffs guests in embarrassing places, drop a piece of food or two on the ground, just to get his head even lower than sniffing level. Then you can reward him at the same time as you prevent the unwanted behavior. Soon he associates "Leave It" or "Off" with looking for food on the ground – an Alternative Incompatible Behavior which he can't do at the same time as sniffing their private parts.

With a dog who is mouthy, and nibbles or bites during greeting, teach him to carry a toy or other object in his mouth. Grant him permission to greet people only when he carries something in his mouth. This prevents the mouthing and gives him something else to think about.

Every Place, Every Time

Shift context early. Enlist every person willing to help. Most friends are happy to help you teach your dog not to jump on them. Supervise greeting procedure everywhere you go, in lots of different places. Be proactive. Be prepared every time your dog greets someone, not just when you feel like it or when the person is dressed nicely.

Have food handy and give it to everyone who will cooperate. For those who aren't really into helping you train your dog, just stick the food in front of the dog's nose as he approaches to guarantee his acceptable behavior, or pass by that person. Your dog doesn't have to greet everyone. You choose who he can greet and you control his behavior.

Being proactive means being consistent. That means you take control of greeting *every* time, not just when it suits you. This initial investment in consistency, especially if done early (like the entire first month you have your dog or puppy), pays off in reliable behavior in the long run. If sometimes you just can't be bothered or aren't prepared, put the dog away (if the visitors are at your door) or keep the dog away from the people. Avoid having him rehearse unwanted behavior.

Work on Response first – having the dog's feet stay on the ground on cue. Next work on Responsibility – having the dog stay on the ground during the entire greeting procedure. Finally, focus on Reliability – putting both parts of the behavior together most of the time.

As the dog becomes reliable, add a cue (word or gesture) to give him permission to greet someone, like "Say Hi!" or "Go Be Friends." Also teach a cue such as "Leave It," to tell him you'd rather he didn't greet that person – useful with your elderly grandmother or a friend carrying hot coffee. Highly reinforce any attention back to you for this behavior, especially with a very social dog.

Later, you can require that the dog sit as a greeting behavior. But be absolutely sure that behavior is solid, and reliably on cue, before adding the distraction and excitement of greeting procedure. Shouting "Sit" over and over at a wiggling, bouncing dog usually doesn't work.

When you're really into teaching your cute little dog lots of Stupid Pet Tricks (oops, we mean Smart Pet Tricks), just because positive training is so much fun, you can teach him to wave or shake hands as a cute greeting behavior. Both are easy to teach and definitely keep the dog's mind off jumping or sniffing.

Letting your dog greet people is a privilege you grant. That is part of heaven that comes through you. He earns this privilege by offering the correct behavior. Keep control and keep it consistent.

We got a little ahead of ourself here, so let's get back to teaching the basic manners. First things first.

The Name Game

The first step in teaching anything is to get the dog's attention. This means teaching the dog to respond reliably to his name. We call this process the Name Game.

Name recognition means that the *first* time you say your dog's name, he turns his head from whatever he is doing and looks at you. This really is the least he can do for you, since you buy the food and the toys and all that other good stuff.

Just as when you say a person's name, or your child's name, you expect a response, you should expect the same from your dog. Acknowledging your presence and making eye contact is the correct response to a name – human or canine.

You'd be surprised how often this simple zero to one step is neglected. Name recognition must be taught.

Somehow the dog is supposed to know his name once he's heard it 10 times. Dogs need lots of repetitions to learn words and their name is no exception. This is probably the most important word he needs to learn.

Play the Name Game again and again throughout the first few days and weeks, whenever you and your puppy are together. At first, just wait for any moment when the puppy looks as you, say his name happily, praise him and give him a treat.

Once the puppy offers this behavior more and more, put it on cue. Pick a moment when the puppy is close and not looking at you, but is also not terribly distracted. Say his name happily once. If he looks at you, make a huge fuss, praise and jackpot – 10 small pieces of food right in a row!

If he doesn't look at you right away, just touch him or tap him lightly. Most puppies will turn to see what touched them. Repeat his name, praise and feed.

The reason you repeat his name again here, *after* he looks at you, is to associate his name with the correct behavior. The fact that he didn't turn and look at you the first time he heard his name means that he has not made the correct word association yet in his little puppy brain.

Avoid calling the puppy's name when he is really distracted or when he is too far away for you to do anything about it. If you want to attract him, clap or whistle or toss something near him to interrupt his focus and get his attention. Call his name from a distance only after he responds reliably at close quarters. Then add distance gradually, as well as distractions, one by one. Remember to ackpot as soon as he turns and looks at you on his name.

Name response is an important behavior that can earn privileges. It is the beginning of the dog being responsible. It s the beginning of recognizing your authority. And it is the beginning of coming when called.

Teach the Name Game positively and thoroughly. It is the foundation of relationship, as well as future training. Remember, you can't train without attention and name response *is* attention.

Wait

After responsibility comes self-control. While it can be counter-productive to insist on long, motionless stays with puppies or young dogs, they are certainly able to learn the beginnings of self-control. Wait is one behavior that helps teach the concept that all of heaven comes through you.

Teach the puppy to wait at doors, at stairs, to come out of the crate, to go in and out of the car and anywhere else in your lifestyle where there is a specific physical boundary that the dog can observe. Many people make the criteria for wait just to stop and hold still. But both the relationship and future training benefit if you release him from wait only when he makes eye contact with you, especially when he really wants access to where he is going.

For housetraining purposes, it is sometimes difficult to make the very young puppy wait to come out of the crate, especially if you've left it too long. We explained how to be proactive in the housetraining schedule with the crate (see Chapter 14: The Puppies).

But whenever you are proactive, and get to the crate early so you know the little fella doesn't have to go out urgently, teach him to wait for permission to come out of the crate. Initially, just say "Wait," and toss a piece of food or a couple of kibbles into the crate as you begin to open the door.

Only open the door an inch or two at first – no need to slam it on his head if he tries to get out. But do use your other hand (the one not holding the door) to prevent him from coming out before you give permission. If your hand has a piece of food in it to help him wait, all the better.

Being Quiet

If your puppy is very vocal, and barks or whines whenever you come near the crate, avoid letting him out in response to this behavior. As you approach, toss several pieces of kibble or other tiny treats into the crate.

While he is being quiet (because he's searching and eating), begin associating a word (such as "Quiet") with that behavior. Open the door while he is still looking for or eating the food and then begin the routine to teach wait.

As soon as the puppy exhibits even one second of self-control, put the word on it, "Wait, Wait. Goooood." Give the puppy another treat. Just as he's done eating it, give your release word clearly (like "Let's Go" or "Free Dog") and open the door wide so the puppy can come out.

Keep working this up the approximation ladder for slightly longer times, up to a few seconds, before releasing. Then go back to a shorter time, but begin opening the door wider. Work up to where he waits for at least two seconds to come out, even when the door is wide open.

Continue to put the word on the desired behavior as often as possible so the puppy hears it over and over while he is waiting. Always praise and offer food treats in the crate for staying there. Use the word "Wait" every time the puppy exhibits the desired behavior.

Shift Context

Practice the same behavior at the house doors and the car doors. Have the pup on leash (to prevent the unwanted behavior) and reinforce wait with food and praise, then finally with access to passing through the door after you release him.

Should the agile little pup manage to dash through the door before you give permission, simply close the door behind him. He's on a leash so he can't go anywhere.

Give him several seconds to let him process what went wrong and why he's out there all by his lonesome, on the wrong side of the door. Then open the door and invite him back in to try again.

As soon as the puppy starts to offer the desired behavior, and wait automatically even for two seconds, add the criteria of eye contact for permission to go through the door. Avoid stretching the waiting behavior too far. Don't push the threshold.

Keep it short and successful. For a puppy to wait even a few seconds shows great self-control, especially if he is excited about going out, or perhaps urgently needs to relieve himself. Some things just won't wait that long!

Raise Criteria

As the puppy gets older and more able to control himself, raise criteria. When he waits and gives eye contact, tell him to "Wait" again as you take one step forward, going in front of him before you release him. Increase the distance you go in front slowly, one or two steps at a time, and only when he clearly shows he's ready to handle more distance.

Shift context to help the dog generalize the cue for this behavior. Take "Wait" everywhere, adding one new place every few days. He can wait while you to go through the door first or up the stairs ahead of him. Perfect this waiting behavior at doors or stairs, especially if there are any leadership issues with the dog.

With the pushy or dominant dog, teach him either to climb the stairs behind you on cue ("Behind Me") or make him wait at the bottom until you get to the top. Then release him to come up.

Charging up the stairs ahead of you is a control issue for the dominant dog. Modify this behavior and set clear rules if you see any leadership challenges looming with this dog.

Teaching the puppy to wait in the crate, or at doors and stairs, does take a few extra minutes out of the day. But it is an investment of time well spent.

Once these behaviors become habits, they affirm the relationship and enhance the pleasure of living with your dog. They also provide added safety because he doesn't dash out the door or jump out of the car.

Walking On Leash

Walking on a loose leash falls into the same category. The initial few steps take a little extra time each day, but life is so much easier and safer once the behavior is learned properly. Besides, your wonderful puppy is certainly worth the time you invest now.

We already talked about a constructive introduction to the leash (see The Leash). Now we need to take those first few steps. Bring your really good food. This program works best if you begin it with a hungry puppy on his first walk.

Have your puppy wait at the door for a second (with you feeding him) before releasing him. As you release him and step through the door, show him that you have more really good food in your hand.

If he pays attention to you and doesn't pull on the leash, feed and praise and put a word on it, like "With Me" or "Right Here" (or even "Walkies!" if you must). Use your chosen word only when the leash is loose and, at first, when he's paying attention to you.

Equipment Check

Just a word about equipment. Use a regular, well-fitting buckle collar. No choke chains please! (Jean Donaldson appropriately refers to them as "strangle collars.") If I were God, I'd outlaw choke chains, along with the sale of puppies in pet shops, as is the rule in many European countries.

These two simple laws would be a giant step toward humane treatment of animals. (Sorry, stepped back onto the soap box there for a moment.)

The best leash is cotton web, light nylon or soft leather, less than an inch wide with a snap that suits the size of your dog. Leashes should be light and flexible, not chain or heavy webbing or thick, stiff leather. If you want your dog to feel like a feather on the leash, don't put an anvil around his neck or a chain in your hand!

Flexi-leads won't work here. The very nature of Flexis require the dog to pull and then reward that behavior by letting him go further away. They promote the exact opposite of what we want to teach right now.

Later, you can use a Flexi at specific times, such as letting the dog relieve himself. But first, he must learn to be responsible and responsive to you and not pull on the leash.

When you do graduate to a Flexi, keep the puppy fairly close. Work on the Name Game and leash etiquette. He earns the privilege of going to the end of the Flexi only by exhibiting correct leash manners.

So now you're a few steps out the door and puppy sees or smells something interesting. He hits the end of the leash. You just stand still and wait. Do not move. Allow him to make the decision to release the tension on the leash.

As soon as the leash goes slack, associate the cue, "With Me, Good" and take another step forward. Whenever the puppy checks in and looks at you, or comes close to you, praise and feed.

Slower Is Faster

As you can see, this first walk might get you half way down the front path. Understanding comes slowly the first few sessions. This is definitely one of those times when going slowly is actually going faster.

The pup is just learning to learn. Maybe by the end of the week, you'll get to the end of the driveway, depending on how food-driven and how curious and bold your puppy is. But keep building the right behavior and associating a word.

The goal is to teach the pup to walk on a leash, not to go for a mile-long walk the first day. Once the puppy grasps the right concept, it lasts a lifetime if properly and regularly reinforced. This is an investment that pays off in the long run.

Keep it fun, and stay calm. Be prepared to wait. Bring your patience and your perseverance. Take the time you need. Enjoy the time with your puppy.

Watch him closely and keep smiling. He can't be doing anything wrong because he doesn't know anything yet. Reinforce and praise what you like. Ignore the rest.

The most important thing for you to bring to these first few sessions is a patient attitude. It is absolutely vital for you to believe that the pup can do nothing wrong. Remember, his behavior isn't good or bad – it's just acceptable or not.

For a dog who already pulls hard, you can try one of the halter or martingale type of head collars, just to prevent the initial unwanted behavior. Be especially proactive with this dog – reward any attention to you and any attempt to walk without pulling.

But avoid becoming dependent on these special collars. Don't use them as a crutch. Use them just to prevent the unwanted behavior for now. Take the time to teach the desired behavior through positive reinforcement and be sure to put it on cue.

Putting the dog on leash is not an excuse for him to check out and forget where you are, just because you are attached. The leash does not end his responsibility. Use the leash to reinforce your leadership, not to abandon your position. Remember that whenever the dog pulls on the leash, he takes control.

Reliable Recall

Every owner expects his dog to come when called. What's amazing is how few dogs really do respond reliably to this request.

Many people say their dog has a "100% recall." What that usually means is that he comes 100% of the time when he wants to, and refuses to come 100% of the time when he is interested in something else, like a squirrel. In most cases, the owners simply did not take the time and make the effort to teach the young dog to come when called – every time.

Contrary to popular belief, this is not something dogs are born knowing. They don't come to you just because they know their name or because you wrote a check for them and now have the ownership papers in your desk drawer.

One of the reasons that come when called is so often neglected is because young puppies (up to 12 weeks old) tend to hang around. That's their nature. In the wild, sticking close to the den, and to the pack, is a survival tactic. Those who wander away rarely live to pass on their independent nature.

One informative, but sad, nature show follows a family of golden-backed jackals in Africa. The small litter includes one precocious member, known as "Bold Pup." This one is too confident for his own good. While still too young, Bold Pup tries to follow his parents when they leave to go hunting one evening. He fails to catch up to them and they don't hear his cries when he is finally alone.

The next morning they find him, but his night alone has cost him one of his rear feet. Amazingly, it heals and he gimps around for another month, but his boldness is gone.

Eventually, he becomes a mortality statistic, along with so many other pups who fail to survive their first year in the wild. This one doesn't live long enough to pass along his "bold" genes.

The same holds true for wolves. During the first year of the history-making Yellowstone Wolf Recovery Project, an "impressive and assertive" young male (nicknamed "Ah-nold") became an early casualty.

This truly magnificent specimen quickly dispersed beyond the Yellowstone boundaries with his mate. He was subsequently gunned down and beheaded by a trophy-hunting local. "Ah-nold" did manage to sire one litter, orphans who then had to be rescued. But many of the less bold wolves are still passing along their genes today.

Courage and independence are not usually assets to the genetic survival of wild canines. Bolder isn't always better. The smartest and most wary canines are more often the ones who live long enough to become alphas in the wild.

Bold Is Beautiful?

But it's the Bold Pups that people like. Breeders select for confidence and independence and "boldness." Often, their goal is to eliminate all shyness and unsureness in the temperament. Along the way, sometimes we lose the very nature that makes dogs dependent on us – the trait that made them so prone to domestication in the first place.

The public often reinforces these breeding goals. Most buyers tend to pick the pup who unties their shoelaces first. So if you happen to have one of those Bold Pups, who is not still hanging around close to you at 12 weeks old, then you need to start today to teach him to come when called – absolutely.

For the normal puppies, who do stick close for those several weeks, the owners start to take it for granted. They assume the dog is going to follow them around like that forever. Wrong. Even the most dependent, people-oriented puppy usually starts to explore on his own between four and six months old.

These are the "terrible-twos" of puppydom. This is the age when the pups in the wild start traveling with the pack, sometimes testing the waters on their own for brief forays. This is the age of teething. Hormones begin to flow and most puppies assert their independence in a variety of ways.

If the first few declarations of independence go unnoticed, or are accepted by the owner, the terrible-twos get worse and worse. What we accept we train. This puppy is on his way to taking over the household.

Hostile Takeovers

If your puppy has moving up to CEO on his mind, pay special attention to the little things. When the little things are in order, the big things never happen – like maybe a bid for a "hostile takeover." Get more proactive.

"Don't sweat the small stuff" is a common maxim for human relationships. In canine relationships, it's exactly the opposite. Control all areas of this puppy's life.

Use the little things to convince him of his subordinate status. Janitors don't contemplate hostile takeovers. If he's pushing the parameters, time to lose privileges. It isn't that he understands this connection, but his unacceptable behavior is a symptom of his misguided view of the relationship.

Make his world smaller. Attach him to your waist with the leash. Make him follow you around the house so you can monitor his behavior.

Food comes only from you – and only for his acceptable behavior. Get most of it out of the bowl and into daily life. Toys and games too come only from you. Control everything this dog wants and make sure he understands that he must have permission from you to get them.

Reward the acceptable, but stop the unacceptable right away. If you don't like what's happening, change it. When behavior improves, add privileges one by one.

All dogs benefit from understanding "Wait" and "Place" and "Behind Me" and "Off" and "Leave It." But for this dog, it is critical that these daily parameters be strictly enforced, every day, preferably before he reaches adolescence. When he doesn't comply, then he doesn't get to do what he wants. He gets a short time out in his crate.

Be especially proactive with such a puppy. Just as with children, it works best to establish the relationship early, before they get to be teenagers. Instead of saying, "Gee, he never did that before," adopt the attitude of, "He'll never do that again." Getting away with something twice means the dog is learning the wrong things. What you accept, you train.

Get Proactive

When you start really being proactive, incidents that once were disciplinary problems now become management issues. When a dog exhibits an unacceptable behavior once, it's more than likely he'll do it again if nothing changes. The answer is to process the valuable information he has given you and prevent the unwanted behavior next time through correct management.

If you're unsure about whether to accept a certain behavior, ask yourself whether a subordinate wolf would act that way with the alpha. Would he be allowed to body check him or lean on him? Would he bite him or growl at him? Would he steal his food or bark at him? This can give you a clearer idea of how the dog is perceiving the relationship.

With this type of dog, the one who has an agenda all his own, manage the little things in his life. Then try to make training a challenge for him.

Figure out how to get him to *want* to do what you want. Put something in it for him and challenge him to figure out how to get the valuable rewards he wants. Try to pose a question for this dog, instead of staging a fight.

Often, these are the dogs of character. The trainer of the great racehorse Seattle Slew said that this horse would fight to the death if you tried to make him do something, but he would die trying to do what you wanted if you posed it in the form of a question. Seattle Slew was obviously a horse of character.

Training works better with these types when they view it as a challenge instead of coercion. Why would anyone ever want to break or inhibit such a wonderful spirit in the name of training?

The Light Line

Back to the recall. Proactive management is also the best way to teach a reliable recall. The first step is to prevent the unwanted behavior. That means extending the leash to a light line.

This light line is, like the leash, not an instrument of control. It is merely a tool to prevent the unwanted behavior of the puppy getting too far away. The line is made of thin, strong cord (venetian blind cord works well for most breeds) with a small snap attached to one end and no knots or loops or handles to catch on anything.

Wherever the puppy goes, he drags such a line. Often, because we are doing such positive training and always have food with us to help reinforce desired behavior, our puppies become stuck to us like Velcro. We don't complain.

They want to be with us because we have all the good stuff. This is one of the wonderful side-effects of positive reinforcement training. Even so, they always wear a light line outside.

This prevents us being caught off-guard that first day the puppy decides that something else might be much more interesting than we are, and thus declares his independence. You never know when the terrible-twos might strike.

If the puppy is showing independence, or exhibiting undesirable behavior in the house (such as chasing the cat or jumping up at the windows), then he gets to wear a line in the house too. The house line can be shorter – about four feet works fine unless you live in a mansion.

The line for outside should be about 25 feet long. There is no reason any puppy (or dog) should be any further than 25 feet away in these formative months.

Remember the Three Rs as criteria for behavior. By being Responsive and Responsible and Reliable in coming when called, the dog can earn the privilege of a longer line, or even (much, much later) running free. But this privilege, like all others, must be earned through consistently correct behavior.

Keep It Safe

Be sure to practice outside only in a safe area, not near a road. Lines can break. Remember that raising a puppy is as much about protection as it is about exposure and training.

Attach the line to a well-fitting buckle collar (no chokers!). When the puppy is on the line, inside or out, begin with the same procedure as in the Name Game. Just as the puppy is getting distracted or interested in something, but while he is still fairly close, say his name. If he doesn't turn and look, step on the line. His response controls the outcome.

The Right Response

Most puppies, even after a few days of the Name Game, are turning and looking almost every time. Simply extend this program to all sorts of different places and situations, but only if the puppy is being totally successful and responsive in quiet places and at home. As soon as the puppy turns away from a distraction and looks at you, this is a moment for much praise. Get excited.

Tell the pup how much you like that behavior – "Wow! What a dog!" If he happens to come all the way to you on just his name, get excited about that too, with petting and food and lots of positive energy. This is behavior you like!

If for some reason the puppy does not turn and look when he hears his name, stand on the line to prevent him from running away and reinforcing himself. We don't want him learning how much fun it is to chase those squirrels.

Standing on the light line prevents that. Avoid calling his name over and over. That only teaches him to ignore his name and your presence.

You are now standing on the light line. Without saying a word, walk down the line. When you get close enough to touch him, do so. As he turns to look at you, remind him what his name is. (He's obviously forgotten.) Then praise and feed when he looks at you.

Make a big fuss now that he has turned away from something interesting and given his attention to you. Make yourself more fun than the distraction. Spend a few fun seconds with the puppy. Then let him loose again, but not to go as far away as before. The puppy has just made it clear that this is too big a step for him.

An important part of coming when called is for the pup to learn that it doesn't mean confinement or that free time is over. It never means anything negative happens.

Just as the puppy is moving away, or even looking away, call his name again. If he doesn't offer the appropriate response – turning and looking at you – take him away from the distraction and work in a quieter location, such as back in the house. Remember to jackpot when he responds correctly.

If your puppy does turn and look while he is moving away outside, get excited again and praise. Toss him several pieces of food. That's enough for now. Getting the right Response is a major step, so quit while you're ahead.

Earning Freedom

Your puppy has given you the Response you want, so you now give him what he wants – access to freedom. Walk around together and just let him explore. No more calling his name. If he gets too far away, like more than 15 feet, step on the line. Don't say or do anything else, just let him be free. This is his reward. Get involved with what he wants to do.

If you don't think you're quick enough to step on the line before the pup dashes off, then hold the end in your hand as a safety measure. But there must never, ever, be any continual tension on the line. The pup just drags it around.

Should he happen to stop and look at you or come back to you in between exploring, praise and pet him and give him a food treat. We want a dog who checks in and is responsible for knowing where we are, instead of vice-versa. Reward any step he makes in that direction.

When your puppy is winning at the Name Game – consistently turning to look at you when you say his name, indoors and out, and around mild distractions – begin to train come when called. Go back to a quiet setting. As your puppy is exploring a few feet away, say his name.

When he turns to look at you, praise him. Kneel or squat down and open up your arms in a welcoming gesture. Kneeling or squatting is a much more inviting posture to a pup than bending over.

Call "Come" once. If he begins to move toward you, clap your hands and encourage him with "Yes! Yes! Good! What a dog!" Avoid using the word "Come" again until he arrives close enough for you to touch him.

Receive him and pet him and praise him and make a huge fuss over him. Remind him that this is "Come" (to help him associate the word) and jackpot – feed him small pieces of food continually, from alternating hands, for at least 20 to 30 seconds. Then let him go back to exploring.

End On Success

Three repetitions are enough for any session. End on success. If his first recall is just perfect, leave it there for this session. Let him have extra free time to explore while he drags his line, as you watch and follow.

Now, for one week, do only three recalls each day when you *know* your puppy will come to you. When he does, jackpot – give him small pieces of food continually, from alternating hands, for at least 30 to 60 seconds.

This is from Leslie Nelson's puppy program, and it works like magic. In fact, you'll probably have trouble getting your pup to leave your side. He's trying to figure out what earned him that full 60 seconds of yummy food!

After one full week, begin to increase the distance you allow your pup to go before being called. But stick to doing just three recalls per day, *only* when you are sure he will come, with a 30 to 60 second jackpot as reward. Your puppy is learning to earn the privilege of being further away (up to 25 feet) because he is being responsive.

Once the puppy is consistently coming from 15 or 20 feet away in a quiet place, move to a different place and shorten the distance back to a few feet. Whenever you shift context, back up a step or two. Increase the distance only after the puppy reliably shows the correct Response.

We are working on the puppy's agenda here and letting him show us what he is ready to learn, when and where. Every puppy is different and each has a different time frame for learning.

Once Is Enough

Remember in the Name Game to call his name only *once*, ever. Do not teach him to respond on the second or fifth repetition. Do not teach him to wait for a louder voice. Do not teach him to wait for a scream to respond.

Teach him to respond reliably to a calm, happy tone of voice the first time you call his name. Responding to his name is not coming when called. If he turns and looks at you when you say his name, that is enough for him to get reinforced and rewarded with praise and excitement, and maybe even a piece of food tossed to him.

He should come when he hears the word "Come." For now, add squatting down and clapping as encouragement to help him get the right response. But as soon as he is coming consistently, drop these signals and help him less.

Only call him once to "Come." Do not teach that this can be obeyed the second time, after he ignores the first call. He only gets one chance. If he fails to come the first time, stay quiet and walk down the long line to the puppy. Back up all the way, as you lure the puppy back to the place where you called him. Use a food treat, but keep your hand closed.

When you get back there, back up a few feet more as you tell him "Come." When he follows, feed and praise and make a big fuss as you remind him that this one is "Come."

Should he fail to come more than once, go back down the approximation ladder. Return to a quieter place, like where he was last successful. Shorten the distance.

Get more excited when he comes next time. Get better food. Be sure he is hungry. Play the Name Game more often and in different places. Rebuild the foundation and then go forward more slowly.

The puppy can't be wrong. He doesn't know this yet because it hasn't been taught completely. He's just a puppy. He forgets. He gets distracted – that's why he drags a line. And it takes time to teach this thoroughly! With a little more training, he'll get it.

Come when called is not something taught in one week. It is an ongoing process that often takes months for the dog to understand completely.

Distraction Recall

When the puppy is coming most of the time, the first time you call, the next step is distraction training. He's got Response. He's being Responsible and coming all the way. Time to teach Reliability. This is the step that assures a true 100% recall, not the kind we mentioned earlier.

Enlist the aid of a friend. Start in a quiet place where the dog is comfortable and where he is most reliable in his recall. Give the friend boring food, like a biscuit or kibble. You keep the really good stuff, like roast beef or cheese.

With the dog wearing his long line, let him get interested in the food your friend has in his hand. But the friend keeps his hand closed. He never lets the dog eat his food for now. You stand near the dog, just off to the side. While he is still sniffing the other person's hand, play the Name Game.

Give the pup a couple of seconds to respond. Allow him time to make the right decision. If he looks at you, get excited. Praise him, tell him how wonderful he is and give him some of the good stuff you have.

If he doesn't respond, touch him or tap him to get his attention, or show him what good food you have. When he looks at you, say his name again, praise and feed. Repeat this step until he is responding reliably to his name the first time, even when you are standing a couple of feet behind him instead of off to the side.

That's enough for this session. This is a tough concept for a dog – to leave what's in front of his nose to find better stuff somewhere else. Soon the Consequence will begin to drive his Behavior.

At the next session, repeat the previous step once to make sure the dog responds quickly and correctly to the Name Game. When he does, pet and praise and feed. Get him interested in your friend's boring food again.

You go a few feet away. Call his name. When he turns to look at you, squat down, open your arms and call him "Come" in an excited, inviting voice, as well as clapping your hands. The moment he takes one step toward you, praise with "Yes! Yes! Good! What a Dog!," but don't say "Come" again.

Rejoice! This is a difficult step for a dog to master. When he gets close enough to touch, pet him and remind him that this is "Come" as you feed him the good stuff.

End the session here. Sit on the ground and play with him for a little bit. Take him for a nice walk, letting him explore while you follow. (Yes, of course your friend can come too, he just can't feed your dog yet.) If your dog likes it better, play fetch. Throw a toy or a stick for him. Give him what *he* wants for a reward.

Should the dog not respond, there are two options. The friend can lead the dog over to you (by having him follow the food in the closed hand). Then you repeat the dog's name and "Come," backing up slightly, showing the dog what you have. Praise and feed the good food when he reaches you.

Or you can go to the dog and touch him to remind him about responding to his name. Then call him "Come" and do a shorter recall as you back up, praising and encouraging and then feeding.

Be careful never to beg the dog to come. Don't plead or coax. Praise and encourage the dog only while he is moving toward you – exhibiting the behavior you want. Only then is it reinforcement for the right behavior.

Let Them Learn

The point of this exercise is to allow the dog to learn that coming when called is always more pleasurable and rewarding than the distraction. The friend does not feed him. He never gets that food. He only gets food from you (better food!) when he does what you ask.

This is a classic example of letting the dog learn, instead of teaching. When people jerk on the line and reel the dog in, they get the right behavior, but no learning.

The dog must be allowed to think about it, work it through and figure it out by himself. He must be allowed to make the right decision.

No, it doesn't happen the first time. It takes patience to stop teaching and let the dog learn. But when he gets it – once the light bulb goes on – the friend will have to hold the dog's collar to keep him there. The dog figures it out for himself and it makes for a powerful experience that he remembers.

Once the dog gets it with this person in this place, add one more step. Have the friend hold the dog by the collar, still showing him the food in his hand and letting him sniff and lick it. You call the dog – name first, then "Come." Have the friend hold on to the dog for just a split second after he turns to look at you and then let him go.

Adding this little bit of opposition reflex to the routine usually causes the dog to fly back like he's been shot from a cannon. It's sure to put a smile on your face.

Now continue the same program, but shift context. Go to a different place. Use another friend. Let the friend have some better food, but never anything your dog likes better than what you have.

Then, when the dog returns to you when called, the friend walks over to you and feeds the dog his food too – jackpot! The dog earned the bonus, and we all know how good that feels.

Do the same exercise with toys, if your dog likes toys. Increase the distance to 25 feet (if you really think your dog will let you get that far away by now). This gets to be a really fun game for the dog when he learns how to control the outcome.

Advanced Recalls

Once the dog responds reliably in all these different situations, you're ready to take him to places of ultimate distraction. These temptations are different for every dog – squirrels, a pond, dogs, cats, birds, woodchucks, whatever.

Be sure to make the situation safe. If using other dogs, have them behind a sturdy fence. Be sure your light line is strong – not worn or chewed or knotted. Preferably find a large area that is fenced and far away from dangerous roads.

Start with the Name Game while your dog is still close, before he ever gets interested in the distractions. Of course he's still on his long line.

Work on the dog's agenda. If he checks in the first time you call his name, try a short recall. If he's successful in both of these, quit for the day and let him explore and enjoy what he loves. If he gets too far away, just step on the line.

Three recalls are the maximum for any session. When the dog responds properly, he's earned the privilege of free time within 25 feet of you. Of course you reinforce any attention to you and show appreciation whenever he checks in. But don't ask for more. He's earned his freedom for today.

Giving your dog access to what he truly loves is a major step in becoming a fair pack leader. Maybe you can't safely let him chase squirrels or cats or deer, but find something he does really like and to which you can grant access.

Be sure to be proactive here. It's often impossible to stop a dog from chasing something if he's already running full tilt, just as it's difficult to stop barking once it's started. It's usually much more effective to interrupt his focus before he gets fixated. Learn to watch his eyes and his body posture.

When he notices something, step on the line and play the Name Game. Confirm that he needs permission to pursue everything he wants. And sometimes you grant it.

Get attention. Get a behavior. Then allow him to check it out. Being the one who always stops him from doing what he wants doesn't get you any points as a fair pack leader.

Hide-And-Seek

One game that teaches responsibility to you, and helps with coming when called, is hide-and-seek. This tactic works especially well with very young puppies – those under 12 weeks who have not yet reached their terrible-twos. Simply hide on the puppy if he gets a little too far away. For this you need a safe place, such as a fenced field.

Just wait until the puppy is a short distance away and then slip into the tall grass (or behind a tree or gate) and call his name. Stand still and keep an eye on him. Puppies can see movement, but not real definition at any distance.

If he starts to go the wrong way, whistle or clap or call him again to help him. When he finds you, make a big fuss and roll around on the ground with him. This is a fun game that is a fine learning experience too.

Whenever your puppy or dog responds particularly well, especially under a difficult distraction, have something special. By now you should know what he likes best – a squeak toy, a fuzzy ball, some really great food, a belly rub or just throwing a stick.

Reward his excellent behavior with what he really wants and you're on your way to having a dog who loves to come when called. You're on your way to Reliability.

Response in the recall is the dog turning to look at you and taking that first step toward you. Responsibility is coming all the way to you without any further help. Reliability is doing both consistently, even under distraction.

One word of caution. Don't take any chances. Keep the light line on all the time, even if you don't use it. Should you need it, there is no substitute.

Prevent any unwanted (and dangerous) behavior until your dog is absolutely reliable under all distractions. A completely reliable recall is rarely fully trained until the dog is at least 16 to 18 months old.

Remember the criteria: Response, Responsibility and Reliability. When it comes to total recalls, there's no substitute for maturity and experience.

Progressive Parameters

Just as the leash becomes a light line, and responsive behavior leads to more freedom for the puppy, so parameters in the house are expanded as he earns our trust. Our responsibility is to help the pup be successful step by step.

The key to success here is management – and that means confinement. Just as the leash became a light line, so the crate can be expanded to a small area in the kitchen, behind a baby gate or an exercise pen.

All puppies should learn to respect such physical barriers. They need to learn not to knock them down or push through them, even when they can. They should also learn to stay inside a fenced yard, even if they could jump over or dig under.

When puppies learn about confinement early, they rarely challenge it later. Like those elephants bound by ankle chains when they were young, they can be tied with a silken thread for the rest of their lives. They never question it.

As with crate training, teaching parameters properly depends on supervision, a regular schedule and consistency. Once the puppy is dependable in a small area, that space can be expanded, perhaps to the entire kitchen with only a baby gate across the door.

Confinement shouldn't mean isolation. This frightens and frustrates a puppy. He feels abandoned. Teach him to be in his own area near where you are.

An oversized wire crate or an exercise pen, so that you can see the dog and he can see you, is one of the best investments you can make in keeping your puppy and your house safe during growing pains. A regular baby playpen works well for small breeds.

Reaping Rewards

Responsibility earns access. When the puppy is clean and quiet in the crate, he gets access to the kitchen. When he is good in the kitchen, he gets access to the family room – with supervision of course. When he is responsible and reliable in the family room, he earns supervised access to other rooms. Acceptable behavior earns privileges. Should behavior deteriorate, privileges are curtailed.

Through these approximations, the young dog can have success in subsequently larger and larger areas of the house. Eventually, when he is responsive and responsible and reliable, he can earn access to the entire house and spend more time with you.

If you want the dog to occupy a certain place in the kitchen while you are cooking, or a specific area in the dining room while you are eating, then consistently feed and reinforce the dog there. Define the space with a rug or a bed. Put a word on that area such as "Place." Toss a few treats there and, when the dog goes after them, put the word on it.

Dogs, like all organisms, gravitate to the places of highest reinforcement. As he goes there more and more, offer better reinforcement. Show him the places you want him to be, instead of nagging him about where you don't want him to go.

Supervision is a key here. Would you allow a toddler to run around the house, unsupervised, to make discoveries about electrical wires, hot stoves or glass decorations? The same applies to the dog.

He can't know the rules until you show him what they are. Once he knows the rules, he must demonstrate that he is willing to follow them before he earns privileges and freedom.

This is natural to dogs. The pack has strict rules that must be followed. Setting parameters makes you a fair pack leader. Until he pays the mortgage or vacuums up his own hair, the dog has no ownership rights to anything. All the decisions are yours.

But give the puppy a break. Put the garbage away. Pick up the kids' socks. Keep your slippers out of reach. File the dirty laundry in the hamper. Supervise the dog around food. Avoid the unwanted behaviors until the puppy is more responsible and understands the rules.

And avoid being in a hurry to give him free run of the house. The overwhelming desire to chew lasts much longer than visible teething. Rarely can dogs be trusted alone in a large, valuable area of the house until they are about 18 months or older.

Barking

Inappropriate barking can be annoying. Sometimes it is difficult to stop completely because it is such a natural and self-reinforcing behavior. Barking is especially prevalent in certain breeds, such as Shelties.

So if you really don't want a dog who barks too much, research breed specific behavior. Evaluate the dog or puppy to see how vocal he is, then choose the quietest one.

The answer to barking is to teach the word "Quiet." To do this, we must first identify an Alternative Incompatible Behavior – something the dog cannot do and bark at the same time. Let's face it, in order to associate the word "Quiet," the barking must stop. Food is the one that we've found works best, but if you know another one, please let us know.

We already talked about tossing little pieces of food in the crate when you leave the puppy. If the puppy is vocal, and then settles down when you toss in food, associate the word "Quiet" while he is looking for the food and eating.

The puppy quickly shows when he is prone to bark. The owner's responsibility is to get proactive – *before* he starts the undesirable behavior in that situation.

Let's say your puppy barks whenever you leave him in the car. Take some kibbles with you. Just as you get ready to leave, tell him "Quiet" and drop a handful of kibbles (tiny ones) either on the floor or in his crate. As he goes looking for the food, tell him "Quiet, Good Quiet" and leave.

If you allow this barking to continue, it only gets worse and worse. Why? Barking is self-reinforcing and separation anxiety is a natural fear and frustration that does not disappear by itself. Nip the situation in the bud by teaching a different behavior.

Silence Is Golden

If the puppy barks at other times, such as at puppy class, teach "Quiet" another way. Before the puppy starts barking, firmly press a dab of peanut butter onto the roof of his mouth (nope, no jelly or milk with it) and associate it with the word "Quiet."

This calls attention to the word having something to do with his mouth. It also prevents the barking while he is preoccupied. The idea here is not to use peanut butter his whole life, but to prevent the unwanted behavior (barking) so we can reinforce the proper behavior (with food and petting and praise) and associate the word "Quiet".

I have had amazing success with this in teaching a friend's dogs to remain quiet in their kennels while another dog walks by. Initially, all three dogs would go crazy barking in the kennel at the sight of another dog.

I got proactive. When another dog was going to be brought in, I tossed a handful of small kibbles into their runs and said "Quiet." While the other dog walked by, I kept repeating "Quiet, Good, Quiet" as they were vacuuming up the kibble.

They made the positive association – see dog, get food. That broke the pattern and prevented the unwanted behavior. Then they started to make the word association between "Quiet" and getting food.

Eventually, I could show them one small biscuit, tell them "Quiet," and walk another dog past. They would wait quietly for me to return and give them each their cookie.

Now, I can toss one small cookie into their kennel runs first, and they are quiet most of the time. (This specialized skill has been termed "Biscuit Bowling." It's nearly impossible to get even a tiny cookie through two-inch mesh from six feet away – it must be "bowled" under the kennel door.)

When I say "Quiet" now, the dogs either start to drool or look on the floor for food. They've made the right word association. But it is critical to be proactive here. I don't pretend to be able to stop them once the barking festival is underway. They're having way too much fun! (Remember self-reinforcing behavior.) But I can prevent the behavior before it begins most of the time.

Teaching "Quiet" is especially important because barking can lead to unwanted aggression. Barrier frustration and barking at other dogs, such as when the dog is in the car or crate, can trigger the start of a serious problem.

Alarm Barking

Many puppies, especially those from the guarding breeds, show an early tendency to alarm bark. This is where the puppy sees something and starts to bark frantically, usually in high-pitched hysterics.

Whether at another dog or a person, this behavior is never acceptable and should be stopped right at the start. (The only exception might be if you want the dog to bark at people outside your house for protection purposes.)

If the object of alarm barking is a person, and the situation is safe, the solution is simple. Drop the leash, let it drag on the ground, and *you* approach the person.

Alarm barking is a tactic to get pack support. It's an alert designed to bring the pack running. Once the leash connection is gone and the puppy is on his own, the barking usually diminishes. If it doesn't, at least it isn't getting pack support from the owner.

Pay no attention to the puppy until he exhibits more acceptable behavior. Alarm barking is based on suspicion and fear. It has nothing to do with confidence or protection.

Ignoring the puppy means no eye contact and no reassurance. You just stand calmly laughing and talking to the person who instigated this frenzy.

Should the puppy become quiet and start to approach, praise him for that behavior. Avoid calling the puppy with "Come" because he probably won't comply when he's afraid. Set up only for success with that word.

Try to lure him closer with food, but be quiet. Any words of reassurance sound like reinforcement to the puppy. Drop a trail of food on the ground, toward the person, and see if he'll follow it. If he won't come close, just walk away.

Set up the situation next time. Feed the pup far enough away from the person, before the barking starts. Be aware that the situation will probably happen again. The puppy has given you some valuable information.

Get proactive. This puppy needs exposure to lots of different people with yummy food treats. He needs time and experience to make the correct association, "See person – get food." Teach him to approach everyone expectantly.

Dog Meets Dog

More often, alarm barking occurs toward another dog. When this is allowed to continue, and if the owner tightens the leash and holds the puppy back, it becomes the beginning of dog aggression. No, it's not play behavior – it's aggression.

This type of learned aggression escalates even faster if the owner reassures the young dog with "It's OK, Good Dog" and touches him as well. Now the dog has all the pack support he needs to assert himself. He's really afraid, but he can become a punk, like a juvenile with his gang behind him.

The first time this happens, if the situation is safe and you know the other dog is trustworthy, just drop the leash and walk over to the other dog. Very few puppies continue barking and carrying on when abandoned by their pack and left alone. Praise the puppy if he approaches nicely and stops barking.

If you are not sure of the situation, say the puppy's name immediately and walk the other way. The puppy won't bark at what he's not looking at. He's on a leash or light line, so he has to follow where you go.

Once you identify this behavior, as soon as possible set up safe situations. Use a steady dog who is experienced and trustworthy with hysterical puppies. Again, be proactive.

Begin feeding the puppy far enough away from the other dog, before he reaches that critical distance where he begins alarm barking. Should the puppy alert on the other dog and bark, back up and feed at a distance where the puppy feels safe.

In subsequent sessions, lure the puppy closer to the other dog with food, feeding continually. Should he start to bark, drop the puppy's leash and you go over to the other dog and feed *him*. As soon as the puppy exhibits acceptable behavior, and approaches even one step closer without barking, praise and toss him a piece of food.

Should the puppy approach all the way to the other dog, this is the time for calm petting and praising. Just be careful, if using food, that the two dogs don't get into a contest over getting the food.

Be sure to reinforce the older dog with food for allowing you to feed the silly puppy. You need to use a very reliable older dog for this and then reward his tolerance.

Follow this program only with a young puppy. Dogs with fully-developed canine teeth and a history of biting need a much different program supervised by a professional.

Proactive Prevention

With some puppies, you need to set up this situation a number of times. They need to learn that this behavior is not productive. You do not back them up when they behave this way. In fact, you abandon them in favor of the "enemy."

In a situation you cannot control, say the puppy's name (clearly and happily) and get out of there. Walk in the other direction. He's on a leash or a light line, so he has to come with you. If you've been doing your homework, he will.

If you must stay for some reason, like at class, go to the car and get your now-ever-present jar of peanut butter. Sit at the side and begin to teach "Quiet." Aggression management could fill an entire book. But the best thing is to prevent any escalation in this behavior by extinguishing it at the fist signs.

Just a special word about equipment. With an older dog wearing a prong collar, be aware that prong collars incite aggression. They are used in some protection training to *increase* the level of aggression. This is not the appropriate collar for a dog who shows any signs of aggression.

For an older dog who has a history of barking and aggression, the halter or martingale type of collars that shut the dog's mouth and control the head can help prevent unwanted behavior and make the situation safer.

But avoid using these collars as a crutch. Take the time to modify the behavior through the systematic use of positive reinforcement. And put a word on it like "Leave It."

If the puppy has already shown that he is prone to alarm barking, be proactive in management. Don't leave him where he can reinforce himself by barking at another dog. This includes the car, the crate, the X-pen or even your own fenced yard, if other dogs walk by.

If you must leave him in a crate near other dogs, cover the crate with a sheet so he can't see the other dogs. Visual stimulation is often the trigger for alarm barking.

Especially avoid putting the puppy in a situation with another dog who joins in the barking. That only provides the vital pack support he wants.

Remember that two dogs constitute a dog pack. They get everything they need from each other. Why on earth would they need to obey you?

Second Dogs

Speaking of double dogs, remember that when you introduce a new dog into the household, your investment lies with the resident dog, not with the newcomer. The older dog has already earned his privileges and is part of the family.

Too often, owners are captivated by the new puppy, who then receives all the attention without having done anything to deserve it. The resident dog gets jealous – and justifiably so.

When you get a new puppy, take the time to make the proper introduction on neutral turf. Put the pup in a wire crate or X-pen – somewhere not on the resident dog's home turf. Ignore the puppy and provide everything the resident dog wants – food, petting, praise, attention, toys, whatever. Provide these things closer and closer to the puppy, but keep ignoring the puppy.

If the older dog shows interest in the pup, reinforce any calm attention or curiosity – provided the resident dog is being gentle and friendly. Then go back to doing whatever the older dog likes best.

Repeat this introduction in the house. Get the resident dog to make the proper association – "See puppy, get food. See puppy, get petting. See puppy, get attention" – so the older dog sees the intruder in a positive light. Then he wants to include the puppy in the pack because it always brings him what he wants.

Dogs Will Be Dogs

If your dog is the politician type, one who just loves the sound of his own voice, basic management is the best approach. Give him a time when he can bark productively, like for a toy or for his food or to go outside. Put it on cue. Then also teach him to be "Quiet" on cue.

Acceptance also goes a long way here. He's a dog. Dogs bark. He isn't gossiping or lying or bad-mouthing you to your friends. He's just barking. He's a dog and he's doing what dogs do. Next time, get a Basenji – they don't have a true bark.

In any area, whatever behavior your dog exhibits, modify it into the behavior you want right from the start. When behavior becomes acceptable, only then does the dog earn privileges – such as getting on the sofa (only when you give permission), or sleeping on the bed (same rule), or sitting in your lap, or access to any other place or thing that he enjoys.

If you have two dogs, remember that each needs some individual time to cement the relationship and prevent dog dependency. Two dogs makes a dog pack. They need you, and respond to you, only if you require that they do so. Otherwise, they find everything they need in each other.

Why?

When modifying behavior, some folks become obsessed with figuring out why the dog acts a certain way. There is certainly a place and time for asking why, but the truth is that you don't need to know the answer to be able to modify the behavior.

Simply determine whether the behavior is acceptable or not. Then proceed to modify or encourage it, using the principles of positive reinforcement. Reinforce it, or teach the dog an Alternative Incompatible Behavior.

If you aspire to become a behaviorist, or a serious dog trainer, by all means explore and consider the various opinions at every opportunity. Start by watching the nature shows on TV with the sound turned off. The animals can show you more of the facts without you being influenced by the commentator's opinions.

But feel free not to have to figure it out. It's just dog behavior. Get what you want, put a word on it and keep reinforcing it!

Reinforce your position with your dog by requiring acceptable behavior before you grant any privileges. You had to earn your freedom as you grew up. Allow your dog to do the same. Then he is on his way to being a responsible canine citizen as well as a delightful companion.

FOCUS ON BEHAVIOR !

16

The Paradigm

" Dogs are not obedient to commands;
they are obedient to the laws of learning."
– Jean Donaldson

Now that you know the significance of the laws of learning, training becomes simple – just put any behavior you want to teach into the Positive Training Paradigm.

1. Establish a goal. Make a plan. Set up for success.

2. Prevent or ignore unwanted behavior.

3. Teach topography first. (Technique, skill and form.)

4. Associate the word with the desired behavior.

5. Shift context early. (Place, direction, wean prompts.)

6. Plan approximations. (Move up and down ladder.)

7. Raise criteria, raise reward.
      (Eye contact, longer, faster, more intense. Add toys.)

8. Premack it for access to favorite places and things.

9. Be unpredictable in providing Consequence.
    (Vary reinforcers and schedule of delivery. Be creative.)

10. Continually evaluate the plan.
    (Back up when necessary. Cement foundation.
    Consider temperament. Work on the dog's agenda.)

Remember:

Be Proactive.

Forgive Forgetting.

Keep Them Trying.

Follow the ABCs.

Let Them Learn.

Do No Damage

Keep It Simple.

Keep It Clear.

KEEP IT FUN!

SECTION III:

The Behaviors

17   The Sit

" Nobody can go back and start a new beginning,
but anyone can start today and make a new ending."
    – Maria Robinson

Let's face it. This is really a pretty silly chapter isn't it? Everybody knows how to make a dog sit, even if they never trained a dog in their life.

Simply keep shouting "Sit,Sit,Sit,SIT" as you hold the dog up by the neck (preferably on a strangle collar) and push down on his butt until the dog's resistance wears down and the joint support system collapses and the dog ends up in a heap that resembles a sit. Right?

Wrong! Now we don't want to focus on the negative here, but one of the great advantages of writing a book is that you get to air some of your pet peeves. You guessed it – this is one of mine.

In the above scenario, every time the dog hears the word "Sit" he is using all his natural opposition reflex to resist sitting and remain standing. The word ends up meaning to lock up all your muscles and get ready to resist because someone is going to try to push your butt down.

If you are unlucky enough to witness anyone making a dog sit in this manner, note the expression on the dog's face when he is suffering this indignity. Some roll their eyes or look away. Some adopt a particularly eloquent expression. Some are annoyed and others are stoic. Many are outraged and some even look embarrassed. But almost all are offended and resistant.

The fact that dogs taught in this way ever learn to sit at all is a testament to their cooperative, forgiving nature and bright minds. They sure aren't getting any help from the teacher. (We're always amazed at the number of dogs who actually do manage to learn, despite this type of "training"!)

But those dogs who do learn it this way often respond with a sit that is slow and stiff – a leftover from all the initial physical resistance. This is certainly not the type of sit we want to teach for competition, or anywhere for that matter.

The more serious side of this training method is that it can damage the complex rear end assembly of puppies and young dogs. Ligaments and tendons are like rubber bands in juveniles and connective tissue is still soft.

That's why puppies (and toddlers too) tend to bounce when they take a fall that would surely result in serious injury to their older counterparts. Pushing down on a young dog's rear while he is resisting, (which they almost all do because of their instinctive opposition reflex), can injure those tender joints. But the major problem with this type of training is the damage it does to the dog's mental outlook. It's just so totally unnecessary.

It's A Natural

Most eight-week-old puppies learn to sit quickly and happily for a food reward in a few short sessions. The photo on Page 202 was taken at this pup's first session!

A consistently square, tight, tucked sit for future competition might take a little longer to teach – depending on the pup's physical ability at a specific age. But if you begin reinforcing only a perfect sit right from the start, you'd be surprised how quickly most pups get it.

Sitting is a perfectly natural behavior for most dogs. Every healthy, sound pup we've taught offers this behavior almost immediately and continues to offer it reliably.

In fact, we recommend teaching one or two other behaviors at the same time. Otherwise, puppies can get stuck in offering sit as a "default" behavior. They learn it so well, and it is so natural, that they offer this one first, whatever the cue, and then go on to try something else.

So we suggest also teaching the puppy to lie down, as soon as he begins to understand the idea of the sit. This way, very early in his training, the puppy learns the concept that he is being asked for a specific behavior and that he needs to pay attention to the cue.

Behaviors that are not under specific stimulus control do not constitute learning. Like the computer program where you have to try several different key strokes to produce the desired result, it's useless. If you can't produce the behavior on cue, it isn't learned and can be of no use to you.

The game plan here is to teach the dog the cue and associate that with the desired behavior. Since sit is so easy to teach, we'll put it into the Positive Training Paradigm right away and use it to help the puppy learn these concepts.

Topography First

First teach the topography, or technique. The puppy must learn *how* to use his body to get into a sitting position. This is the easy part.

Teach this as the first behavior in kitchen training. The puppy is hungry. You've prepared his food and he's paying attention, ready to learn. Put a tasty tidbit between your thumb and forefinger. Hold it right in front of his nose.

When he shows interest in getting the food, raise your hand – very slowly – up and slightly back. When the pup's head follows the food up, his butt naturally drops solidly on the ground (Photo on Page 202). If the puppy tries to jump or paw or offer some other behavior to get the food – say nothing. Just close your fingers tightly and withhold the food.

Then either wait, or adjust the way you present the food to manipulate the puppy into a sit. It might take him a few seconds here to figure out how to get what he wants. He needs some time to identify which behavior is *not* earning him his reward. This is the waiting game that is so hard for some folks – just hang in there.

As long as the pup is still interested in the piece of food, keep offering him a chance to get it. Keep quiet. No verbal help is necessary. Begin to make words meaningful – by saying nothing right now.

Stop teaching and let him learn. When he learns it by himself and gets the food reward for the right behavior, he's on his way to grasping the first concept – offering behavior for reinforcement.

Word Association

Just as the puppy's butt hits the ground, begin the word association. Tell him calmly "Sit, Sit, Gooood Sit" as you release the food. The piece should be small and soft enough so that he swallows it right down and doesn't chew it or drop it on the floor.

Give the puppy the food *as soon as possible* when he sits. The faster you provide the food, the faster the puppy learns which behavior produced it. The best trainers are the ones who reinforce the fastest!

As soon as he's eaten that piece of food, remind him "Sit" if he's still sitting, and get another piece of food ready. You can have the food on the counter nearby or you can put several pieces in your hand so that you can get the behavior for a longer period of time.

If the puppy remains sitting, get another piece of food in there as quickly as possible. Between pieces of food, for as long as he's sitting, keep making the word association of "Sit, Sit, Good Sit." Give him more food while you praise.

If your puppy remains sitting the first time, long enough for you to feed him four or five pieces of food, fantastic. You've got a focused pup and you're presenting the food properly.

If you have an eye toward future competition, be sure to associate the word "Sit" only with a square, tight, tucked sit right from the beginning. If the puppy is not physically capable of that yet, then put a different word on it as an informal cue for everyday sit behavior. When he starts sitting properly, then you can introduce "Sit."

Release

If your pup has made the connection, and his butt is now riveted to the floor, teach the release right away. The pup should learn that there is a beginning and an end to every behavior – from the cue to the release.

Begin teaching this concept right away. Instead of just letting the pup get up from the sit because you have stopped feeding him, give him a clear and happy release.

Say "Free Dog!" or "Let's Go!" and move him out of position by you moving away. Lure him with food to get up only if absolutely necessary.

Release should be a happy, energetic cue. Use the same words and energy every time you release your dog from a behavior.

However, release is not a time for continual petting or feeding. And save the exuberant play for later, after he learns to be calm and focused in training and work for his release. Keep the high reinforcement within the behavior, not in the release afterward. Your dog should see training as the fun part, not the aftermath.

Keep him focused on you. Soon you'll be asking for more behaviors in succession. So keep his attention and concentration, even after the happy release.

Keep Them Trying

If the pup doesn't sit right away, no problem. Remember, he can't do anything wrong because we haven't taught him how to do anything yet. Keep smiling. Be creative. Avoid using the word "Sit" until he's in the right position.

Depending on how the puppy is reacting, tune in to how to make this work. Every dog is a little different.

If he's jumping, change the way you offer the food – keep it lower or get less appealing food. If he's losing interest, get better food or different food, or go to a quieter place. Make the pieces a little bigger, or maybe a little smaller. Try at a different time of day, when he's hungrier.

Adjust the plan to suit your dog. Be patient, persevere, and get the behavior you want. There is no cookbook formula here. What works for one puppy is a little different than what works for another. It can't be auto mechanics.

You're working with a living, thinking, reacting being. Take stock of what he's showing you.

Is he too excited about the food? Is he not interested enough? Is he jumping up? (If he's biting, go back to Chapter 13: The Beginnings.) You're getting your first taste of reading your dog and using your brain to train him instead of your brawn.

It's fun – and you can't be doing anything wrong as long as the puppy is still paying attention and trying to get the food. He'll get it. You just have to perfect your teaching technique to suit his learning capacity and physical capability. And you have to learn to wait!

Up The Ladder

If the puppy pops up from the sit after taking the first piece of food, fine. Reinforcement ends behavior. He gave you the Response you wanted and he heard the word and got his reward. Game over. You did a fine job. You got him to sit.

The next step up the ladder is to teach him to hold the sit for a few seconds. Take some more food and repeat the steps that worked the first time to get him into a sit.

Now have two or three pieces of food in your hand and offer them one at a time between your thumb and forefinger, while the dog is sitting. Use alternating hands if your pup really needs faster reinforcement in the beginning.

For that second between the food rewards, keep repeating "Sit" whenever he is sitting properly. Remember that it takes hundreds of repetitions before the dog actually recognizes these first few words. Once he understands the concept of words as cues, he will learn future words faster. But this is his first real training word!

Be sure to use the release cue every time you get him up. Watch the puppy closely and get your release cue in there *before* he gets up. Be proactive here. Release him before it's his idea.

These first few approximations might take some pups a few sessions to learn. Some get them quickly and others take more time. Build these first steps slowly and completely. So much is going to be built on the concepts the dog learns in these first few training sessions.

The most important requirements for these first sessions are a healthy, hungry puppy and your fun, patient attitude. Remember that the pup definitely can't do anything wrong because you haven't taught him anything yet!

Behavior vs. Learning

Soon, the puppy sits solidly and rivets his attention on you as you prepare his food. He's offering the behavior even before you have given him the cue.

This is his first attempt at spontaneous rehearsal. Smile and tell him he's being a fine dog. He's paying attention and not jumping up on the counter trying to get at the food.

Rejoice that you are doing such a good job with this beginning training. Remind him that this one is "Sit" and praise him. But don't offer any primary reinforcement (such as food) for behavior offered without a cue. We want the dog to learn the cue. Otherwise, we have lots of behavior, but no real learning.

He's showing he's ready, but first he's got to think and respond correctly before getting his high magnitude reinforcement. The behavior must be offered on cue for him to earn the reward he wants – food.

Shifting Context

Once the puppy's food is prepared, get out your treats and move to another place in the kitchen – just a few feet away is fine. Remember, you are doing this in the kitchen only if it's a quiet place. If not, take your "kitchen training" somewhere else.

When the pup is paying attention to you, hold your hands at your side this time and ask him to "Sit" in the same tone of voice you've been using before – not harsh and commanding, just clear and definite. If he does, praise calmly and feed right away. Keep on associating the word while he's sitting, in between feeding, before you release him.

Release and rejoice! He's showing you that he's thinking and learning. Recognize that this is the only behavior he knows at this point, so he is likely to offer the right one. Understand that he hasn't really learned the cue yet, but he's on his way. He's already got the behavior.

Shifting context is the fastest way to promote learning. Here it means simply moving to another part of the kitchen and dropping the prompt of your hand over his head. That helps the pup focus on the cue (the word "Sit"), instead of just offering behavior because of place conditioning. He's starting to learn that words have meaning.

Hand Signal

If you also want to teach your dog to respond to the sit with a hand signal, introduce it a little further along, after he knows the word cue. Learning hand signals is much easier for the dog because it is a more natural cue for him.

When you teach a signal and word together, it takes the dog longer to process the word cue. He always learns the physical movement first. He'll always respond to the physical movement instead of the word, again because that is more natural for him.

For this reason, we want to wean the puppy very quickly from depending on the food in front of his nose as the signal to sit. The food must be the Consequence, not the Antecedent. Remember the ABCs. First must come the cue, then the behavior, then the consequence. If this order is changed, then there is no learning, only behavior.

So as soon as the puppy shows the willingness to plunk his little butt down into a sit when he sees food, begin to fade the hand help of putting the food in front of his nose. Keep your hands at your sides and ask him to "Sit," being careful to keep your tone of voice the same as you used to teach the word association when he was already sitting.

If he responds correctly, lavish him with praise and positive energy and, of course, the food reward. Repeat the word a couple of times too, just to help him further along in his word association. Then clearly release.

If he doesn't sit when asked, go back to manipulating him into position with the food over his nose and then saying the word again – *while* he is sitting, not before.

He just hasn't had time to make the word association yet. Remember, this is his first real introduction to a word as a cue for behavior. This concept might take a little while for your pup to master, but taking the time to build this solid foundation is well worth it in the long run.

After the puppy has clearly learned the word cue, add a hand signal if you want. After many, many repetitions, you'll be able to use either word or signal to cue to sit. But teaching the hand signal first makes the word cue harder for the puppy to learn.

Raising Criteria

Once you have the correct Response, work on Responsibility and Reliability. Time to raise criteria and raise rewards.

First, decide exactly how you want to raise the criteria. Know exactly what you expect at the next approximation. Keep it simple and specific. Your criteria depend on your future goals for your dog. That's an individual matter.

For companion: It's probably more important that the dog remain sitting longer, and more calmly, than whether his sit is straight or not. So start lengthening the time he can remain sitting before released.

For competition obedience: It is important that the dog learn to sit straight and square. If the puppy is physically capable of that, build it into your criteria right from the start. Reward *only* that type of sit.

For Schutzhund: What's important here is that the dog sit quickly and show good attitude in his work. So begin rewarding the faster sit. Then add the criteria of ears up and eyes bright.

For any type of competition work, you probably want to build in a cue for eye contact too. Raise your expectations slowly, step by step.

For agility: This dog must eventually sit and wait at the start while you walk away, so begin working toward that goal. This dog's sit must be solid. Begin to lengthen the time he can sit still and watch you. Increase your distance from him slowly, step by step. (See Chapter 19: The Stays.)

Raising Reward

Raising reward means using something the dog really likes when he's successful at the next approximation. That means better food, or more energy and excitement from you, or more petting, or even a favorite toy and a game of tug or fetch after he's released.

Raise all criteria slowly. Be sure the puppy understands the present step before going on to the next one. The best way to test this is to have the puppy perform the behavior in different places, at least twice in a row, for no reinforcement. That doesn't mean absolutely nothing, but it does mean just calm praise and release, instead of food or petting or play.

Be prepared to go backward as well as forward, down the ladder as well as up. If the puppy shows confusion, or that he's not ready for the next step, back up to the last successful step and perfect that.

Work on the dog's agenda. Cement the foundation. Build on success. Proceed slowly.

Pair Reinforcers

Remember to pair reinforcers along the way. If you praise with "Good Dog" just before you offer a piece of really good food, the two become linked in the dog's mind – hear praise, get food. This makes a powerful association that can work for you in any number of future situations.

If you aspire to competition, be creative with pairing your reinforcers. Using a special (but subtle) breathing cue just before producing a toy in training can become a reliable attention-getter in the ring.

Let Them Learn

As you climb the ladder of approximations, sometimes the waiting becomes the hardest part. You must allow the dog the time he needs to process this and learn it.

If you jump right in there and help him, and guide him or steer him with your hand or with food every time, he offers the right behavior, but he never truly learns the cue. He only learns to follow the prompt.

The young bear fishing in the river learns how to catch a salmon as much by the many times he comes up empty, as by the few times he manages to land one. Let the puppy experiment with his behavior to see what doesn't get reinforced and what does. Let him learn.

You have permission to withhold reinforcement when the pup offers less than you want, as long as he hangs in there and keeps on trying. Just because you have a piece of food in your hand, doesn't mean you have to give it to him. Put it back in the container and start again.

Along with waiting, withholding reinforcement is one of the hardest parts, especially when your cute little pup is trying all his new behaviors, cocking his head and looking at you with such question in his eyes. Praise him and tell him how great you think he is, but let him work to figure out which behavior produces the reward he really wants – food or toy or petting.

Be prepared for your dog to get creative. Keep a smile on your face and enjoy his puppy antics. This is exactly what you want him to do – offer behaviors.

If he offers jumping or barking, ignore it. Turn your back on him as a clear signal that this is not what you want. Then turn back to him and start over, giving the puppy the cue again. When he does get it right, praise enthusiastically with "Yes!" and reinforce with food and petting and excited emotional energy.

Things can't go too wrong. If your puppy is still with you and paying attention, then you're doing it right. Just let him keep trying. Occasionally, reinforce him just for that. Remember to reward effort all along the way.

Consider Temperament

Always, always consider your dog's temperament when teaching him anything. Work on your dog's agenda. Tune in to his capabilities and limitations. This is not a race to see who can teach what the fastest.

If your puppy is a bouncing ball of energy, with a concentration span of a nanosecond and extreme food drive, then working with his food dish on the counter might be, shall we say, counter-productive. If you've just arrived home from work and your dog has turned into a Mexican jumping bean, this might not be the ideal time to train.

Take these dogs out for a long walk or an intense play session. Let them blow off a little steam before you ask them to concentrate. By all means, ask them to sit at the door for at least one second first. But that's possibly all they can master right now. Work on long recalls outside (Chapter 15: The Manners).

When they are tired, that's the time to introduce them to the focus of formal training. Initial training should be fun and easy for the young dog, so work with him, not against him. With this type of dog, keep training sessions quiet and focused and always reinforce calmness.

On the other hand, if you have a lethargic or inhibited pup, train at a time when he is most active or attentive. Save his energy for training and don't exhaust him beforehand.

Be sure the laid back puppy is hungry and eager to learn. With the worrier, be sure he feels safe and comfortable. Keep his learning environment totally free from any sort of distraction that might concern him. With this dog, make training exciting and reinforce effort and energy.

And if you're trying to teach a straight, square sit for example, be sure the footing is good enough to support the dog's feet. He can't be expected to get it right on a slippery kitchen floor.

If you have a small dog, or a very young puppy, feel free to sit on the floor with him, or you can elevate the pup by putting him on a table or bench (just not the kitchen counter, please!). Be sure to get him comfortable on the bench first (photo on Page 255) before attempting to teach any behaviors. Use both the floor and the bench in your training sessions. They provide a convenient shift in context, get you closer to your pup, and save your back too.

Always watch your dog and tune in to what he is telling you. Training is a team sport, so be sure to start out with both of you on the same side.

Premack It

Once you have Response, Responsibility and Reliability to your satisfaction, in different places, this is the time to Premack the sit. Simply ask for the behavior at places where you control access to what your dog wants most.

If you start at the front door, place your hand on the doorknob. Turn to the dog and say "Sit" in your normal tone of voice. Use his name first if he's not paying attention.

If he sits, praise momentarily with "Sit, Good, Sit." Then clearly release him as you open the door. If he doesn't sit when you ask, give him a second or two to figure it out. Say nothing and do nothing. If he doesn't respond, simply take your hand off the doorknob and back away, a few steps from the door.

Get your dog's attention and approach the door again. If you repeat this three times and the dog still does not sit, take your hand off the doorknob and get the dog to sit as you face him. If he does sit, praise and release him to go out the door. But go back to different places and cement Response.

Premacking a behavior like this means you are changing a number of things all at once. The place is different and your body posture is different (hand on the door).

Your tone of voice may also be different (more excited or stronger) and your dog's attitude is different (excited about going outside). So don't be surprised if the dog doesn't respond correctly. He hasn't generalized this behavior yet.

He's telling you he's just not ready for all those shifts in context together. Work on them one at a time to cement to cue. If the dog understood that simply sitting would open the door for him faster, he'd do it. Guaranteed.

Back to Basics

Go back to basics. Work a session on sit at the door, rewarding with food and praise and petting as usual. But do not use going out the door as a reward just yet.

Work up to the approximation of Premacking the behavior for going outside. This might take a few more sessions, but you'll be surprised how fast and eager he is to sit when he realizes how he can get out the door faster.

Once this is going well at one location, use other places of high desire. If he loves to ride in the car, ask for a sit before you allow him to get in. If he really wants to come out of his crate, ask for a sit before opening the door and releasing him. If he doesn't respond correctly, just close the door. Return a little later and give him another chance.

If your dog adores sitting on the couch with you (and you allow that behavior), put it under stimulus control. He should ask permission for this privilege. Having him sit first (or down or some other behavior) is the perfect prelude to granting permission for appropriate privileges.

In each new place, you might have to do a little training there before the dog understands the Premack Principle. Once he does, be creative about where you use it and what behaviors you request, just like Vino learning to make eye contact on "Wait," before being given access to rest areas. (High reward follows compliance with high criteria.)

Attention Sit

The Attention Sit falls perfectly into the category of high reward and high criteria. This type of sit is necessary for any credible competition work. In an Attention Sit, the dog sits squarely at your left side, with his feet facing the same direction as yours, but his head turns to the right to watch you and make eye contact, as in the photo on the next page.

This can be a difficult maneuver for a young dog. It's hard enough for most youngsters to get all their feet pointing in the same direction, let alone turn their head in another. When their head goes right, their butt tends to swing out to the left. The answer is to get back to the dog's agenda. Be sure the dog has perfected a fast, square, solid, tucked sit before asking him to turn his head and look at you.

When the dog is sitting perfectly, you step into position beside him so you are both facing forward. Check your feet and align them with his. Now slowly, step by step, inch by inch, over several training sessions, use food to teach him to bring his head into position for an Attention Sit.

This can be a tricky maneuver for some dogs, so build it slowly and be patient. Sit the dog against a curb, or a wall to his left, to help him understand and to prevent the unwanted behavior. Check *your* position continually.

Each time the dog gets it right, put a word on the eye contact, reward and release. Many trainers find it is easier to teach a word for eye contact first Then they just add this cue to the sit and let the dog figure out how he is most comfortable using his body to combine the two behaviors. (For more detail on the Attention Sit, refer to the *Schutzhund Obedience* book in the Recommended Resources section.)

However you choose to teach the Attention Sit, go slowly. Understand that while you might have a clear idea of what you want, it makes very little sense to your dog to have his head go in one direction and his body in another.

Be patient, and incredibly enthusiastic and appreciative when the dog makes the effort to get this right for you. The Attention Sit is an integral part of a number of exercises (such as heeling, the recall and the finish), so be sure to teach this element thoroughly.

Be Unpredictable

By this time, your dog knows a couple of behaviors – probably down and wait and eye contact, as well as sit. Time to start mixing everything up.

Sometimes ask the dog to sit before he goes out the door and just reward with opening the door. Sometimes have him lie down, then give him a food reward, and then have him wait while you open the door and release him.

Should he ever miss a cue, offer no help – no second chances. Close the door or walk away. Return and give him another chance in a few minutes. Sometimes he has to lie down before he comes out of the car. Sometimes he must wait and give eye contact. Every shift helps him learn that he always needs to pay attention to the cue to get it right.

The combinations are endless, but being creative can be challenging. You have to bring your brain to training. Being variable and unpredictable for most folks is almost as hard as waiting. It sounds silly, but make a plan to be creative.

Decide ahead of time. Most of our dogs know exactly what we're going to do before we do it. If only we could learn to tune in to them as well as they tune in to us!

Behavior not under stimulus control (meaning the dog responds appropriately to the first cue) is useless. Remember the random computer program – pretty useless.

Make more drastic shifts in context. Sit in a chair and ask you dog to sit. Raise your arms over your head and ask him to sit. Ask for the behavior outside, *after* you go through the door.

When a friend is around, make a test. Turn your back to the dog and ask him to sit. (It's surprising how few dogs can figure this one out the first time.) Your friend tells you how he responds, which, of course, dictates his reward. All these changes help cement the cue. He learns that the word "Sit," and only the word "Sit," is the cue for this behavior.

Vary Reinforcement

Once the cue gets clearer for the dog, time to vary the Consequences. Keep your cue a ritual, but vary the types of reinforcement and put them on a variable schedule.

In your kitchen training, or other specified training time, change the reinforcement style. Have the food on the counter nearby. Ask the dog to "Sit," then go and get the food and bring it back to him. Vary where the reinforcement comes from. Have it in your back pocket one time and in your top pocket another time.

Remember the Cookie Jars? Have a couple of canisters with dog cookies in various rooms of the house. When your dog is in a room with you, go to the cookie jar, put your hand on it and ask the dog for a sit or down. If you get the right Response, give him a cookie. At first, practice right near the cookie jar.

Progress to getting the behavior in another part of the room. Then release the dog and take him with you to the cookie jar to get his reward. Should he ever offer the wrong behavior or fail to respond, just show him what he could have had, but put it back in the cookie jar.

Later, you can ask him to hold his position while you go and get the cookie and bring it back to him. Much further down the line, when he's getting proficient at stays, ask him to sit and stay in one room. Then you go to a cookie jar in another room and retrieve a cookie for him – just another way of being unpredictable.

Also vary the type of reinforcement. Switch from food to a favorite toy, especially when his effort is the best one that day. Be sure to make it a surprise to the dog.

Very early in training, the dog must not see the food or the toy before he complies. Remember the sequence. The only correct order for learning to occur is Antecedent-Behavior-Consequence.

If you are showing the toy or food first every time, then your Consequence becomes your Antecedent. ABC produces learning. CBC produces only behavior. Always follow the ABC rule as soon as the dog knows the cue for the behavior.

When we say to be variable and unpredictable, we mean to use all kinds of reinforcers (see Chapter Five: The Reinforcers). Use them intermittently and creatively, at different times and for different behaviors.

Your dog should never know quite what's going to happen next, except that it always follows the same rule – something great happens when he pays attention to the cue and responds correctly.

KEEP THEM GUESSING !

18

The Down

" You think dogs will not be in heaven?
I tell you, they will be there long before any of us."
— Robert Louis Stevenson

Positive reinforcement provides an easy and effective way to teach a dog to lie down on cue. The basic steps are the same as in teaching the sit.

Lying down is also a natural position for dogs and they offer this behavior frequently in everyday life. In the past, however, getting the dog to lie down quickly and willingly when told could often be a little more tricky than teaching the sit.

To the dominant dog, lying down is a more submissive position than sitting. The worried dog feels more vulnerable when lying down. Both need to feel that they are safe, and in the presence of a trustworthy pack leader, before they will down readily. This harks back to all those relationship issues discussed earlier.

For the more dominant and independent dog, refusing to lie down on cue can become a way to challenge authority. Ironically, militant techniques used in the past to force the dog into a down position created even more resistance and refusal in this dog, and sometimes led to open rebellion.

We'd rather avoid a power struggle here. We don't want him responding with, "You can't make me." Instead, we prefer to get the dog to *want* to lie down when we ask in order to get what he wants.

Trying to wrestle the dog to the ground by jerking down on his leash invokes strong opposition reflex in most dogs. In the willing or worried dog, this method can result in the poor dog flipping himself over on his side, tail slammed between his legs and eyes averted, hoping to inhibit the aggression he believes is imminent.

None of these methods do anything to improve the relationship or to establish the owner as a fair pack leader. The sad part is that it is all so totally unnecessary, not to mention unfair to the dogs.

Not So Natural

Lying down might not be as natural an act of compliance as sit, but dogs can learn to love it. Many of our positively trained dogs actually offer this behavior as default, instead of the sit. The irony is that most of those who do default to the down position are the more dominant and independent ones.

With these dogs, the rewards for down have been made so valuable and powerful that they short-circuit any resistance. Down becomes the most pleasurable behavior for these dogs (and sometimes the most manipulative).

They repeatedly offer the down to try to get us to give them what they want most. Through positive training, you can turn the lions into the lambs.

Some dogs are strong-willed and have their own agenda about life. They arrive with an attitude, and always seem to be contemplating a hostile takeover. These dogs know what they want and they want it now.

When a dog has this attitude, it makes sense to provide him with exactly what he wants – just as soon as he complies with your simple request. He gets what he wants when you get what you want. It helps make for a fair and balanced relationship.

Now there's no power struggle, no fighting over who's in charge – just a simple exchange. All you have to do is make sure that the dog considers what you are offering worth the work.

You become a respected pack leader in the deal because you provide all those things the dog wants. To this dog especially, all of heaven must come through you.

Since many of these driven dogs are true working dogs at heart, they're tickled pink to have a job to do that earns such valuable rewards. It's another one of those win-win situations that makes everybody happy.

Topography First

Start teaching down when the puppy is showing eagerness for kitchen training and has begun to respond to the verbal cue of "Sit" without any prompt from your hand with food. This means he has begun to grasp the concepts – offering behavior for reward and that words having meaning.

The first step is to teach the pup how to get into a down position so we can reinforce it. Put a few pieces of food in your hand. Get the puppy interested in the food while he is standing up, not sitting. We don't want him to get stuck in the sit here.

While he is standing, slowly lower your hand to the floor – down and back slightly – toward the puppy's chest. Lower your hand all the way to the floor and keep it there, as in the photo on Page 222. The pup's nose naturally follows the food to the ground.

Now comes the waiting part, again. Keep your fingers closed around the food while the puppy tries a variety of antics to get at the food. Keep your hand *right on the ground* in a closed fist with fingers facing the floor. Smile and be entertained. There's really no hurry. He can't be wrong. You haven't asked him to do anything.

Sit or kneel on the floor the first few times to make the waiting easier and more comfortable for you. Also, begin this on a slightly slippery floor, which assists the puppy in ending up in the desired position.

Just keep your hand with the food there, right on the ground, as long as the puppy is trying to get at it. If he really seems to be getting stuck, try moving your hand back slightly a few times, between the pup's front legs.

Most puppies slide their front legs out so their elbows are on the ground, but they tend to leave their butts up in the air. When they are young, they barely know they have a leg at each corner! They aren't even aware of what their rear end is doing.

Hungry puppies usually get around to lying down in about 30 seconds or so. Some can take a minute or two. This can seem like a long time to wait for the right behavior, but let's face it – it really isn't!

You can raise the food back up and try again if you like or you can get another piece of even better food and try with that. But this step is mostly about waiting. Say nothing. Let the puppy figure it out. Give him time to learn.

Word Association

As soon as the pup lies down properly, as in the photo on Page 222, release the food piece by piece, right on the ground, and begin the word association of "Down, Down, Good Down." Release the food *as soon as possible* when the puppy does lie down to help him learn faster.

The better your timing, the faster he makes the association. Place each piece of food on the ground to keep his focus there.

When you are out of food, release the puppy clearly and move away to help him get up, just as you did in the sit. The release is an important part of teaching down.

He should understand right from the beginning that a cue both starts and ends the behavior. Letting the puppy get up on his own teaches him just that – to get up whenever he wants. Remember, what you accept – you train.

Once the pup gets the idea of lying down to get the food, we want him to stay there longer so we have more opportunity to make the word association. After you get Response, work on Responsibility – lying down until released. You guessed it! Get more food.

Start to wean away from the hand prompt while the pup is lying down. Have several small pieces of food in your hand as you lower it to the ground. Just as the pup gets all the way down, tell him "Down, Good, Down" and release one or two pieces of food *on the ground*, directly between his front legs and right in front of his nose. Place the food on the ground, not in his mouth.

During the few seconds he is eating the food from the floor, withdraw you hand a couple of inches as you remind him "Down, Down." The moment he has finished eating, way before he even thinks about getting up, get your hand back in there and place another piece of food on the floor in front of him.

Should he get up at any point when there is a piece of food there, try to snatch the piece off the ground fast enough so he doesn't get it. Wrong behavior. No reward.

If he should succeed in getting the food after he stands up, process what he has told you. Be very careful next time not to release the food unless he is lying down solidly and calmly.

Use every opportunity to repeat the word "Down" *while* he is lying down in the correct position. Use the word especially if he looks up at you for one second while he is still lying down. Use the word as much as possible here while the dog is in the right position.

Keep in mind that he learns the word faster if he hears it while he is not eating. But at first, continue to say the word when he is eating, because that's when you're sure he's staying down.

While he's eating, he doesn't really hear the word, so the effect is more subliminal. But it can't hurt – might help – and it's good timing practice for the handler.

The goal is for the dog to hear the word between pieces of food, with your hand withdrawn a few inches away. Start that progression as quickly as possible, before the pup gets attached to the hand prompt as part of the cue.

He needs to learn that this behavior is not dependent on your hand being on the floor, nor upon food being between his front legs. The behavior should get linked with the verbal cue of "Down." So the more times the puppy hears that word when he is in the right position, the faster he can make the right association.

Keep Trying

Just as with the sit, these first few steps take the longest. Bring your patience and your sense of humor. Smile and enjoy the training. There's no deadline here.

Avoid holding the puppy down or otherwise touching him for now. Later, petting can be used as a distraction.

If the puppy seems resistant, or just isn't getting it, put the food underneath your leg. Monica Percival, a top trainer in agility, introduces this technique right from the start to teach agility dogs to slide into a fast down for the table.

Kneel on the floor with one leg and put the other foot on the floor. Make a sort of bridge under that leg, suitable to the height of your dog, so he has to duck his shoulders to get under it. Lure the dog underneath with the food. Keep your hand on the floor until he lies down, as in the photo on the next page.

If your coffee table is the right height, you can use that to get him to duck his shoulders and lie down. At this point, concentrate on letting the puppy figure it out himself. He can't do anything wrong because we haven't taught him anything yet.

If he gets up, so what? No big deal – just start over with more food in your hand. Process the information the puppy is giving you. The down is going on too long for his attention span. Release him sooner next time. Then build up to a longer time step by step, over the next several sessions.

Each puppy has a different threshold for how long he can concentrate. Work within that agenda and get to know your puppy. Around the house, repeat "Down, Good, Down" whenever the pup lies down. There is no wrong time to make the word association if he's exhibiting the right behavior.

Hand Signal

Once the pup is offering good Response, begin to wean away from the initial hand prompt. As he's on his way down, repeat the word and stop lowering your hand. Be prepared to wait. Give him time to think it through, but avoid saying the cue again before he is down. Once is enough. If he is looking at you, keep your focus on the floor, not on him.

The second the puppy does lie down, praise and feed on the floor. Weaning from the hand prompt to just the word is one of the biggest learning steps for the pup. He'll always rely on a physical signal rather than a verbal.

If he doesn't go all the way down when you do this, just don't reinforce. Start again and give him another chance to try harder. Wean from the hand prompt and food lure step by step, lowering your hand just a little less each time.

Remember how long it takes a dog to process the meaning of words in those few little brain cells he's beginning to devote to this task. Give him time. Watch your puppy to know how quickly to move forward. Just because he gets it right once or twice, doesn't mean he's learned it. What he is learning to do is experiment with his behavior to get his reward – a most valuable concept.

Shifting Context

When you begin to see a glimmer of understanding in your puppy, and he's offering the right Response with less hand movement, shift context. In the beginning, it never helps you look like a better trainer, but it does cement your dog's understanding of the specific cue. That always pays off in the long run.

If you've been sitting or kneeling on the floor, do the other. Stand up if you have a larger dog. With a small breed or very young puppy, put them up on a table or bench, as you did for the sit.

When the dog masters this shift and responds there, move to another place in the room. Then move to another room. Next, find somewhere with different footing. Go from slippery to solid (like carpet). As you vary the place, change your body posture too. Wean from the hand prompt totally.

It's okay if the pup misses a few times. He just doesn't get reinforced. Turn your back and walk away a few steps if you get no response. Avoid saying "Down" more than once when using it as a cue.

Just come back and ask again. If the pup fails to respond three times in a row, the approximation is probably too far along for his learning level. Return to a successful repetition and keep building word association with correct rehearsal, using as little hand prompt as necessary.

Raising Criteria

Once the puppy has figured out how to lie down, and is beginning to associate it with the cue, raise criteria. Remember, that means raising rewards too! On to the liver treats or leftover roast beef!

Now you must decide exactly what your criteria are for the down. This depends on your plan for your dog's career.

For companion: To lie quietly and calmly when told is probably a major goal for his training, so start reinforcing calmness. Slowly lengthen the time he remains lying down, to the extent that his age and temperament allow. You've got Response, now teach Responsibility.

For competition obedience: You probably want the dog to lie down in what is known as a Sphinx position, with all his legs under his body, instead of flopped over onto his side. So reinforce *only* that type of down. (See photos on Pages 222 and 229). Take a little more time to manipulate him into the proper position with the food and then make the word association.

With competition in mind, you should decide whether to teach two different words: one for a quick, Sphinx down with all four legs underneath, ready for recall, and another for the long down, with the dog rolled onto one hip. Also choose an informal cue for down, such as "Relax" or "Settle," which can be used around the house and by family members. This avoids breaking down the competition cues through lack of reinforcement and attention to all the specific criteria.

For Schutzhund: The same basic criteria apply as in competitive obedience, except that the dog must lie down quickly and happily. These dogs are judged on the joy they show in their work, so concentrate on Response. Train a quick down to insure success in the moving down and for article indication in tracking.

For agility: The down on the table can become the nemesis of some teams, especially when it creates a power struggle. Focus on teaching a quick, cooperative down by keeping rewards high. And for heaven's sake, keep the behavior away from the table until the dog has a thoroughly reliable and enjoyable down on cue.

No Sit First

Competition training is one of the reasons we teach the dog to lie down from a standing or moving position, not from the sit. When we teach the puppy to lie down from a sit, it is very easy for him to process the sit as part of the down exercise.

When he hears the cue "Down," he sits first and then lies down. This is called superstitious learning. The dog believes that this is part of the exercise.

That's also the reason we avoid the popular "doggie push-ups" of sit-down-sit-down-sit. These two behaviors can become too closely linked to each other. That makes them hard to separate later.

Before teaching position changes, wait until the dog knows the stand as well. Incorporating three positions prevents any two from becoming too closely linked.

For competition, there are two reasons to teach down from the stand and not from the sit. First, both obedience trials and the Schutzhund sport have exercises that require the dog to go directly to a down position while moving. (It can be a time-saver to do it that way in agility too!)

Second, lying down from a sit requires that the dog move forward to position himself. Our goal is for the dog to stop his forward motion immediately and lower his front and rear simultaneously, making for a faster and smoother down in motion. Teaching this topography first, even to a young puppy, helps insure future success.

Raise criteria slowly. Spend as much time as your dog needs to master the basic physical technique for down and to learn the word cue. Always consider the temperament and physical capability of your particular dog.

This exercise provides more challenge to a Greyhound or a Newfoundland than it does to a Belgian or a Border Collie. For the larger sighthounds, the sit and down can be difficult, so they usually take more time to develop the necessary technique. The stand is easier for them, so teach that first. (See Chapter 20: The Stand.)

If you want to teach a hand signal for down, do so after the dog understands the verbal cue. Remember, once he comes to rely on a hand signal, the word is more difficult for him to learn.

Raising Reward

The down is one exercise where it always pays to keep the rewards high. In fact, the more difficult this behavior is for your dog, physically or emotionally, the more important it is to reward with really good stuff.

So when you're asking the dog to lie down faster, be sure you have the truly good treats. Praise sincerely and appreciate his effort. The same applies when asking for a longer time between feeding. Make the food reward worth waiting for and worth working for.

Be sure the dog understands the present step before making the exercise more difficult. To test this, ask for two repetitions for just praise and release – no food. Then return to quality primary reinforcement.

Once the dog has mastered Response, Responsibility and Reliability, in a variety of locations, occasionally use a favorite toy as a reward. Give it to the dog just as you release him. Then reward with a play session.

Keep the toy reward for special moments, when the dog has done a really great job in a more difficult situation. Be sure he is calm and solid in the down before using the toy as a reward. Avoid showing him the toy first – let it be a surprise. He should never know when it is coming. That way he learns to pay more attention and work harder.

Be sure to release clearly and happily. The down is one exercise where the dog should understand that he has to hold the position until the release, without being reminded to stay. That's his Responsibility. But back up a step and work on foundation again when needed. The down is not always as easy for the dog to learn and perform as the sit.

With the down, work up the ladder more slowly. Build a solid foundation of understanding and cooperation in this exercise. It always pays off in the end.

Premack It

Since you have already been Premacking the sit in various places, add the down at random. Now that the dog must make a choice between these two behaviors, he must pay more attention to the cue.

Just as with the sit, don't be surprised if the dog makes some mistakes here. He has to really use his brain now to concentrate on what is being asked of him. That's hard when he's focused on how much he wants to go out the door or get in the car. Avoid giving him a second cue.

He must concentrate and get it right the *first* time to earn what he wants. Simply walk away from the door and the dog if he doesn't get it right. If he offers the wrong position, just shrug your shoulders and release him – no positive emotional energy or praise. In a few seconds, try again. Be sure the dog is paying attention this time before you ask.

If he's not getting it right most of the time, go back to foundation training. Do a few sessions just on sit and down in front of the doors, but without letting him go through.

This type of training leads to a dog who pays attention and concentrates on getting it right the first time. Why? Because it always results in him getting what he wants – such a good deal all around.

Down With Recall

The competition down with recall exercise requires new topography for the dog. He knows how to lie down, but now he must learn how to go down at speed.

This is just like you learning to hammer the nail with your left hand. You know what to do, but it's going to take a little time to get the topography right.

To teach this, have the dog run beside you, but not in any sort of formal heeling. Start slowly at first, not at a flat out run. As you say "Down," lower your hand (with food in it) straight to the ground, between his front legs.

Use either your right or left hand, whichever is more comfortable for you. Switching hands later becomes a shift in context. Keep your voice quiet, but make it a little quicker and sharper to encourage a fast down.

If the dog doesn't go down, or overshoots your hand because of his speed, show him what he could have had and start again. Let him learn what does not get reinforced. Avoid helping him to get it right after he's done it wrong. Next time, just run a little slower to set up for success.

The faster the dog goes down, in the place where your hand is between his front legs, the faster you release the food and praise him and get excited. The first time he gets this right, release all the food in your hand on the ground – jackpot! Reward his great effort in this difficult task.

The minute he finishes eating, release him to jump up and get his toy. We don't want to penalize a fast down by making him stay there for a long time.

We also want to teach him to leap up from the down and be ready to run for when we add the rest of the recall (much, much later). For more detail on teaching a fast down in motion, refer to the *Schutzhund Obedience* book listed in the Recommended Resources section at the end of this book.

Adding Distance

At the same time as teaching the dog to down in motion, begin teaching him to down at a distance from you. Start this after he knows to stand on cue (Chapter 20). Leave him in a stand on the edge of a step, or behind a board, to discourage him from coming forward. Go just a few steps in front of the dog and face him.

Give him the cue and when he lies down properly, go to him and reward. Release by turning him to the back or side, not forward. Lengthen the distance you go away from him by small increments, moving up and down the ladder.

Once the dog has mastered the topography of lying down quickly at speed while running beside you, and he also drops quickly at a distance without coming forward when you are facing him, put the two together.

Begin with the dog in a stand at the top of a single step with you facing him. Have him down on cue. Return, reward and release. Then move him back from the edge of the step a little distance.

Call him and ask him to down just before he reaches the top of the step or curb. At first, step toward him as you ask him to down. Return to him, reward and release. Next, instead of a step or curb, use a visible board on the ground and do the same exercise there.

Wean away from the step and the board by using just a thin stick or a white line on the ground, like in a parking lot or tennis court. The idea is to teach the dog to slide smoothly into a down from speed, without crossing the visible barrier – soon to become an invisible barrier.

Again, teach topography first. He has to learn how to get his body to do this before he can be successful.

Keep Rewards High

Always make the place he goes down a place of high reinforcement. Go to him and praise and pet him. When he's especially good, use a jackpot – lots of pieces of food, given in quick succession. Sometimes use a toy. Let him jump up and play tug, or throw it behind him as you release him. Should he ever miss the mark, go there and show him what he could have had. Then give him an opportunity to try harder to earn those rewards.

Once the dog masters this step reliably, begin to add random downs, anywhere he is moving at a reasonable speed. Again, start with a little less speed in the beginning.

As you tell him "Down," move toward him. Should he overshoot the mark, go back to where he should have dropped and place your hand with the food in it on the ground. Show him what he could have had, but don't let him get it. Give him another chance to get it right.

If he fails to down quickly and properly twice in a row, go back to teaching. Improve the weak part – either the drop at a distance or the down from movement.

Build the foundation for the parts of this exercise properly and eventually the dog puts them together. When your dog does get it right, add high rewards in a variable manner.

Be Unpredictable

Once your dog learns down, you can invent all sorts of ways to use it. Ask for the down in different places, including outside. As with the sit, try asking for it in different postures: sitting in a chair, hands over your head, turn your back (this can be a tough one for the dog), close your eyes.

Try being further away and then throw the food to him as you release him. Try standing behind him. The more variable you can be, the more solid your dog's understanding of the cue becomes.

Vary reinforcement too. Sometimes, go to him and feed him in down position and then release him to play tug with a toy. Another time, when he's been really solid, release him to a toy thrown behind him. The more you can vary exciting Consequences, the more driven the Behavior becomes.

By this time you're really starting to have fun watching your dog learn. And the teaching should be just as much fun.

You can put all sorts of behaviors into this Positive Training Paradigm. Teach him to wave, or to sit up and beg, or to roll over, or to play dead. Training together is not only fun, it builds a strong relationship based on communication and fairness. This is what having a dog is all about.

MAKE TRAINING FUN !

238

19   The Stays

*" Wolves seem to have a more highly
developed sense of fairness than humans."*
— Jim Brandenburg

Everyone wants their dog to come when called and stay when told. Very few realize how much easier one is to train than the other.

The reason is that one makes so much more sense to the dog than the other. Once the relationship is established, and you convince your dog that you deserve his respect because you are a fair pack leader, teaching come when called involves more management than actual training time.

It's natural for puppies to want to stay with the pack and hang out with the pack leader. Reinforce this behavior over and over, every time it happens, and it happens more and more often. Come when called gets rewarded with everything the puppy wants – great food and good lovin'.

Come when called makes sense. The only challenging part to training a reliable recall is to figure out how to make yourself more interesting than what is most distracting for your dog.

A distraction recall takes time only because young dogs have difficulty controlling themselves. It takes maturity and experience for the dog to develop a sense of responsibility, even to the terrific pack leader you're now in the process of becoming.

With proper management and guidance and effective training sessions, even a high-level distraction recall can be reliable by the time the dog is 18 months old. As with kids, for some things we just have to wait for them to grow up!

But the stays fall into a completely different category. As soon as the young dog starts to get it right, you leave him. This makes no sense at all to him.

Not only does this seem stupid to the dog – it's also completely unnatural and frightening. For a young pup to be left alone in the wild means death. To the dog, this looks like an exercise in abandonment.

So look at the stay exercises from your dog's point of view. They aren't really difficult, but they take a lot of time because the dog has so much innate resistance to overcome. Nothing about staying away from you is natural. It just doesn't make any sense to him.

Even when the dog does come to understand the point of the exercise, to him it's still a stupid, boring and frustrating exercise. So always recognize how your dog feels about the stays. Take the extra time to be a fair pack leader and make success worth his while – stay close at first.

Think of the stays as an exercise in building your dog's trust. To perform a reliable stay, he needs to become confident in his belief that you always return. He must feel safe. He must trust that you won't let anything bad happen to him while you're gone. So always associate stays with pleasant things, like frequent high rewards and lots of support and appreciation.

Many trainers who actually do use some motivational methods seem to revert to punishment when it comes to stays. What is really appalling is that they think it is justified, even with young puppies, who are the most insecure. How unfair!

Consider Temperament

Stays take time. It takes time for the pup to grow up enough so that he can physically control his body. It takes time for him to learn to control his emotions and time for you to convince him that this exercise makes any sense at all.

For the dog who is unsure and dependent, the owner must first build a trusting relationship and develop the dog's self-confidence. Leaving him on a stay next to a big, nosey dog only undermines his trust in the pack leader and shakes his confidence.

The confident, bold dog must learn to control himself. The minute he's left alone, even a few steps away, he's going to want to be sniffing and exploring and escaping from the leadership which only inhibits his adventurous nature.

For either dog, the stays are challenging. Teach them carefully, step by step. Keep rewards high. Make it worth your dog's while to engage in what he considers to be pretty stupid behavior.

Work on the dog's agenda. For most, the down-stay is the easiest to learn first because there is less temptation to move. But if your dog is particularly nosey and likes to sniff, then sit-stay might make the concept clearer for him, without offering so much temptation. Adjust training to suit the dog.

Private Time

Convince your dog that it is safe for him to stay where you leave him. Protect him from any disruptions until he is older and secure in the stays.

When a dog breaks a stay, understand that it makes sense to him. He's either coming to get closer to you or he got distracted and needs to check out something. He's not doing it to annoy you, and he's certainly not doing it to earn a correction.

Whenever your dog breaks a stay to come to you, you should rejoice. Just do it internally, not externally. He's not running away – he's coming to find you. He's making a valid mistake. Maybe it's a confidence issue, or a safety issue for him, but be thankful he looks to you for support and safety. This indicates a strong relationship.

Of course, put him back where he should have been, but do it nicely and with an understanding heart. Proceed to Show and Tell – Show him what you want and Tell him he's a good dog. Be pleased with him, not angry. Appreciate where this behavior came from. Lighten up and keep it in perspective.

Teach stays far away from any sort of distraction. Start when the dog is calm and quiet, not when he's excited about eating or going outside. Wait until he is confident in the sit and down position, and knows the difference between them.

Begin when the dog shows Responsibility for holding a position until released. Train stays only after you have worked out most of your management and relationship issues. Begin only when the dog shows he is ready.

Place

Teach the puppy the concept of staying with the placemat method. This teaches the beginnings of self-control.

Use a bathmat or small rug to teach the word "Place." That means to go to the rug and hang out there. Toss him some food treats every time he goes there, or give him a favorite bone to chew there. Remember that every organism tends to gravitate to the places of highest reinforcement.

The pup doesn't have to sit still or lie down on place, but he should keep at least one foot on his placemat. This is easier for a young dog than a formal stay, and it introduces him to staying away from you and controlling himself.

If he gets up off his placemat, just calmly take him back and remind him "Place" when he gets there. After a few moments, reward him there. Then go to him and clearly release him. Never call him to you off this place.

Don't expect him to stay there too long at first. Build the time slowly, and don't leave him alone when he is on his placemat. Abandonment is not part of this exercise.

Once he understands about one placemat, add a few more. He can have a placemat in the kitchen, one in the dining room, one in the family room and one in the bedroom. Teach him to run to the nearest "Place" when you tell him and point to it, and then reward him with what he likes.

Go and sit with him sometimes and feed him and pet him there. Intermittently toss him small biscuits while he's on his placemat.

Make "Place" a very pleasant place to be. Don't use it as a punishment or a time-out. Keep it a positive place where your puppy can learn confidence and self-control, way before he's ready for a concentrated stay.

The First Stays

Once the puppy is offering Response, and shows that he can control himself and stay on his placemat for short periods of time until released, begin to work on stays. Add some sort of visual barrier to help him understand the concept.

One innovative trainer, Nancy Beach, uses a hula hoop. The dog learns stays within a hula hoop. All the rewards come within the hoop, so the dog makes a positive association.

This helps the dog get the concept that staying away from you, in this place, makes sense because it earns him high rewards. If the dog makes a mistake and moves, it's easy for him to make the connection that he has to get back inside the hoop to earn his valuable rewards.

When the dog is ready to leave the placemat or the hula hoop, leave something of yours with him. At first, put it in front of him.

This gives him something to focus on and provides a visible barrier. A rolled up leash is fine, and makes a good antecedent to transfer to the competition ring later.

Time

The two elements of teaching stays are time and distance. Work on them both separately.

Once the dog shows good Response to sit and down, work on Responsibility. Teach him to remain in position until you release him. Lengthen the time between reinforcement. Build the threshold exponentially. Do this by being proactive.

For example, if your dog can sit for 5 seconds before getting up, praise and reinforce at 4 seconds. Give another cue (because reinforcement ends behavior) and allow him to remain for another 4 seconds, then release. He's just done an 8-second sit-stay!

Next time, try for 6 or 7 seconds, praise and reinforce. Give another cue and go for another 5 seconds before release. You've just raised the time of your sit-stay to 11 seconds.

Build these time periods between food rewards slowly, and avoid going up and up and up. Remember to be variable. Sometimes reinforce at 3 seconds, and sometimes and 7. Backing up can move you forward much faster.

Here you are just working on time. Stay close to the dog – close enough to reinforce every few seconds. Remember to use praise, as well as food, to reinforce.

Be proactive. If the dog breaks the stay at 9 seconds, that's the handler's fault. Obviously, the dog needs to be reinforced or reminded or released at 7 or 8 seconds. Build time slowly, always considering age and temperament.

Distance

Once the dog is staying for 10 or 20 seconds with only one food reward, start working on distance. Go 2 steps away for 5 seconds. Return, praise, feed and release.

Do the same thing again, but instead of releasing, remind the dog to "Stay" again and go 3 steps away for another 5 seconds. Return, praise, feed and release.

Build the distance the same way you build the time, but build them separately. When working on distance, keep the light line on the dog, just in case.

Even though we always want Response to the first cue, it helps teach the dog Responsibility when we repeat the cue while he is exhibiting the correct behavior. This reminds him to concentrate on what he's doing and helps confirm word association. Telling him "Sit, Good, Stay, Good" reassures him that he is right and helps teach that praise does not mean release.

Go slowly, step by step. Shorten the time when adding another step away. Reduce time when adding distance and reduce the distance when adding time. When shifting context, shorten both time and distance. The same rule applies when working around distractions.

Keep Him Guessing

Be variable and unpredictable. That means going back a step or two as well as going forward. Keep the dog attentive by varying when you return and reinforce. It pays to keep him guessing.

Reinforce with praise too. The great part about praise is that you can reinforce from a distance, but the dog must clearly understand that praise is not release. Don't reinforce with food if the dog ever gets up when praised. Just calmly put him back and remind him what he was doing – Show and Tell.

Once your dog demonstrates Reliability on the stays, vary reinforcement style. When you're a few steps away, after a few seconds, release him and throw a bunch of treats to where he was staying.

It's okay – he can get up and eat the food! You released him. Keep him thinking it's in his best interest to stay in this spot because something really good might happen here.

Establishing Criteria

For companion: Teach that "Stay" means to remain in place until released. Add that cue whenever the dog is where you want him to be. Moving a paw here is no crime, as long as he stays in place. Focus on Responsibility and Reliability.

For competition obedience: Teach that "Stay" means to remain absolutely still and concentrate on his position. That means no barking, shifting his feet, sniffing or sleeping. Competition stays means concentration, not relaxation.

For agility: Work on significant time and distance for "Sit, Stay" under high motivation. Once the dog loves agility, having him stay while you lead out can become the most challenging part of the course. It makes no sense to him to let you get out on course to play by yourself – without him!

Don't expect too much too soon. Fortunately, you can remind him of what he is supposed to be doing. There's no penalty here for helping him be right.

Make the stay worth his while. Return often and reinforce with food (only if he didn't break). Throw a toy behind him sometimes as you release him. Send him over the jump *behind* him. Keep him guessing. Look at it from the dog's point of view and keep the rewards high.

Once he's far enough along in training to know what's really expected, if he breaks the sit – let him miss his turn. Take away what he wants most – Premack the stay to being allowed to run the course. Then it makes sense to stay.

For Schutzhund: Forget teaching the word "Stay." It's not permitted anywhere in the rules in any exercise. Once the dog is told to "Sit" or "Down," he is expected to hold that position until told otherwise.

This is the way we prefer to train our dogs. "Stay" then becomes a reminder to concentrate. But in reality, "Sit" works just fine, provided the dog understands the concept of holding a position until released or given another cue.

Shifting Context

Shifting context early helps the dog understand the stay exercises, but do this with caution. Change to another quiet room at first. When going to any new place, stay close to the dog and shorten the time. Keep it successful.

Solidify the stays in every room in your house, when it is quiet, before adding even the slightest distraction. Wait for your dog to exhibit the confidence and concentration that come with maturity before adding distractions.

Use the Cookie Jar method explained in Chapter 17: The Sit. This is a fine way to make the stays solid – waiting for the handler to return with a cookie. At least it makes some sort of sense to the dog.

When you want to go outside, start in your driveway, near the garage door or on the front step. Having a solid barrier at his back makes the dog feel safer. Again, stay close and shorten the time. Teach him that he can trust you. Make him sure that you won't go too far until he's ready.

Group Stays

In obedience class, stay close to your dog and reinforce frequently. Make any excuse to the instructor (or show him a copy of this book). Better to have success here and foster trust, than to make your dog think you want to abandon him in the midst of all this chaos.

The point of an obedience class is for *you* to learn how to train your dog and for him to have some positive exposure. The goal is not to have the dog perform all the exercises perfectly in class in six weeks to please the instructor.

Take the information home and work on it there. Make class a positive experience for your dog. Work on stays at home, not in class. Look for the good things your dog is doing in class and reinforce those. Reward any and all attention to you.

Listen to the instructor with your ears, but keep your eyes on your dog. Always reinforce calmness. Sit off to the side if your dog is too bold or too worried.

Bring along his placemat and practice with him right next to you. Remember to keep him safe, always. That's your responsibility.

In class, feed and praise any and all good behavior your dog offers. Obviously, if the instructor doesn't allow food and toys, find another class!

Practice Shows

A word to the wise about taking your dog to practice shows for competition. By all means, when your dog is ready, take him to the trial grounds. Let him investigate the entire place, then ask for a few behaviors off to the side.

Your dog clearly shows whether he's ready to work here. If not, just walk him around some more and reinforce the behaviors you like – especially attention to you.

If your dog seems relaxed and attentive enough to try a little routine in the practice ring, go for it. Smile and breathe and do your part. Stay connected to your dog and be there for him.

But when it comes to sits and downs, do them outside the ring and stay right next to your dog. This is not the place to allow an unpleasant experience.

The dogs at a practice match are there because their training is not far enough along to be ready to compete. It only makes sense that their stays won't be so solid either. Make it a rule to practice your group stays only in the company of reliable dogs!

Avoid putting your dog in any negative situation, especially in the context of the show grounds. Practice your stays outside the ring. Work on time, not distance. Stay close and protect him from anything negative. Be his protector.

By the way, one of the best ways to start group stays with a young dog is to put him beside an older, reliable dog whom he knows and trusts. If you have such a dog in your household, or your friend has such a dog, this is the perfect partner to start group stays.

Yep, just the two of them at first. Not only does the youngster see a good example, but he also feels less abandoned because he has been left next to a trusted friend.

Antecedents

For competition, there are so many antecedents that differentiate the stays from any other exercise. Be sure to show them to the dog in training so he clearly knows what is coming.

Long before you practice with a group of dogs, show the dog the procedure of how you walk in (without the line of other dogs) and how you set up. Practice how you remove the leash and where you place it behind him.

Rehearse your posture and behavior for this exercise. Build all these antecedents into the stay, long before the dog is ready to walk in a line or sit in a group.

For the Novice sit-stay, be sure to stand differently than you do for the recall. Fold your arms and look above the dog, not directly at him. Relax your body and breathe gently.

Avoid fidgeting. If you can't concentrate on standing still for one minute yourself, then you shouldn't expect this of your dog. Practice your behavior too.

Likewise for Schutzhund, practice the antecedents for the long down. Approach the flag area the way you will at a trial. Stand up straight. Practice taking off the leash, without actually removing it. Switch it to a long line you have already placed on the ground.

Practice putting your leash away. Stand up straight again. Breathe deeply and relax your body posture.

By the time you give your dog the "Down" cue in a trial, he knows what's coming. He knows this is the long down, not heeling or a recall or a motion exercise, because all the Antecedents are there.

Consequences should be unpredictable.
Antecedents should be ritual!

All this preparation not only shows your dog what to expect on trial day, it also gives you specific things to focus on. Rehearse correct presentation without your dog first. After you know your routine perfectly, then practice with the dog. If you do your part, there's a good chance the dog will do his.

Preventing Unwanted Behavior

For dogs having difficulty learning the stays, the handler is probably moving forward too fast. Return and rebuild foundation. Put him back in the hula hoop.

As you start to increase distance, prevent the unwanted behavior of the dog coming to you by restraining him. He should already know how to hitch. (Chapter 12: The Leash.)

Attach a long line to a post behind him. No tension – just to stop him from reinforcing himself by getting to you. Have a friend help you. Walk back to your dog *only* when he is sitting and staying. If he breaks, walk away.

Have your friend help the dog get back in the correct place and position. When the dog learns that sitting and staying bring you back to him, he sees more point to the exercise. Wean from the hula hoop by just putting a board on the ground in front of him, then graduate to just lines on the ground.

With a dog who whines or barks, prevent that behavior by pressing a dab of peanut butter or squeeze cheese on the roof of his mouth before you leave. Away from the stay exercise, teach "Quiet." (Chapter 15: The Manners.)

Never forget that breaking a stay, whining or barking are symptoms. The dog is trying to tell you something. He may be anxious or stressed or afraid or annoyed. Build a positive foundation to change his attitude.

While you are still close, have another person go up and feed your dog while you praise him for staying. Far too many folks have strangers correct their dog for breaking a stay, or for moving or whining. This is so totally unfair. Now the dog truly does have something to fear when he's been abandoned on a stay.

As you go further away, or for longer, have other people go to the dog and reinforce him with a kind word (calmly) or a tasty treat or gentle stroking. These can actually be distractions, as well as reinforcers, so watch how the dog reacts.

Work within each dog's limitations. You can't change temperament, even when you modify behavior. Understand each dog's individual personality. Remember who chose this career for this dog.

Be fair in your expectations. Make sure your dog feels secure. Let him grow up and mature before asking so much.

Be Unpredictable

Once you have taught the dog all the antecedents for the stays, it's time to mix things up and cement his learning. Even if you are only interested in competition obedience, where you always walk away from the dog in a straight line, teach him to hold position even if you leave to one side or the other. This shift in context helps him understand the concept of stay.

Leaving to the side makes it more difficult for the dog to hold position. He wants to turn and look in the direction you are going. If he moves his feet, return and reposition them. Remind the dog of his job with Show and Tell.

Leave at an angle next time, instead of directly to the side. He's telling you he's not quite ready for that step. Once you can leave to either side, this is good preparation for those future stays out-of-sight, where the handlers often leave the ring to one side or the other. Avoid leaving directly behind the dog until he is really solid.

When it's time to practice going out of sight, do not take this shift in context for granted. Return to shorter time and distance and build each gradually with you out of sight. Go to a place close by, where you can still watch your dog, or have a friend watch for you. Be proactive and prevent any unwanted behavior right from the start.

Stays tend to become boring. Keep in mind how stupid and senseless they seem to the dog. Be creative in making stays fun.

We already mentioned about releasing the dog from several steps away and tossing food treats at him. You can do this just as you walk away too. Keep him guessing.

Once the dog knows the stay, interrupt the exercise at different times and with a variety of different reinforcers. Release him and throw the toy to him. Release him to go find a favorite toy. Let him jump all over you. Release him and roll around on the ground with him.

Be creative. Keep the stays interesting. Build them slowly. Reinforce calmness and concentration. Take your time. Let your dog mature. Listen to what he tells you. Let him learn at his own pace.

PROTECT YOUR DOG !

20

The Stand

" A dog is a good friend.
He wags his tail and not his tongue."
           – Chinese Proverb

By the time your dog starts to understand the cues and behavior for sit and down, you're getting pretty familiar with how the Positive Training Paradigm works. You're also getting to know your dog better, and how he reacts, as you get more involved in the intimate dance of training.

By now you've also figured out that we're going train the stand by putting it in the same paradigm. The real decision with this behavior is exactly when to train it.

Obviously the dog knows how to stand – he does it perfectly well all by himself. True, we want to put it on cue, but we also want to teach him to stand *still*. For the wriggly puppy, this is obviously going to be a challenge.

Unless you need to teach the stand for some specific reason, wait until the dog is older to teach this exercise. It is easier for the dog to learn the stand once he is more focused and more concentrated, and understands to stay in the sit and down positions until released.

Waiting until the dog understands the concept of stay makes training a solid stand much easier. The sit and down are better anchor positions to help the dog learn to remain still and hold his position until the release.

When the dog is standing, it's just too tempting for him to move his feet. This makes it harder to teach and more challenging for the young dog to master the exercise.

So wait to teach the stand until the dog matures a little bit and has a little more training under his belt. Wait until he understands the concept of holding still in the sit and down before starting the stand.

Even if you're in an all-fired hurry to show your youngster in Novice, where there is a stand for examination, you'll have more success, and produce a far more solid stand in the long run, if you teach this exercise at the end, instead of at the beginning. Those few extra months of maturity and training make the stand easier for the dog to learn.

Fortunately, in Schutzhund, the moving stands are not required until the third and final level. Whoever wrote the rules understood – it's harder for the dog to remain standing absolutely still than it is for him to hold a sit or down.

Preventing Unwanted Behavior

The easiest way to teach the dog to stand still, without moving his feet, is to remove most of the options. Find a place where there is a step down and a wall along one side, like the top of a stairway.

Begin teaching the stand with the dog at your left side. The wall, or similar barrier, should be on the dog's left side – to prevent him from moving sideways, away from you. His front feet should be at the edge of the top stair, so that even one step forward would result in him stepping down the stair.

If you have a small dog, teach the stand with him on a table (such as a grooming table) or a bench. Put the table against a wall for a solid side barrier. First, feed the dog to make him comfortable there, as in the photo on the next page.

If you cannot find anywhere suitable, put a platform or bench against a wall. Making it difficult for the dog to move forward, by being at the edge of a step or on a table, helps him learn to stand still right from the beginning. It clearly removes the option of moving forward.

Trying to hold the dog in place only invokes his opposition reflex and thus produces resistance and stiffness. We want to train the dog to be relaxed and comfortable in the stand position.

Companion Criteria

If you have no plans to train your wonderful companion for competition, there is no reason to teach any sort of steadfast stand. A sit-stay or a down-stay suffices in most situations.

However, if you want to teach the dog to stand on cue, simply follow the directions, but allow him to walk forward into the stand from the sit.

This is easier for the dog. There is no need for him to master the difficult technique of standing up without moving forward, which is necessary for competition.

With the companion dog, establish suitable criteria. As long as he remains standing in one place, and allows you to touch him all over, it doesn't really matter if he walks into it or moves a paw or two here and there.

If he wags his tail so hard when you praise him that his back feet move, so what? All the better for his positive attitude to training. Be fair in your expectations.

Why This Way?

For competition, the dog needs to learn how to get into a stand from a sit without moving his front feet forward. There are three reasons why to teach it this way.

First, it makes it clear to the dog that standing is different from sitting.

Second, it teaches him the concept that the stand has something to do with the position of his rear end.

Third, not moving his front feet forward is important for advanced competition, such as the signal exercise in Utility or the moving stands for Schutzhund. We want the dog to learn to stand by keeping his front feet still, not moving them forward. Teaching correct topography from the start avoids retraining later.

One other advantage of this method is that it solidifies the dog's understanding of sit because he does two sits for every stand. In other methods, when the dog learns the stand, the sit can get shaky. Sometimes it even disappears entirely!

This is often seen in SchH. III dogs, who down and stand perfectly, but miss the moving sit – only to stand instead. Most did the moving sit just fine in SchH. I and II. But somehow, in learning the moving stands, they lost the sit along the way.

Incidentally, we've yet to see that happen using this method. When the dog does two sits for every stand, the established behavior is enhanced, even while teaching the new one at the same time. This method clearly serves to help the dog differentiate between the two positions and cues – a difficult task for some dogs.

Teaching Topography

By now the dog is attentive and ready for training, eager to earn his reinforcement. Take him to the top edge of the stair, so he is at your left side with the wall on his left.

When his front feet are close to the edge of the stair, ask him to sit. You might have to spend a few sessions perfecting the sit here, so he sits close enough to the edge of the top stair.

If he sits back from the edge, it is too easy for him to move his front feet forward as he gets into a stand. His front feet should not move at all. He should also be close enough to the wall to prevent movement sideways, but don't crowd him.

Once he is sitting in the correct position at your left side, praise and reinforce. Put one finger of your right hand in his collar, facing downward, to stabilize his front end.

Bend at the knees, but keep facing forward as much as possible. With your left hand flat and fingers together, calmly slide it under the dog, just in front of his stifles.

For a body sensitive dog, this is often enough to make him stand up right away. If he does, praise calmly and slowly stand up yourself. If necessary, gently position his rear legs so he is standing in a comfortable position.

Once he is standing comfortably, begin the word association of "Stand, Stand" along with calm praise. If he knows "Stay," you can alternate the two words with praise, while he is standing correctly.

After a few moments, remain quiet for one or two seconds and then clearly ask him to "Sit." This one should be easy for him by now! Praise sincerely, feed and release calmly and quietly, sideways or back.

Keep the dog at the top of the stair, even after the release. Don't give him the idea that the end of the exercise is to leap forward, as this can cause confusion later on.

If the dog remains firmly planted in the sit as you slide your hand underneath him, just raise your hand and arm up and back slightly – against his stifles – to raise his rear end to a standing position. Begin the word association once he is standing comfortably. Avoid having the dog standing in a roached or stretched position.

Avoid forcing the dog into a stand here. This is Show and Tell again. Give him as little help as possible to let him figure out how to use his rear end to stand up from the sit without moving forward. Use your hand and arm calmly and gently to produce the desired effect. Keep your hand flat and open, with fingers closed, using the edge of your hand against his stifles.

This exercise is best taught before the dog has had extensive training on stays and long before doing any proofing or distraction work. We certainly don't want to confuse the poor dog, who might think this is some sort of new test to see whether he remains sitting while someone pokes him!

Word Association

If you want, you can do an earlier step to begin word association. Simply use the word whenever your dog is standing still, adding praise (and a treat if that's possible without him moving). This begins the word association and is a good zero to one step. But you'll still need to teach him the technique of how to get into a stand from a sit.

Tone of voice is critical for the position exercises. "Sit" should have a happy, short, upbeat tone. "Down" should be in a deeper, more serious tone. "Stand" is best said in a calm, steady, medium tone of voice.

The greater the difference in the phonetic sounds you use for the three words, the easier it is for the dog to identify each one. (See Chapter 7: The Words.)

Raising Criteria

The stand is one exercise where it is often easier to raise all the criteria and cement learning in one place, before shifting context. Besides, most houses have a limited number of stairs with walls in the right place.

Once you have Response and Responsibility, you can add another little wrinkle. When the dog understands that he is to remain standing for a certain period of time, stroke him gently along his back.

This is both reinforcement and a mild distraction. Stroke him only once or twice in each stand, praising and reminding him to "Stand, Stay, Good" in a calm, quiet tone.

Once he stands quietly during this petting, end one stroke with *very gentle* downward pressure on his hips, just for a moment. If your dog is in good weight, you'll feel his two pelvic bones a few inches in front of his tail. They are the highest point of his rear assembly, just as his withers are the highest point of his shoulder assembly.

Since we have never, ever pushed down on the dog's rear end to make him sit, this becomes an effective way to solidify the stand. The dog's opposition reflex kicks in and he sets up his rear in an even more solid standing position.

Remind and praise with "Stand, Good" as you use this opposition reflex in your favor, instead of fighting against it. But do this only if your dog seems comfortable and it has the desired effect. Always consider temperament.

Raising Rewards

Adding reinforcement in the stand can be a bit more tricky than usual because this is such a static exercise. The really good food we usually use can excite the dog too much and cause him to move.

Depending on the dog, this is often an exercise where less appealing food can be more effective. Put off using food as a reinforcer here until the dog is holding position calmly and quietly. Use praise and stroking while the dog is in the stand. Reward the sit at the beginning and end with food, being variable in when and how you reward.

Evaluate Response and Responsibility before raising rewards. Once the dog begins to stand up on his own as soon as you start to reach down, and he stands solidly (without moving his feet) until you ask for the sit again, try adding a food treat.

Start with the least appealing food – small pieces of kibble or a tiny, dry biscuit. But if this low grade food excites the dog so much that he moves his feet, put off feeding in this exercise until learning has progressed further.

Sometimes food can inhibit learning. Some dogs get so obsessed with getting the food that they fail to think. Rejoice that you have such a food driven dog.

But keep the food out of the static exercises until later, when he understands more about what is expected of him and how to earn the food. With this dog, always reinforce calmness around food.

This is a prime example of where each dog is different. What works for one can sabotage another. Tune in to your dog. Use whatever works and process the information the dog is giving you.

Be calm and deliberate in teaching the stand. And for heaven's sake, stand still yourself! You can't expect the dog to do what you can't do yourself.

Fading the Prompt

One of the biggest steps in the stand is to fade out the body prompt of reaching your hand down under the dog. Do this when the dog is beginning to stand *before* you actually make contact with his body. First, begin to say "Stand" a little earlier, just as he begins to move.

Substitute touching him gently with your left foot to prompt him to move. Just as you start to reach down with your hand, stop the movement earlier and move your left foot instead, so that it touches the dog where you normally put your hand – against the front of his stifle.

That should be enough to remind him which part of his body he needs to move. Now you don't have to make such a big body movement toward him. This helps the dog learn that the cue is the word, not your hand and body movement. Get the word association in there *as soon as* he begins to stand up with his back legs.

Once the dog shows he really understands how to get himself into a stand, use a slender stick (like an arrow with the sharp tip cut off) to touch his stifle (only if necessary) as you give the word cue. It works best if you reach behind your own body to touch him with it. Obviously, your foot and the stick are used simply to remind the dog of what he has already learned (which part of his body to move), never to provoke him into movement.

If he does not respond to a gentle touch, return to foundation work of Show and Tell – Show him how to get into the stand and Tell him he's good when he does. Cement foundation. This is not an easy physical maneuver.

Some dogs need more time to learn how to perform the stand properly. Some need to leave it alone for a day or so between sessions. Work on the stand all by itself. When he makes progress at one session, end training there and give him quiet time for his brain to process this new information.

Remember the analogy of learning to hammer a nail with your left hand? Sometimes even when the dog knows what to do, it can still be hard for him to do it.

Shifting Context

Shifting context with the stand is more difficult than with other exercises. For quite a while, practice the stand where the dog can't move forward or out to the side as he's getting into the right position. If you're observant, you can find more places (like curbs and doorways) that have the necessary configuration to insure success.

Once the dog learns to stand up by himself from the sit, without moving forward or sideways, move away from the wall and the stair. Use lower barriers, like curbs or parking lot stops, to help define the stand.

Sometimes use just a barrier in front and other times one at the side, depending on what your dog shows he needs most. Eventually, just a board on the ground, or the white line in a parking lot or tennis court, is enough to help the dog define the space and prevent movement in that direction.

Climbing the Ladder

Climb the ladder of approximations slowly with the stand. As your dog understands "Stay" better with sit and down, take one step forward (you go down the first stair) as you remind him to "Stay." Step back beside him right away.

After a few seconds, have him sit. Release clearly and calmly – to the side or the back. Work up to where you can take one or two steps in front of him, and one or two steps sideways, while he remains standing without moving his feet.

Once he has learned to stand up by himself from the sit, move away from the barriers. Practice walking in front of the dog while he stays, so you can change from his right side to left side and back again.

For Schutzhund, walk past him and repeat your cue for stand as you pass by. This prepares him for the picture of you leaving as he hears the word in the walking stand.

Avoid walking behind the dog at this point. Going behind encourages him to turn his head to watch you. This can make him move his feet to stay balanced. Build on success. Avoid doing anything too soon that breaks down training, especially with a more difficult exercise like the stand.

Even though the dog is standing solidly now, it's a good idea to practice the stand with a visual line (such as in a parking lot), even after you no longer need a physical barrier. As you begin to move around him, sometimes it is difficult to tell whether the dog moved his feet or not and the lines can help.

As your dog shows more Reliability in the stand, begin changing what you do at the end. Sometimes release him right from the stand, without the final sit. Release back or sideways, rarely forward. Always release calmly and quietly.

Position Changes

Once the sit and stand are sure, have him down after the stand. Return to the top of the stairs to prevent him from moving forward as he goes into a down.

When the dog shows that he clearly understands which position is which, add the most difficult transition. Back at the top of the stairs, ask the dog to stand from a down position. Be prepared to help a little here. Guide with food in front of his nose and a helping hand at his stifles, if necessary, to teach this new topography.

Ideally, the dog should rise to a stand from the down without moving any of his four paws. His feet should remain in exactly the same place. The dog should simply straighten all four legs at once and come to a standing position.

After using Show and Tell a few times, (Show him how to do it and Tell him how good he is), say the cue and give him an opportunity to figure it out himself. A few seconds is enough. If he fails to respond correctly, that's okay. He just doesn't get his reinforcement. Smile and interrupt the exercise. Give him another chance later.

If he doesn't get it right the next session, go back to Show and Tell. Obviously, the teaching phase has not been long enough. He doesn't really understand this one yet. It's difficult, so give him time.

When the dog can rise into a stand directly from a down, not only does it cement his understanding of all three positions, but it is a delight to watch. Vino took almost a year to learn this maneuver, but now he thinks he's a real cool dude when he rises to the challenge (so to speak) and gets it right. I tend to agree with him.

Once the dog masters these changes of position, ask for any one of the three positions in random order, but avoid doing sit/down or down/sit too often. And don't do too many changes at one time unless your dog seems to like this exercise. Most dogs think it's sort of stupid and pointless to do changes of position over and over.

Keep the dog at the edge of a stair or behind a low barrier to practice position changes. Even after spending a lot of time teaching the desired technique, creeping forward is a strong temptation. It makes the exercise easier for the dog, and nobody ever said they were stupid. They'll usually find the easiest way to do something if left to their own devices.

Hand Signal

If you want to teach a hand signal as well, introduce it after the dog clearly knows the verbal cue. When you use the two together, the dog always responds to the hand signal instead of the word. It's more natural for him.

If the dog learns the hand signal first, you'll have to fade the signal entirely for him to learn the word. And he'll keep looking for the body signal.

Best to teach the word first – the hard part. Then the hand signal association is easy. He remembers the word cue because he learned that first, with no hand signal.

Teach a small signal. This requires the dog to pay close attention. Give the signal a distinct movement, since dogs see motion better than form. You can always make the signal bigger in a distracting situation.

Premack It

Once the dog knows sit, down and stand, vary which behavior you ask for to allow the dog access to what he wants. However, be careful where you ask for the stand. This is usually the more fragile one, so ask for it in places that help the dog get it right, like at the top of a step.

Moving Stand

Some important approximations are still missing for the dog to know how to lock up into a stand while moving. To teach this, go back to the stair. If possible, use a different step from the one where you did the foundation work from the sit. The place association to start with a sit could be strong enough to override your verbal cue to stand.

Now, instead of starting in a sit, walk the dog to the top of the stairs and ask for "Stand." Be sure to give the cue *before* the dog reaches the edge of the top step. Timing here is very important. The dog needs to hear the word and have time to process it before he reaches the step.

When he stands, lavish him with calm praise and gentle petting and food if you can. If he doesn't stand the first time, help him out with Show and Tell – Show him what you want and then Tell him how good he is.

Once the dog is standing reliably on cue at the top of a stair, without sitting first, give him the "Stand" cue as you reach the top of the stair while you keep walking – just down the first stair. This is a real test.

If your dog does it perfectly – praise, return, release and get happy. Your dog's brilliant and you're becoming a great positive trainer.

When the dog is showing Reliability in his Response to the walking stand, shift context to a new location. Find a location where the dog really wants to go forward, like down the steps to the yard or out the door, if there is a step there.

Use the Premack Principle to get him to lock up for two seconds in a solid stand. Praise, then release him to go out and do what he wants.

Gradually start to add a little more speed to your movement into the stand at other locations where there is a natural barrier. Once the dog learns to stop the forward movement of his front legs when you say "Stand," even when going at a brisk pace, he's on his way to truly understanding what you want in this behavior.

Running Stand

When teaching the running stand for Schutzhund, more topography is needed. Just because the dog can get into a stand from a sit, and can stop in a stand from a walk, doesn't mean he can lock up in a solid stand from the run. New muscle memory must be learned.

Even when the dog knows what to do, the running stand can be a challenge for some dogs. Remember the difficulty of learning to hammer with your left hand? That's probably easier than getting four legs to come to a dead stop from a run! So even though the dog can recognize the cue and knows what to do, he still might not be able to perform it to your satisfaction for awhile.

Teach him slowly. Go back to a stair or low barrier and just keep increasing your approach speed as the dog gets more successful. Give him time to learn *how* to do what you are asking, especially with a younger dog or a larger breed.

Once he masters the technique and you are getting consistent Response, use natural barriers in places he wants to go to Premack it. The doorway to the yard is perfect – even better if there's a step or two.

Be sure he gets it right the *first* time before he gets what he wants. Second chances don't count. If he misses, close the door for a few seconds and then start over.

The Big Guns

As well as using the Premack Principle, start to reward a steady stand with the big guns – toys. Introduce this only after the dog is showing Response, Responsibility and Reliability, even while you reward with his favorite food treats. We certainly don't want to tempt him into making a mistake.

Introduce the toy back at the top of a step or behind a low barrier. The urge to move forward becomes even greater when you raise the reward.

Stay beside the dog as you walk him into a stand and remain beside him. Produce his toy while reminding him to "Stand, Good Stand." Slowly lower the toy to just in front of his nose, while reminding him to stand. Release him with "Get It" and play a little tug-of-war or just let him have it.

Progress up the ladder of approximations. Eventually he should hold the stand solidly, even while you walk a few steps in front as you show him the toy. Then toss it back to him as you release him to get it.

Toss it behind him sometimes too. Using the toy this way, first as distraction and then as reward, can add some positive body tension to the dog's stand.

Done properly, when the dog truly understands what is expected, he rivets his feet to the ground. Many dogs tense up their muscles when they see the toy and develop a much more concentrated stand.

If at any time the dog shows that this motivation is too much for him in the stand, go back to using food or release him to the toy while you are still beside him. We're not trying to trick him here. For more on using play drive to reward the stand, see *Schutzhund Obedience* (Recommended Resources).

Zero to One

One note about teaching changes of position (sit to stand to down to stand, etc.) for competitive obedience. Many dogs learn these positions within each exercise, such as the drop on recall, or signals, or the motion exercises in Schutzhund.

But these same dogs can rarely perform the basic stationary changes of position when asked. And many can't get the position right when the pattern is changed. Instead of a drop on recall, try to get a sit. Try mixing up the order of the motion exercises for Schutzhund, or the signal exercise for Utility. Very few dogs actually understand the three positions on just a verbal cue or hand signal.

The trainers missed the zero to one step. If the dog can't do changes of position, then he doesn't actually understand which position corresponds to which word – sit, down and stand. He's just pattern trained to the antecedents within each exercise – a perfect example of behavior without true learning. Shift context and it falls apart.

All competitive obedience dogs should be able to perform changes of position easily, before being asked to do them while moving or in the context of a complete exercise. Otherwise, how can they be expected to perform them reliably in every trial?

I learned this from watching the dogs in Belgian Ringsport. There, the sequence of position changes is picked at random at each trial. A box is marked with white lines on the ground and the dog must remain inside it. The handler goes about 10 feet away, often behind some sort of obstruction so only his head is visible.

In one championship, the handler had to sit in the cockpit of a small plane! The handler must then ask for three to five position changes.

These dogs fully understand the verbal cues for each position. Once your dog can perform this type of exercise, he's far more ready to put them into the trial exercises consistently because he has a clear understanding of each cue.

Once the stand is really solid, test the dog by mixing up which behavior you request (sit, stand or down) for any privilege he wants – whether it's going out the door or eating his dinner. The more you shift context, the more you promote his understanding of the specific cue for each different position. Remember, he must get it right the first time to earn what he wants.

Probably one of the hardest tasks you dog will encounter in this training game is to differentiate reliably between these three verbal cues – stand, sit and down. Take the time to teach these cues properly. Let him learn, and be sure always to forgive forgetting.

BE FAIR TO YOUR DOG !

21 The Heeling

" An animal, especially a dog,
is possibly the purest experience you can have."
– Audrey Hepburn

Heeling is attention. The entire heeling exercise is a study in attention. Does the dog really want to stay with the handler every step of the way? If he does, he pays close attention.

Nowhere is the training dance more elegant, or inspiring, than in precision heeling. Watch the invisible silver thread link the smiling eyes of dog and handler moving in unison – both there only for each other in this moment in time.

To see such a team is to realize the transcendent nature of dog training. Patty Ruzzo and her magnificent Terv, Luca, were such a team. If you never had the privilege of seeing this kind of teamwork, we suggest you find such an example before setting your own goals.

Nowhere is the power of positive training more evident than the sheer joy a dog can show in heeling next to his master. The prancing gait, the focused eyes, the waving tail, the intensity, the concentration are all part of the perfect picture.

Heeling starts with attention. For those who aspire to teach great heeling, reinforce any and all attention to you. When you get consistent attention, begin to reinforce eye contact – any and all eye contact. Follow The Golden Rule here!

As you are walking, encourage the dog to stretch his head up as high as he can to reach the food in your hand. Teach him to walk with his head held high, as though he is trying to bring his eyes closer to yours – to shorten that silver thread.

Reinforce all this behavior. Put a word on it and ask for more and more effort, higher and higher head carriage, better and better position. Get excited when you get it.

Real attention from your dog means real effort and concentration. Show him you appreciate it! Give him your undivided attention in return.

This is totally unnatural behavior. When did you last see a dog walking around gazing up into the sky – except when there was a squirrel in a tree? So if you aspire to flashy heeling, start making yourself at least as interesting as that squirrel in the tree.

The Basics

The basics of motivational heeling are covered in detail in the *Schutzhund Obedience* book (listed in Recommended Resources), so we won't take up the space here. Some of those basics haven't changed, but a few major ones have – and we do mean major.

Teaching heeling seems like a simple exercise – just walk and feed the dog at your left side. Simple, but not always easy. We still carry food, but now we use really good food and lots of different types of food too.

The dog never knows what to expect. We can train longer now. Each change in food seems to spark the dog's interest in working harder. It doesn't necessarily have to be better food – just the change seems to make a difference.

We still wait for the dog to pay attention and then we reinforce that attention. And we still feed the dog when he hits the right position.

But before, there was a lot of food steering and luring the dog with food. The result was lots of great behavior but, unfortunately, not much real learning. The ABCs were mixed up. Keeping them in order lets the dog learn.

Often, in the past, the food became the Antecedent. It was supposed to be the Consequence. Rehearsing CBC produces Behavior, not learning. The dog looked great, but when the food disappeared, often so did the heeling. The dog had lost his cue. With the food always present, he didn't bother to learn the other cues – the relevant Antecedents.

Now we know how important it is for the dog to understand these Antecedents, or cues. For heeling, there are lots of cues. Now we know to get these Antecedents in there *first*, so the dog can learn them. We wean from the food prompt early and get the Behavior before providing the Consequence. Then we let the Consequence drive the Behavior – true to the laws of learning.

Body Posture

The most important Antecedents for heeling are your body posture, energy and the way you walk. These provide your dog with the most information.

Practice walking properly without your dog. Perfect your part – right from the start. Square your shoulders. Walk a straight line.

Use your eyes properly. Divide your focus between where you are going and where your dog's eyes are when he's in perfect position. Then you can keep that silver thread connection with him at all times. You can also guide him with your eyes. The dog soon learns to follow your eyes.

Put your hands where you intend to carry them. Avoid letting them interfere with your dog. Walk briskly and with purpose. One of you has to be the leader. One of you has to know where you are going – and it can't be the dog.

Learn to make precise, consistent turns. Look where you are going. Turn your head, but your head only, about one stride before you turn. Keep your feet directly underneath you. Keep your shoulders level and square as they turn in the direction you are going – just after you turn your head.

Keep your eye contact with your dog as you make the turn, but without looking back. Keep focusing forward. Learn to let your dog know where you are going.

Your normal focal point should be just a few strides ahead. Shorten the focal point for turns and for the slow pace. That gives your dog a chance to know what's next.

Ease into the fast and slow paces. Incline your body slightly forward as you start the fast. Straighten up a little and open up your shoulders before the slow.

Learn to walk perfect circles for the figure eight and group exercises. Keep your shoulders square and level, turned slightly in the direction you are going. Keep your body upright and your feet underneath you. Don't lean in on the circle. Avoid looking back. Stay focused on where you are going, but without losing eye contact with your dog.

Practice all this without your dog. Get your posture and movement correct before you ever ask the dog to heel. Then you're half-way home. Far more than half of all heeling difficulties stem from the handling, not from the dog.

The Real Antecedents

Your body posture, your demeanor, your attitude and your breathing are all powerful antecedents to your dog for heeling. Just how significant are they? They are so important to your dog that, when they are used consistently and conscientiously, the word "Heel" becomes irrelevant.

How do I know this? Back in the days when I showed in Schutzhund, I walked my pattern several times each week. The routine is always the same in that sport, so it is possible to practice the actual heeling pattern before the trial. At the park, I would let my two marvelous German Shepherds run free while I walked my pattern. Often this was at night, and I used this particular park because it had a single light at the side, just bright enough for me to get my bearings in the shadows.

Without fail, as soon as I started practicing – setting up at my chosen start position, squaring my shoulders, placing my hands and taking a deep, calming breath – within seconds both dogs would be at my side, jostling each other to get into heel position. Keep in mind, this was in the dark and no words had been spoken.

To Espe and Charra (both Schutzhund-titled), this looked like heeling, so it must be heeling. The words were irrelevant, and it obviously wasn't dependent on the presence of food, since I had none.

So get your body cues going. Focus. Breathe. Set your posture. Muster the energy. Smile. Be relaxed, yet deliberate. Know where you are going. Give your dog all that help.

Another story illustrates the importance of your part in heeling. One June, a friend came to me from over 100 miles away for help in obedience. Her female German Shepherd had just failed her first try at a B, the Traffic Safe Companion Dog title that is a prerequisite to enter a Schutzhund trial. The exercises are similar to the Novice routine, but much longer.

When she arrived, I spent about five minutes watching her work with the dog. I asked her to put the dog back in her car. We then spent well over an hour – fixing her posture, her walking, her breathing, her focus – rehearsing all the things the dog needed to see in training.

Because we lived so far apart, I did not see them again until our club trial in October, where the pair presented one of the finest B routines I have every witnessed. When the handler did her part, the dog was magnificent!

Hardly anything had changed in the dog's training – except the handling. If you can't master the handling part of heeling, how can you expect the dog to follow you in any sort of respectable manner? Do your preparation; do your homework. It's only fair to the dog.

The Start

Once you have learned how to walk and turn and focus and carry your hands, invite your dog to join you. You've already mastered the entire routine, so going back to walking just a few steps in a straight line is easy.

Your dog already hangs out close to you by now, so there's no reason for a leash, unless you're in a dangerous place. If the dog wants to leave, the relationship issues need to be worked out first.

Begin at the beginning. Wait for attention. Start when the dog shows you he is ready. This can take the most time, but it's worth the wait.

If you have a nosey sniffer, start on asphalt or pavement. Take that distraction away. Why fight about it? Practice heeling on the grass only *after* heeling and attention are reliably on cue. Go to the grass only when this dog has learned which behavior leads to the best reinforcement.

A word about sniffing. It is not only natural behavior for the dog, it is also necessary. A dog uses his nose the way you use your eyes. To ask him to enter a new area and then tell him "No Sniff" is like putting a blindfold on you before you enter a new place. How secure would you feel? The dog perceives his world through his nose. He uses it just the way we use our eyes – to get oriented to where he is.

Give him plenty of time to sniff around wherever you go. First, let the dog be a dog and check out the area, then ask for attention. He is much more ready to perform once he feels comfortable and safe, and has satisfied his curiosity.

The Word

Back to heeling. Of course you have good food. Your dog knows you have good food because you always have good food at training time. And by now he seeks eye contact with you to get it. Great! You're ready to start heeling.

Put a couple of pieces of food in your hand and position yourself so your dog is on your left side. There is no need to start from a sit. Walk slowly at first, and when he comes into position with his head up, tell him this is "Heel" as you reinforce with praise and a piece of food.

For the first few times, have the food close to where you want his nose to be, so he stretches his neck to get his head up high. This is just to manipulate him into the behavior we want so we can begin to make the word association.

Associate the cue with the behavior that gets him his reinforcement. But be sure you are only saying "Heel" when the dog is in *exactly* the position you want.

Experiment to see whether he heels better if you start from a sit or not. For some dogs, just getting up out of the sit to follow you is the hardest part – so leave that until later.

If the dog already understands that attention, carrying his head up and eye contact earn him great reinforcement, he offers these behaviors more and more frequently. When he hits the correct position, begin to associate the word "Heel."

Don't worry about other behaviors like jumping up or pushing at your hand, they'll extinguish eventually – provided they don't get reinforced. Why dampen the dog's enthusiasm right at the start?

Smile and enjoy it. He can't be doing this wrong because you haven't taught him this yet. Only reinforce the behavior you want – the right position. Praise effort, but feed position. Keep him trying, but save the high magnitude reinforcement (and excited emotional energy) for when he gets into the precise position and makes strong eye contact.

When he hits the right position, tell him "Yes! Heel, Good" and feed. Stop walking for a few seconds while you feed him if that's more comfortable for you.

Associate the word whenever you can, but only when he is in the perfect position and making eye contact. As you reinforce this behavior more, the dog offers it more. He knows the game by now.

Teaching Topography

To walk in a straight line close beside you, carrying his head up high, is not an easy task for a dog. He's used to looking where he's going – leading with his nose and letting his rear end follow along any old way it can.

If the dog swings his rear out to the left, the handler may be reinforcing when the dog's head is turned too far to the right. Formal heeling is easier for this dog once he understands the Attention Sit (Chapter 17: The Sit). Then he already has the concept of his head going in one direction and his body in another. This is much easier to master when sitting still than while moving.

Try doing some very slow heeling with a curb on the other side of the dog. This helps him learn how to carry his body in a straight line to avoid stepping on the curb. Give him enough room. Don't crowd him against the curb.

Praise any effort he makes to straighten himself out, even if it's only two steps. Keep him trying. Let him get completely comfortable with this new way of walking at your side, before adding changes of pace or turns, and be careful not to reinforce when his head is too far to the right.

For dogs who swing their butts out to the left, do most of your heeling in a big circle to the left to help them be straighter. With those who want to lag behind a little, heel in big circles to the right to make them work harder. Reinforce effort and energy.

Be sure to keep your focus forward at all times. Looking back encourages lagging by reinforcing the wrong behavior with eye contact. Do your part!

As heeling progresses, ask the dog to carry his head higher and higher, by making him reach and stretch more for each food reward. Teach him to incline his head slightly more to the right in small increments, by varying where you feed him and which behavior you reinforce.

These are all physical techniques that the dog needs to master for proper heeling. Teach them slowly and in small steps, just as you would develop certain muscles by adding small weight increments at the gym.

Dogs aren't born knowing how to heel properly. They must be taught, physically as well as mentally. Teach the physical techniques first, slowly. Wait until he has mastered his body before asking for turns and changes of pace.

Small Dogs

To be able to maintain correct posture with a small dog, and still be able to reinforce properly (and avoid an aching back), use benches. Teach the dog to be comfortable walking along a bench, one that is wide enough to be safe. This is easy if you have already started teaching the sit, down and stand on a table or bench. (See photo on Page 255.)

After you have practiced by yourself walking alongside the bench, put the dog on the bench to heel with you. This brings him up close enough for you to reinforce without changing your total body posture.

Heeling along the bench also eliminates his fear of being stepped on. The small dog feels safer when he is up higher and occupies his own space. He can also learn to walk a straight line instead of swinging wide to avoid your feet. And if you've done your homework properly, the dog gets to see the picture of perfect posture for heeling right from the start.

When the dog is ready for turns, put four benches in a square. Teach right turns with you inside the square and left turns with you on the outside.

By now your dog is getting really comfortable in heel position, so you can teach the about turn back on the ground. Before you do, start back on the ground slowly. Every few steps, bend at the knees to reinforce.

Let your dog get comfortable with this new picture. Avoid leaning down or hovering over the small dog. Keep your feet close together, underneath your body and out of his way, so he doesn't worry about being stepped on.

The transition to slow pace can be taught on the bench, but teach the fast pace on the ground. It's just too risky to teach on the bench.

When working on the ground, to save wear and tear on your back and knees, put some peanut butter on the end of a stick or a wooden spoon. Reinforce with that (with praise, of course) to avoid bending down every time. At the moment the dog offers the precise behavior you want, lower the stick into the proper position – so he stretches up to reach it with his head high. This also keeps your position correct.

Working with the small dog is a physical challenge. It is also a mental challenge for you to make these little dogs feel safe and confident in training. You must become a dependable pack leader so they can show their best work.

Shifting Context

Shift context early and often while teaching the basics of heeling. This doesn't make you look like such a brilliant trainer at first, but it does help your dog learn the cues better.

You eventually want your dog to be able to heel anytime, anyplace. Build the basics in a variety of settings, obviously without distractions. By building a foundation everywhere, you insure greater success in the future.

Practice without other dogs until your dog has the basics. Leave that group heeling stuff for those who have no aspirations to truly attentive heeling. There are no trials yet where group heeling is an exercise.

If you teach a group class and want to introduce heeling, let each team heel individually. Both dogs and handlers can concentrate better when the rest of the class stands still. This also allows the teacher to provide much clearer direction to each team and offer more personal instruction. The others learn by watching too.

At first, have the participants line up along one wall. The first person heels around three sides of the room and ends up at the back of the line. Once they learn the about turn, they can heel across the room individually, do an about turn and then return to their original place in the line.

Group heeling can be frustrating and futile. Set up for safety and success with individual practice.

Distractions

Once the dog shows intense attention, and has deemed you to be even more interesting than the squirrel in the tree, (after all, he can catch and eat what you've got!), introduce mild distractions. Keep them far away and just wait for attention.

Reinforce every movement toward attention and position. If you want energetic heeling, be exuberant and exciting. Encourage his enthusiasm. Appreciate his efforts. Do your part. Stay connected to him.

Gently push him away and then you run away. Make him chase you, like he would chase the squirrel. Make this a fun game – to find heel position – and thus receive all the energy and attention and great food as his reward. Make attention to you, and heeling, worth the effort. Be a fun mate. Be active and animated. Be a squirrel up a tree!

Teach Touch

For competition, teach your dog how to "Touch." That means to reach up with his nose and touch the open palm of hand wherever you put it.

This makes a fine way to set up your dog for the start of each exercise. Just put your open hand where you want him to be and tell him "Touch." When he hits that ideal position, you can reinforce with praise and lots of good positive energy.

Make "Touch" a fun game. First, put a piece of food between the base of two fingers in each hand. As he touches his nose to your palm to get the food, associate the word.

Then have food only in one hand. Show him your open, empty hand. When he touches your palm with his nose to check it out, associate the word. Then feed him from your other hand.

This gives you both something to focus on and is a positive way to connect between exercises in the trial ring. It also gives you a way to help your dog set up perfectly the first time. Then you start every exercise with a positive connection.

Be Unpredictable

The most important part in the heeling program is to get the food out of sight early. As soon as the dog is trying to get into heel position to get the food, use the food only as a Consequence, never as an Antecedent. This only inhibits and prevents learning.

Carry the food in different places – your top pocket, your mouth, your back pocket, either hand, a pouch around your waist (or around your neck). Praise and make the word association for "Heel," but keep the dog guessing about when and where the food is coming from. Being unpredictable is often the hardest part.

Pushing and biting at your hand are not behaviors that earn reinforcement. Getting into the right position, with head up and eyes riveted, is what gets him what he wants. Watching the food won't get it. He gets it only for watching you with ears up and eyes bright.

Focus on getting Response first. Then lengthen the time between reinforcement until you get some serious Responsibility for remaining in position and attentive. But remember to move up and down the ladder, constantly varying the reinforcement schedule.

Once your dog is consistently in the correct position, add a game of tug as a reward, or a favorite toy. Keep the toy close to you – don't throw it away as a reward. Heeling is all about focusing on you.

For Schutzhund, keep heeling well away from the protection phase until it is reliably on cue and fully understood. Practice obedience during protection with long downs and Attention Sits instead.

Away from protection, introduce heeling for a burlap bite roll so the dog discovers that you can play exciting games with burlap too. Reward his most intense heeling with an energetic game of tug on the bite roll.

Be variable about when you reinforce, and with what. Save the toys – the big guns – for when your dog is really giving you what you want and trying extra hard. There's more on using play drive to shape and reward animated, accurate heeling in the *Schutzhund Obedience* book.

Stop teaching and let the dog learn. Allow him to experiment. It's okay, he just doesn't get reinforced when he's wrong. But be sure to let him know the instant he gets it right.

Make heeling exciting. Keep him guessing. Make it fun.

DO YOUR PART !

284

22   The Recall

" Dogs come when they are called.
Cats take a message and get back to you."
                                                   – Mary Bly

The recall we are talking about here is the formal exercise for competition. There's absolutely no reason why this type of recall should be slow or dull.

The dog should fly to the handler as fast as possible and slide smoothly into a front sit – head up and butt planted firmly and squarely on the ground. For a dog, this should be a joyous moment – arriving close to his master after being apart, even if separated only by the length of a trial field or obedience ring.

The basis for this recall can be taught long before the stay is reliable. This is also a fine introduction for teaching a reliable distraction recall as explained in Chapter 15: The Manners.

Have someone hold your puppy by the collar. The holder says nothing and pays no attention to the pup. Show your pup his favorite toy (or some really great food) and run away in a straight line. Make sure he can still see you, but go far enough away so he gets up a full head of steam. He should be running at top speed when he finally reaches you.

Attract him with his toy. Then stand up straight and still, hands at your sides. When the puppy is looking at you, call his name and your recall cue.

Just after the cue, preferably when he is straining to go forward, your friend lets him go. The puppy runs full tilt to you, as fast as his little legs can carry him.

285

Hold your position perfectly still as the puppy runs to you. Just as he reaches you, drop to the ground and open your arms to welcome him. Play wild and silly games. Feed him a jackpot.

Express your delight in his reaching you. Convince him that this is the finest place to be in the universe. Show him you appreciate his desire and effort.

These long-distance recalls make a wonderful imprint on the puppy. They are the first step in teaching a flying recall. The recall is one of two exceptions to the rule of teaching topography slowly. (The other is the retrieve.) Right from the start, the dog learns to come as fast as possible.

This introduction, and the formal front-sit techniques, are thoroughly explained and illustrated in the *Schutzhund Obedience* book (Recommended Resources), so we won't duplicate them here. We will, however, expand on them and offer some new concepts from the Positive Training Paradigm.

The Words

As discussed earlier, whatever word you use for an informal recall, use a different word for your formal recall. The informal word means to stop whatever you're doing and come on over here.

The formal recall word cues your dog for a flying run into a perfect front sit. This gets rewarded with all the best stuff – always with a smile, appreciation, positive energy and super food treats, or his favorite game. Keep competition cues for that training only, where criteria and rewards are high.

Right from the start, use this formal word for your blazing puppy recalls, even though no front sit is required. Dropping to the ground as he reaches you effectively interrupts the exercise. By hearing the word when the pup has a great desire to get to you, with no other prompts, he can begin to associate the word with running in at top speed.

Later, associate the same word with the front sit and, amazingly, the dogs manage to put the two together all by themselves – with a minimum of training. They're getting really good at figuring things out by this time.

Teaching Topography

The physical technique of a smooth, square, straight front sit is something the dog must learn. It depends on the dog lifting his head as high as possible as he plants his butt solidly. (See photo on Page 284.) Not many dogs walk around watching the clouds roll by. Most keep their noses close to the ground whenever possible.

Teach the front sit after your dog clearly knows how to sit squarely on cue and pays attention to your face during heeling. Start the front sit before the dog becomes entrenched in heeling. This avoids him continually trying to get to your left side for reinforcement.

Show the dog that you have food in each hand. Put both hands together in front of your body, at your waist, or wherever the dog's nose lands at the highest point the dog can reach and still keep his feet on the ground. Walk backward a few steps. As the dog follows, praise and feed a treat from each hand, just for following you with his nose up.

Then put both hands behind your back and stand still. Wait for attention to your face. If you have a word for eye contact, use it. If the dog goes around to sniff or push at your hands to get the food, say nothing. Keep your hands low and closed and perfectly still. He's experimenting. He's trying to figure out which behavior earns the reward. This one doesn't.

Let Him Learn

When your dog follows your hands around to get at the food (and most do), smile and be quiet. He's doing exactly what we want him to do. Just let him learn it by himself.

Remember that the young bear learns to fish as much by what doesn't work as by what does. Remind yourself that the waiting is the hardest part.

Every time the dog follows your hands around behind you, just wait a few seconds. Keep your fingers closed tightly around the food as he noses at them. Then simply turn to face him again. There's no rush. He's not getting reinforced for that behavior, so pretty soon he'll try something else.

As some point, when you turn to face him, he looks questioningly at your face, if only for some clue as to why you aren't producing any treats for him. Praise instantly with "Yes!" and feed him a treat from one hand or the other.

Make him work hard for the reward. Bring your hand to the front and place it where he has to stretch as high as possible to reach it – close to your body and in the center, as in the photo on Page 284, but he doesn't have to sit at first.

If the dog gets stuck, occasionally show him what you want by bringing the food up in front of your eyes, repeating your word for eye contact and praising. Then lower the food in a straight line from your eyes to his mouth.

Do this only a few times. By now, he doesn't need this type of luring. Just wait, and give him the time he needs to figure it out by himself.

Put both hands behind your back again and wait. Stand up tall, square your shoulders, and lean *back* instead of forward. Leaning over the dog inhibits him from coming in close to you.

You'll be surprised how quickly the dog figures out that attention to your face is what produces the reward. He learns it sooner if your body posture is inviting – leaning back.

And he learns it even faster if your timing is good and you get your excited praise word in there ("Yes!") the first second he looks at your face. Don't miss your moment.

Spitting Food

This is one exercise where teaching your dog how to catch food that you spit to him is very useful. Patty Ruzzo has elevated food-spitting to an art form. If catching food is a skill your dog knows, use it to reward front sit.

The basic behavior to develop here is for your dog to raise his head as he looks at your face. Then he has to stretch up even further to get the treat when you produce it, unless he knows how to catch food when you spit it to him.

Once you get eye contact as a consistent Response, wait until the dog is very straight and square in front of you and ask him to "Sit." If he really knows this cue, he plunks down his butt in a perfect front sit the first time. Praise, reward and release. If you're not spitting the food, be sure to keep your hand high enough so he has to stretch to reach the treat. Make this a habit in front sit right from the start.

As his Response improves, add your recall word when he looks up at your face. At first, couple it with "Sit," such as "Here, Sit." Lean back and keep your hands behind your back to keep your shoulders open.

Soon, just bringing your shoulders back, opening up your chest, initiating eye contact and smiling produces the desired behavior. Now begin to associate your formal recall word with this behavior, just as he arrives in front sit.

Drop the word "Sit" unless the dog forgets and needs a little help sometimes. Helping with a verbal cue is far preferable to using body language or food steering to get the desired behavior.

Adding Distance

Once the dog offers the correct Response to the front-sit cues, ask him to find the position from a few steps away. If his stay is solid, have him sit-stay while you back up – just a couple of steps at first.

Give him the antecedents for front sit – open shoulders, hands behind back and leaning back. Smile and give your recall cue in an encouraging tone of voice. If he comes and just looks in your face without sitting, fine.

Appreciate his effort. He got at least part of it right. Reward that a couple of times. Next time, cue him to "Sit" just as he gets there. Help him get it right as he puts these two movements together.

If he doesn't sit close enough, or rocks back onto his haunches, put the food where he has to stretch his head up to get it (Page 284). Always reward only a square sit, with his nose stuck up as high as he can reach without raising his rear. Teach solid topography here.

Be sure you are opening your shoulders enough and leaning back to encourage him to reach up. Most dogs sit out too far because the handlers hover over them, or deliver the food too far away. This is not Pizza Hut – we do not deliver!

The dog must work hard to get the food by stretching up. No free lunch here. Place your hand high enough, and actually against your body, so the dog is reaching up when he gets the food.

Do this exercise when the dog is walking freely, not just from stays. For Schutzhund, practice from a down position, as in the trial routine. The dog must learn how to get up quickly from a down and slide smoothly into front sit.

Preventing Unwanted Behavior

To prevent crooked front sits, make sure the dog is facing you squarely, and that you are standing squarely, before asking for front sit. If necessary, change your position so the dog is facing you correctly.

The dog only needs to learn how to do a straight, square front sit. Why teach him how to straighten up a crooked sit? If he never has one, he never needs it.

If he does happen to offer one, just don't reinforce it. Let others get obsessed with solving a problem that doesn't need to exist.

"Good trainers solve problems. Great trainers never get to the problems." By teaching your dog a correct front sit, and reinforcing only that, your dog learns only that.

Recalls are always done straight on. Even in the advanced Utility exercises, the handler turns to face the dog's approach in both the directed retrieve and directed jumping. Lots of dogs have learned front sit using this method – rewarding only correctness. Very few ever offer crooked sits unless the handler sets himself up in the wrong position.

So teach your dog what is right. Leave what is wrong to the folks who want a problem to solve.

Raising Criteria

Once the dog masters front sit – raises his head to make eye contact and tucks his butt neatly underneath – now put it together with the recall. After Response, work on Responsibility.

Add a little more distance to the recall. Do this from the stay only if that exercise is really reliable, but avoid doing it from a stay too often. For Schutzhund, practice from the down sometimes so the dog learns how to leap up from that position.

When adding the recall to the stays, be sure to keep high reinforcement in the stays to avoid breaking down that training. The stay is boring. The recall is fun. See it from your dog's point of view and make the stays worth his while.

More often, recall the dog when he is further away, but not on a stay. By now it's hard to get the dog to go that far away during training. Most have turned into Velcro-dogs, pushing and driving with their behavior and eye contact to get the reward they want.

Patty just throws some food on the ground. While the dog is eating, sneak away. Just as the dog finishes eating and looks up, cue the recall. Always face the dog squarely as he's coming in for front sit. Don't try to fool him here – you're both on the same team.

Call the dog just as he looks up from finishing the food. Don't try to call him away from a distraction. Set up for success. Start with a few feet, not 20 yards. Lengthen the distance by approximations.

Adding A Bridge

Just as the dog turns and starts toward you, bridge the behavior with enthusiastic praise, "Yes! Yes! Good!" This encourages him and affirms that he is doing the right thing, but don't use the recall cue again.

As the dog runs to you, assume your recall posture – shoulders back, hands behind your back, lean back and invite him in with soft eye contact and a smile. Just as he gets close, remind him what it is you want with "Here, Sit."

Help him get it right the first few times – but only with word cues, not body help. When he shows Responsibility for finding the right position on his own, praise and reinforce.

Speed and Distance

Lengthen the distance when he shows Reliability in finding front sit, even when coming in at speed. Should he fail to sit properly, no big deal. If he came quickly and made eye contact, reinforce that. Appreciate effort and let him try again from a closer distance.

Once he gets the idea, and slides into front sit even when coming from far away, add even more speed. Go back to having a friend hold him while you run away. Keep the distance shorter at first so he doesn't work up a full head of steam on the recall.

This recall probably won't need a bridge. You running away produces powerful attraction for most dogs. Being held back creates strong opposition reflex to bolt forward, thus using it in our favor again. Just assume your position and give the dog a chance to figure out where he needs to be to get reinforced.

Reward effort (with lower value reinforcement), even if he doesn't get it perfect the first time. Shorten the distance a little and give him another chance.

Right the First Time

The temptation is usually to help the dog out, to manipulate him into the correct front sit in order to feed him. Handlers want to take a step back, into a new position, to give the dog another chance. The dog learns to let the handler adjust, then he gets it right the second time. Wrong.

The dog must take Responsibility to get it right the first time. Let's face it, the second time doesn't count in the trial. The balance here is to help him learn, but without fixing it for him.

If the dog ends up sitting a little too far away, bring your hand to the front, close to your body. Show him where he needs to be to get the food, but don't step back. Stepping back quickly becomes a body cue to the dog for the front sit. We see it over and over.

Helping the dog out a couple of times is fine, but don't make a habit of stepping back and guiding him in. Allow him not to get his reward. You have permission *not* to reinforce less than correct performance. Go back to lower criteria and reinforce foundation work if necessary.

One major key to effective positive training is giving yourself permission not to reinforce. Remember that fishing bear who learns as much from when he fails to catch a fish as from when he does.

Let the dog know you appreciate his effort. Stay connected to him. Always smile and praise him. Show him what he could have earned. Knowing there are fish in the river is what keeps the bear fishing, even if he isn't catching them yet!

Simply give the dog another chance to earn a great reward by concentrating and working harder. Begin with a front sit from the speed and distance he knows. Then have someone hold him again to see if he can figure it out at a faster speed.

If your dog charges in to you so fast that he bangs into you, laugh and be happy. Maybe you don't offer him the high magnitude reinforcement of food or play, but appreciate his wonderful effort. He'll get it right soon enough.

Give him time to learn it himself. Once he does, his understanding is more complete than from any helping and teaching you could ever do.

This type of training feeds into the dog's love of learning. When he figures out a new skill by himself, he can't wait to get it right the next time and get his reward – on the first try.

Raising Reward

When your dog shows Reliability about finding front sit at speed, make it really worth his while. Pull out the big guns. Raising the reward here makes the recall a super fun exercise for your dog.

Play his favorite game. Play tug-of-war. Throw his favorite toy. Scratch his ears. Roll around on the ground with him or let him jump on you – whatever floats his boat.

Giving the dog what he really likes here guarantees a faster recall and more intense sit the next time. Consequence drives Behavior, so be sure you are using the big guns to reward only perfect position and concentration.

The dog must hold his position correctly for you to reinforce with play. Have him stay in the position a few extra seconds, by reminding him "Sit, Sit, Good Sit" as you lower the toy. Release him to "Get It" and then play tug, or let him have it, or throw it for him. A fast game of two-hoses is the ultimate recall reward for many dogs.

When you use play after the release, be sure the dog doesn't jump up and release himself to play. The name of the game is Responsibility, so make it part of the exercise.

If he ever releases himself, the toy goes away. Reward only obedience. The dog has to play by the rules to get the big rewards. Make sure he earns them. Be careful that what you are teaching is what the dog is learning.

Be Unpredictable

Once the dog knows this behavior and is Reliable, vary the exercise. Use different reinforcers. Set up the recall in different places. Be unpredictable and challenge the dog!

Do recalls uphill to make the dog drive harder to get more speed. Interrupt the recall just before the front sit here. Going uphill makes a correct front sit far too difficult. Reward only the fastest recalls. This is great physical conditioning too.

Downhill recalls should be shorter, but with front sit sometimes. This challenges the dog to fight against gravity for an efficient front sit. For other recalls, run out of sight. Hide behind a tree. Keep him guessing.

As the dog is coming, sometimes run away and then turn again to face him for front sit. Sometimes release him early to jump up, either on you or for a toy.

Once the dog has mastered the front sit at speed, do lots of recalls without any front sits. Just interrupt the exercise before the sit. Sometimes toss a handful of treats in the air as you release him and let him scrounge them off the ground, praising all the while and telling him what a great dog he is.

Sometimes throw his toy behind you, just as he starts to slow down for front sit. Release him to go get it before he sits. Sometimes hold the toy out to the side and let him jump up and grab it.

For the long recalls in Schutzhund, use a rolled burlap tug. Just as the dog approaches you, hold it out to the side and let him jump into it as a reward for a fast recall. If you want the dog to do his recall with the same speed as his courage test, then offer a similar reward!

When doing a recall from a stay, return frequently and reinforce the stay. Remember how pointless the stay exercise seems to the dog. Return often, release and play with him there. Just as you leave him, turn and release him as you throw the toy behind him, or to him. Keep high rewards in the stay. Keep him guessing. Practice the recall from the stay very rarely.

If training for competitive obedience, avoid getting stuck rehearsing short recalls. Practice long, motivational recalls, mostly without any front sit. The longer the better – great for physical conditioning too!

Make recalls really fun for your dog. Challenge him occasionally to find a correct front sit from speed and distance. Make yourself exciting. Keep your dog working hard and thinking.

MAKE REINFORCEMENT COUNT !

23

The Finish

" I would not give much for that man's religion
whose cat and dog are not the better for it. "
– Abraham Lincoln

A fast, flashy finish is the perfect way to end any obedience exercise. But getting from here to there (front sit to heel position), and sitting straight when he gets there, can be a challenging maneuver for some dogs.

The first few steps of the finish can be taught early. But when handlers wait until the dogs thoroughly understand both the front sit (Chapter 22: The Recall) and the Attention Sit (Chapter 17: The Sit), it's amazing how quickly their dogs learn the finish.

By the time they reach this stage in training, most dogs can put these two together easily – almost by themselves. All that foundation work in positive training really begins to pay off now.

There are two ways for the dog to finish. He can go to the handler's right side, and around the handler to heel position. This is the easiest one for big dogs to master and the safest one to teach.

The finish done totally on the left side, called a flip finish or a swing finish, requires the dog to have much more control of his body and be quite agile. The dangers are that he can bump into the handler on the way, or he might not get his butt all the way around to end with a square sit. But done properly, it's lots more fun to watch and train.

The steps to teach the basic finish of going around the handler are explicitly outlined and illustrated in *Schutzhund Obedience* (Recommended Resources). The major difference now is that very quickly we stop luring the dog around with the food.

If the dog already knows a solid Attention Sit, and knows how to find heel position himself (by you pushing him away and running a few steps and letting him find the position), then the dog learns this finish exercise very quickly. With just a little guidance from your right hand (and your eyes to get the dog started in the right direction), he soon dashes around to find heel position and earn his reward.

The Words

If you use the word "Heel" for the finish exercise (as you must in Schutzhund, or "Fuss"), then there isn't even another word for the dog to learn here. He simply has to figure out how to get there from here.

To teach both finishes, one in each direction, put different words on them. Then just be sure to practice the exercises enough for the dog to make the correct word association.

However, the flip finish works well with just a hand signal, since that is the initial step used to teach it. So, if you want, you can avoid teaching any new words here (unless you are training for Schutzhund, where hand signals are not allowed).

The Flip

In a flashy flip finish, the dog leaps into the air at the handler's left side and makes a 180-degree turn to land in heel position. This finish can also be done without the jump, which is advisable for a dog who prefers to keep all four feet on the ground.

To start the flip finish, load your left hand with a treat and teach the dog to jump up and get it on cue. Raise your hand higher and higher, step by step, and let the dog jump up and get the treat from your hand.

Eventually, raise your hand so high the dog can't reach it. If that's not possible (like with Patty's agile Whippet, who can jump higher than most people can reach), then just start withholding the food on the jump and adding the turn into the sit at heel.

That's why this is best done after the dog is totally sure of heel position. You can teach the dog to jump for the treat in your hand, and even begin the turn back on the ground. But add the sit to the sequence only after the dog thoroughly understands the Attention Sit and how to find the correct position.

The finish is not a difficult exercise. It simply requires teaching topography, and then raising criteria and raising rewards. Just teach it step by step.

By now, you've come far enough to be able to put this exercise into the Positive Training Paradigm. We'll let you figure this one out for yourself. Wait until the dog is fairly well along in his training program and he usually figures it out quickly and easily.

It's not hard. We know you can do it. Make a plan. Follow the ABCs. Establish criteria. Use approximations.

And remember – you can't be doing it wrong as long as the dog's still trying. This is a fun exercise with which to experiment. Good Luck!

KEEP IT SIMPLE !

24

The Retrieve

" He was one of these dogs
that will play fetch forever."
– Bill Murray

The philosophical debate about the best method to train a reliable retrieve has been going on for decades in dog training circles. For years, we were told the only way to assure that the dog would retrieve reliably was to pinch his ear, or choke the breath out of him, or otherwise use fear, pain and panic to teach the exercise. Yes, even with the dog who would play fetch forever!

In *The Culture Clash*, Jean Donaldson shed some sanity on the ear pinch method. About relying on a motivational retrieve she writes, "So what. You lose an occasional ribbon and keep your soul."

We have some good news for you – and for your dog. You don't have to lose many ribbons to keep your soul. Dogs with a well-trained motivational retrieve are often faster and just as reliable in this exercise. Many get higher scores too! They show a lot more enthusiasm for the work and, best of all, there is no damage done to the relationship with their handler.

For some folks in competitive obedience, their dogs remain at the first level because the retrieve is the stumbling block. Some choose not to hurt their dogs in the name of training. Others just can't get their dogs to retrieve properly. This is a shame and, thankfully, it need not be the case anymore.

301

The Golden Rule

Almost all puppies pick things up and carry them around at some age. This is the time to follow The Golden Rule. Whenever you see this behavior, reinforce any and all inclination in that direction.

The problem with puppy retrieving is that it quickly develops into the keep-away game. Watch puppies playing with each other and you'll see this "I've-got-it-and-you-can't-have-it" behavior, exhibited among human siblings with a meaningful "Nyah-Nyah-Na-Na-Na."

The answer is to positively reinforce any inclination the puppy has to pick up anything and bring it to you. Of course, puppies don't always pick up the right things. So what if it's the kid's sock or your best shoe? It's always better to teach your pup to bring things to you than to run away with them!

Even puppies from non-retrieving and non-working breeds go through juvenile phases of picking things up in their mouths. Too often, they get screamed at and chased – a bad beginning.

Patty reinforced this picking up behavior completely with her young Whippet, Flyer. By the time he was one year old, he would bring her anything – including the car keys, even though they were very difficult for him to pick up and carry. Flyer brings back anything Patty throws – because he has always been highly rewarded for this behavior. And nobody can call a Whippet a retrieving breed!

Two Toys

Another tool to prevent keep-away is the two-hose game, discussed in previous chapters and explained in the *Schutzhund Obedience* book (see Recommended Resources). If you always have another toy of equal value, and you throw it for the puppy *every time* he brings back the one he has, this game cements his desire to return to you quickly and reliably.

However, at the same time as teaching the two-hose game, also teach the puppy to deliver objects to your hand. Dogs can get very locked into spitting out one toy at your feet to get you to throw the other one. This won't do you much good if you eventually want a formal retrieve. So teach both, before the dog gets stuck in one behavior only.

Perfect Balance

The retrieve exercise is a complex behavior chain. The dog has to stay by your side, run out on cue, pick up the dumbbell promptly and properly, fly back to a perfect front sit and present the dumbbell to you correctly. (In Schutzhund, you cannot say "Stay" before you throw the dumbbell.)

The retrieve is one of the most exciting exercises in competition. Performed properly, it personifies the perfect combination of the dog's natural drives demonstrated in willing and eager cooperation with the handler. When trained fairly, the dogs obviously love this exercise too!

For this reason, we aim to teach a full-point, flashy retrieve done with full power and enthusiasm. That means the dog comes back as fast as he goes out, with the entire exercise done at full speed.

Retrieving should be pure pleasure for the dog. He should delight in bringing all his energy to performing this task for his handler.

At the first Schutzhund National Championship I ever attended, the judge for obedience was a respected German. A stranger sitting beside us was watching his very first dog trial.

At one point, the young man turned to my friend, Mary Lou Brayman, and said, "In every critique, the judge says that the dog should come back faster with the dumbbell. How do you train the dog to do that?" Mary Lou turned to the young man and, with a perfectly straight face, replied, "Obviously, nobody knows." We all laughed.

The real irony of the story is that the fellow had asked one of the few people in the country who, at that time, did know how to train it. Just a few years later, Mary Lou won the German National Schutzhund Championship with one of the highest scores ever – one of only two Americans ever to win that title. Her Belgian, Igor, consistently demonstrated intense retrieves with full power at top speed.

The good news is – now we do know how to train it through purely positive methods.

Two Sides

There are presently two basic methods to teach the retrieve – or we should say there are two methods that fall within the realm of humane training. One advocates a play retrieve. This can be somewhat unreliable at times and can produce a dog who plays with the dumbbell, tossing it in the air or mouthing it. The training is humane, but the dog is sometimes having a little too much fun to score well.

The other way is a trade-for-food method. The dog systematically learns to trade the dumbbell for a food reward, effectively shaping retrieve behavior along the way. It works, especially for those dogs with absolutely no innate drive to retrieve. But the exercise often becomes boring for the dog, going through all the repetitions at each stage.

Consequently, even a high-drive dog can end up with a retrieve that is less than spectacular. For Schutzhund, this means the dog cannot earn a high score here, since the dog is judged on his speed and drive for the work. In obedience trials, this type of retrieve often lacks the brilliance needed for a winning exercise.

Finding the Balance

Purely Positive Retrieving combines elements of both these methods. The dog learns how to retrieve with joy and enthusiasm. He learns at his own pace, without drilling on repetitions. The dog is challenged. He has to think, but we capitalize on any innate drive and desire to possess an object.

This is not a prey game. The dog doesn't get to pounce on his prize and toss it around, like a cat with a mouse. It teaches a calm, firm grip, and it encourages the dog to return to the handler even faster than he ran out.

Premacking the stay builds desire, instead of deflating drive with control. Continually raising and changing rewards keeps the dog eager and it means the dumbbell is always associated with fun and success.

Unfortunately, the elements of this method are difficult to explain in words. This is not a cookbook method that tells you what to do on Day 9 or Week 7. Every dog is different, so each dog moves at a different pace and responds to a little different motivation.

We plan to release the Purely Positive Retrieving video soon. The essence of this video is a single, 27-minute session of continuous retrieve training – with unbelievably dramatic results. This is the most exciting 27 minutes of training I've seen in 25 years. Others who see it agree.

Basic Requirements

Although much of the method lends itself to the visual, rather than the verbal, here are some of the basic principles so you can begin. But before starting formal retrieve training, some foundation work is necessary.

First, obviously, the puppy should be encouraged to retrieve anything and everything with high rewards – praise, petting, excited emotional energy, food, play, etc. The dog learns to bring these objects to the handler's hand in a hurry, in order to get his reward. And if what he really wants is the object, sometimes we even give it back to him and let him keep it!

Second, the dog should thoroughly enjoy playing the two-hose game. He should play this with any two toys – balls, socks, sticks, plastic soda bottles, anything he likes – and eventually, with any two items the handler chooses.

Third, the dog should already understand the principles of positive training. He should offer behaviors readily, listen for words, try harder when reinforcement is withheld and love to learn. He should bring to training a great desire to work with the handler and a strong inclination to keep on trying, as well as the desire to get it right.

One warning: avoid any formal retrieve training while the young dog is teething (three to six months). In some larger breeds, teething lasts even longer. Their mouths are sore, they can be overly sensitive at this time and it's a difficult age all around. They are having enough trouble just growing up and learning life's lessons.

Retrieve games are fine during this time, but no tugging or formal training having anything to do with their mouths. If the puppy picks something up and it hurts, that negative association can make a discouraging imprint with the dumbbell.

So let the puppy guide you. If he stops wanting to pick things up, understand why. He's got lots more other stuff to learn at this age. There's no need to start formal retrieve training (with the dumbbell) yet anyway, not until he's much further along in his understanding of the basic concepts of positive training.

The Foundation

The foundation for retrieving is building desire. The dog must *want* the dumbbell. So the first step is to make an intense positive association with the dumbbell. The first time you introduce the dumbbell, have some super good food. Hold the dumbbell in one hand and the food in the other.

By now, the dog knows that he doesn't get the food by poking at the hand, although he'll probably try that initially because the food is so tempting. Withhold the food (by closing your hand around it) and put your attention on the dumbbell.

One of the first things the dog usually tries to offer is eye contact, but you keep looking at the dumbbell. Keep moving the dumbbell around, just out of the dog's reach, looking at it all the while.

Toss it in the air once or twice. At some point the dog looks at the dumbbell. Rejoice "Yes!" and reward with food.

Be energetic and walk around, keeping excitement and enthusiasm in the game. The dumbbell moves from low to high, side to side, with your attention on it all the time.

Keep the right attitude. It's almost like teasing the dog. Your don't want the dog to get it right away, you want the dog to want to get it. Keep moving the dumbbell. Place it so the dog can get it if he wants to, but he has to make a real effort.

Always move the dumbbell *away* from the dog, never toward him. Avoid trying to put it in his mouth. Don't make it too easy for him to get it. Treat the dumbbell like your prized possession. Make a big fuss over your ownership of this particular piece of apparatus. Make the dog wonder what's so special about this thing.

Turn the tables on your dog. Play your own version of the keep-away game. Show him clearly that this is your dumbbell and he can't have it. It's sure to push his emotional opposition reflex button.

The First Step
Remember The Golden Rule. Every time the dog shows any attention to the dumbbell, praise and feed. Keep the dumbbell moving and keep the dog interested.

Nothing can go wrong. You haven't asked the dog to do anything yet. Just keep positively reinforcing any and all attention to the dumbbell.

In between, the dog usually offers other behaviors. He might sit or down or bark. Ignore them. Turn away and put your attention back on the dumbbell – this interesting thing that keeps moving around. Hold the dumbbell in your hand all this time – never put it on the ground.

This foundation continues, over short sessions, until the dog offers the correct Response – strong interest in the dumbbell whenever you bring it out. If the dog loses interest at any point, show him the really good food. Perhaps give him a taste, just for hanging around and trying to figure out what you want.

This foundation can take one minute, one session, or several sessions. Try to end every session just at the peak of the dog's interest in the dumbbell – by taking it away and putting it out of his reach. Build desire for next time by keeping the dumbbell away from the dog.

Step by Step

The big step is when the dog catches on that his reward might have something to do with this dumbbell thing. Once the dog is showing strong interest in the dumbbell whenever it appears, raise criteria. Now the dog has to move *toward* the dumbbell, wherever it goes.

Raise the reward. Show the dog some even better food. Get two kinds of food and let the dog choose which one he likes best and wants to work for. Get him psyched. Develop excitement for the game.

Once the dog is consistently moving toward the dumbbell, raise criteria again. Insist that the dog reach forward and touch the dumbbell with the front of his mouth, or his nose, to get his reward.

Remember to get excited the instant the dog touches the dumbbell. Reward effort once in a while too.

The next step is to get the dog to put his mouth on the dumbbell. This usually happens faster if you raise the dumbbell up, just out of the dog's reach. Keep moving it away and putting your attention on it.

At first, reward the dog just for reaching up and stretching toward the dumbbell. Next, reward only when he actually puts his mouth on the bar of the dumbbell.

Remain at each of these steps until the dog exhibits the behavior reliably and consistently – and eagerly. Start each new session one step back from where you left off last time. Keep the game successful, but also exciting.

The next step is to have the dog grab the dumbbell firmly with his mouth. This is a big step. It works best for most dogs if you keep the dumbbell up high, just above the dog's nose so he has to reach up to get it. To pull it down, he has to grab it firmly. This helps develop a firm grip right from the start.

Move the dumbbell around, but keep it just out of his reach. Tease him with it a little, but always be fair. Don't move it too quickly. When he grabs it with his mouth, praise and reward.

Once the dog is grabbing the dumbbell consistently with his mouth, shift context. Hold the dumbbell so it is vertical instead of horizontal. Hold it at an angle. Put it at all levels – from up high to near the ground, but not on the floor yet. If you're working inside, go outside, and vice-versa, but not to anywhere with distractions yet.

Word Association

Whenever the dog puts his mouth firmly on the bar, begin to associate your retrieve word with that behavior. Use your chosen release word when you take the dumbbell back.

Raise Criteria

Generalize this behavior so whenever the dumbbell appears, any time and any place, the dog tries to grab the bar to get his reward – tremendous emotional energy and excitement, encouragement and appreciation, great food and petting. Reinforce only when the dog grabs the bar, not the bell. Establish that as a criterion early on and stick to it.

It's just a matter of training time now until the dog figures out how to pick it up off the ground and deliver it to your hand. Hold an edge of the dumbbell up off the floor at first. Here again, sometimes the waiting is the hardest part.

Reward with really great food and pure positive energy whenever the dog masters a new step. After he is successful at a new approximation, put him away for some quiet time to allow his brain to process the new information.

If you want your dog to be an enthusiastic retriever, get excited yourself. Should he get stuck, back up one step and reinforce that. Stay on the dog's agenda. Reward effort and attention – with praise instead of food. Encourage the dog as long as he keeps on trying and hangs in there.

If he starts to lose interest, switch the type of food. Show him the new stuff and give him a taste. But note what he is telling you. Shorten the session next time. End while he's still interested.

When your dog makes great strides and masters a new step, that's also the time to change the food again. Give him the best stuff you've got. Then give him some quiet time to process this new learning.

Deliver to Hand

Once the dog knows how to pick up the dumbbell from the ground, get him to deliver it into your hand. At first, your hand is there to take the dumbbell whenever the dog is ready to give it up.

Now the dog has to deliver the dumbbell to your hand, a few inches away, to get his reward. When the dog has Response, work on Responsibility – holding the dumbbell until he delivers it to you.

Be prepared for the dog to drop the dumbbell here. This is why we don't ask for delivery to hand until the dog knows how to pick it up from the floor.

At this level, he might drop it and then come to get his reward. He's lowering his own criteria – back to just touching or putting his mouth on the bar. He's trying to do less work and still get paid. Nice try! Nobody ever said they were stupid.

But now the criteria is for him to deliver it a few inches off the ground and into your hand. Move closer to the dumbbell on the floor and keep looking at it, like you did in the beginning. Keep your hand low and your palm open, close to the ground. Give him some time to figure out what you want. This is a major learning step and can take the dog a little while. Back to the waiting game.

If he doesn't offer behaviors or make an attempt to get it right, then pick up the dumbbell like your prized possession and put it away. Also put away the really good treats. Show him what he could have earned. Show him there are still fish in the river. Give him some quiet time alone immediately after the session – no visual or mental stimulation.

At the next session, bring out the dumbbell with great excitement and enthusiasm. Play a little keep-away first. Show him the really great treats. Go back to having him grab the dumbbell and pull it down. Reward that. Then have him pick the dumbbell up off the floor the way he did before. Reinforce that approximation.

Next, give him another chance to deliver it a few inches to your hand. Allow him time to figure it out. Let him experiment.

Keep looking at the dumbbell with your hand close by, low and open. Take the time to wait. Once the dog learns this piece on his own, once he truly figures out what you want and what gets him what he wants, he's on his way to really reliable retrieving.

Always keep everything associated with the dumbbell fun and exciting. Only reward the dog when he's doing it right, but keep it fun even when he gets it wrong.

Adding Distance

When the dog knows to pick up the dumbbell and deliver it to your hand, add a little distance. First, do a few repetitions of him grabbing the bar and pulling it down. Then tease him a little, but don't let him get it. Teach the dog to explode out to get the dumbbell, bringing all his energy and enthusiasm to the exercise.

This is one of the two exceptions to teaching topography slowly (retrieve and recall). The first time the dog gets to run out after the dumbbell should make an imprint for doing it with speed and energy and enthusiasm.

Hold him by the collar to incite some opposition reflex. Get him really excited about the dumbbell. Throw it a few feet away. Release him just as the dumbbell is about to stop rolling. Chasing and pouncing on the rolling dumbbell makes it too much like play, but don't wait so long that the dumbbell loses its appeal. Timing is critical here.

As soon as he picks up the dumbbell and raises his head, bridge him with "Yes! Yes!" and start to run backward. Show him your open hands as you encourage him to come to you. He should still be driving forward, and you should still be backing up, when you take it from him.

Add the toy here as a reward and play his favorite game, or use very special treats. Rejoice! He's just done his first super retrieve. End the session there.

Once the dog shows good Response and Responsibility, and is Reliable in going out to get the dumbbell, put in some challenges. Throw it as far as you can sometimes. Throw it in a pile of leaves. Throw it down a hill.

Make the game interesting and fun, but always be sure he can be successful. If he ever seems confused, don't hesitate to back up to a step he completely understands.

All these games are done without any front sit. Teach the dog to drive back at full speed to deliver his prize to your open hand and get his great rewards.

The Delivery

Teaching the dog to deliver the dumbbell properly relies on the dog's understanding of front sit. Before asking for a proper delivery, first practice a short recall with front sit, offering the cues and body posture you use to get a correct front sit (see The Recall).

Add this to the retrieve only if the recall front sit was fast and perfect. The dog can only do it right with the dumbbell if he understands it first without the dumbbell. Stand in exactly the same place for the retrieve as you did for the recall.

Duplicate the cues and postures you use for the front sit, especially leaning back. If the dog needs a little extra help, remind him to "Sit" as he comes in. Show him your open hands to remind him how to present the dumbbell. Take it immediately at first, then reward.

As soon as the dog starts offering a correct front sit with the dumbbell, raise your hands slightly so he has to push it up into your hands. This helps prevent any rocking back or mouthing behavior with the dumbbell in front sit.

The dog already knows to stretch up for rewards in front sit. This should be a habit of topography by now. Avoid reaching down to take the dumbbell from him.

He should push it up into your hands. Teach the dog to hold it firmly in the front of his mouth, right behind his canine teeth. He must hold it this way to be able to push it up into your hands for you to take it. Once you reach this step, reward only this behavior.

Be sure to raise rewards as you raise criteria. Once the dog is delivering the dumbbell in a correct front sit, reward with a toy and a game of tug, or play two-hoses. Give your dog more of what he wants here and he brings the dumbbell back faster and faster.

Developing super speed in the retrieve (and in the recall) is a matter of providing the most fun Consequences. Let Consequence drive Behavior.

The Sit

Having the dog sit and wait to go get the dumbbell should build drive and intensity. This control should heighten, not dampen, his desire to retrieve.

First, teach the dog to sit and wait to go get a hose, or a ball, or any other object he really loves. Put a short tab on his collar and hold it, to prevent the unwanted behavior of going out to get the toy before you send him.

Get excited and throw the toy. Ask him to "Sit." The second he does, release him to go and get the toy. If he doesn't sit, you go get the toy. No second chances.

This effectively uses the Premack Principle to get the dog to want to sit and builds his desire to retrieve at the same time. After a few times, the dog begins to offer the sit quickly and willingly. Then you release him to go get his toy. Lengthen the time you keep him sitting a little at a time.

Once the dog sits and waits to get the toy, add it to the retrieve with the dumbbell. Do one retrieve for the toy, with a sit. Then do one retrieve for the dumbbell, in the same place. Chances are he'll duplicate the behavior.

Hold the tab, just in case. Reward the dumbbell retrieve with the toy. Don't ask for delivery in front sit when working on the sit before the retrieve. Just run back and let him drive it into your open hands. Work on one thing at a time.

Attention Sit

One further step is to wait for attention in the sit. Again, perfect this behavior with a favorite toy before adding it to the dumbbell retrieve. The first time the dog offers attention, send him immediately. Then build more and more time into the Attention Sit before sending him.

By this time, most dogs offer the sit quickly and intensely to get permission to retrieve. It makes an impressive picture when the dog watches to mark the spot where his beloved dumbbell lands, then snaps his head up into attention, driving the handler to let him go get it.

This Attention Sit prevents anticipation. It also prevents any inclination toward that reprehensible "vulture sit." That's where the dog leans further and further forward, fixated on the dumbbell (totally ignoring the handler) until his butt almost comes up off the ground (and eventually does), making the sit incorrect.

Using the Attention Sit here puts the relationship back into the exercise. It gets the dog working with the handler, instead of for himself. And it also builds drive for the retrieve through the Premack Principle.

Be Unpredictable

Once the dog shows Response, Responsibility and Reliability, in all the parts, mix up the exercise. Sometimes keep him in the sit a little longer. Feed him for eye contact before you send him. Then grab his collar and build lots of excitement before letting him go.

Sometimes run out with him to retrieve and be there to reward him as soon as he picks up the dumbbell, thereby reinforcing the middle of the exercise too. Make it a fun game to see who can get to the dumbbell first. Keep him guessing what to expect. Avoid rehearsing the same exercise over and over.

Get a friend to help you. Throw the dumbbell near the other person. If the dog breaks the sit before you send him, he doesn't get what he wants to do most – to retrieve. Have the helper pick up the dumbbell and return it to you. Go do something else. Work on it again later.

If the dog does wait for the retrieve command, have the person stand on one bell. The dog must now fight and pull to pick up the dumbbell. It gets to be a great game for him and one that he always wins.

Always consider temperament here. Be sure to build drive, not discourage the dog.

Toss the dumbbell back and forth between two people. When the dog is really interested and frustrated, hold him by the collar and throw the dumbbell as far as you can. As soon as it stops rolling, allow the dog to retrieve, to your great joy and encouragement.

Throw the dumbbell and wait for an Attention Sit. As soon as the dog makes eye contact, whip out his favorite toy and play a little game of tug. Then hold him by the collar, get him excited and send him for the dumbbell. This helps teach him to mark where the dumbbell lands.

When he returns, reward with the tug game again. All the while you are building drive and desire for the dumbbell, and keeping the dog guessing at what comes next.

Once he knows how to deliver the dumbbell properly in front sit, do lots of fun retrieves where he doesn't have to sit in front. Build speed and enthusiasm. Make the game fun for him.

Turn and run away sometimes as the dog is returning to you. Make him chase you to get his reward.

When the dog retrieves really well, as soon as you take the dumbbell, hold it up with two hands and let him jump up and grab it and play tug-of-war with it. Use this sparingly, however, as some dogs can revert to mouthing and keep-away after too much play with the dumbbell.

Play fun retrieve games with a variety of objects. Polish the exercise with sticks or hoses. Challenge the dog to retrieve different items. Work up to the difficult ones – like car keys or a hammer.

Whenever the dumbbell appears, always treat it as your favorite toy, your prized possession. Always build desire by keeping it *away* from the dog. He must work hard for his turn to possess it. One fun retrieve per session is usually enough.

Words fall short of being able to fully explain this method and how much fun it can be, but you get the idea. This might be a little difficult to visualize, but give it a try. It's amazing to watch the dogs think it through and figure it out.

By now you've done so much productive positive training with your dog that this part fits right into the program. Your dog keeps on trying and you keep it fun.

Retrieving should be an exciting exercise for you and your dog. It should be the highlight of a competition routine. Teach your dog to love the dumbbell. Always build his desire. Vary the exercise. Be creative and unpredictable.

HAVE FUN WITH YOUR DOG !

25

The Jumps

" Dogs lives are too short – their only fault really."
— Agnes Sligh Turnbull

All dogs can jump, so this is a pointless chapter, right? Well, sort of. It's true that most physically sound dogs can jump. That means they can get themselves over logs in the woods or other barriers (like baby gates).

It's also true that most sound dogs love to jump. That means they love to hurl themselves into the air at the greatest of speed and leap over whatever happens to be in their way. All this is true – it's just not what we call jumping.

For Schutzhund, dogs must jump a one-meter brush hurdle (slightly higher than 39 inches) without touching it. They must return over the hurdle carrying a weighted (650 gram) dumbbell. Very few dogs, no matter how sound or how athletic or how enthusiastic, can master this task consistently without some sort of constructive, systematic training.

Jump training teaches technique – what the scientists call topography. We want to teach the dog the safest, most efficient way to use his body to clear the jump. My initial background came from horses and I've been applying and adapting those principles to dogs for more than 20 years.

The challenge is the same. Most horses manage to get themselves over a reasonably-sized fence on their first try. But as the fences get higher, or a sequence of fences is put together, they must have learned proper technique to be able to negotiate them successfully.

Dogs, like horses, usually try to compensate with speed. The higher the fence, the more they want to run at it faster and leap into the air sooner. With horses, this is called rushing. It's dangerous and ineffective. A handler should consider whether he'd feel comfortable riding his dog down to a fence, and then train accordingly.

Horses and dogs both need to use their rear end properly to jump efficiently. They don't need more speed to jump higher and better, they need more power. They must learn to harness their speed and energy to create impulsion. That's what technique teaches.

Keep It Fun

Just as with retrieving, jumping should always be fun. There's no point to teaching efficiency if you lose enthusiasm along the way. In agility, the jumping itself often becomes motivational for the dogs, (sometimes so motivational that the handlers lose a little control).

This method of jump training promotes that great attitude, and even enhances it, while teaching technique. As with retrieving, this method works best with a dog who already understands the concepts of positive training.

Jump training can begin with the puppy, but only to teach the idea and the joy of jumping. To be able to jump properly, the dog must be physically capable of being an athlete. That means he must not be carrying any excess weight. (See Chapter 13: The Beginnings).

The dog should be free from physical limitations such as hip dysplasia, and he must be old enough so that his bones are set, his growth plates closed and his connective tissues firm. In smaller, lighter breeds, that might be around one year old. For larger, heavier breeds, 14 to 18 months is a more reasonable time to start. Until this age, no dog should ever jump anything higher than his elbow.

Puppy Hups

The only thing a puppy needs to know about jumping is that it's fun. He can get the idea of jumping up and over something, instead of crashing through or scrambling over. But jumping is really not an exercise for puppies or juveniles. They should never jump anything higher than their elbow, and not even much of that.

When there is an obstacle the right height, preferably half the height of the dog's front leg, call the puppy over with "Come." Avoid making any association with your jump word until he understands correct technique.

If the puppy jumps over the little obstacle, tell him how wonderful he is. If he knocks it down, or just scrambles over, suspend any more jumping for a little while. This is one exercise where it's really best to wait.

Maybe he's just not physically capable yet. Maybe he's not mentally focused enough, or maybe he's just too young and eager. Work on his agenda. Wait until you can set him up for success.

Word association should be linked to specific behavior. So avoid using your jump command for jumping up onto something (like the grooming table) or into the car. These are different movements. The jump cue should mean to jump *over* something without touching it.

The Concept

Many dogs tick jumps with their feet, or use a solid barrier to help themselves get over it, or knock down those flimsy bars in agility. Often, this is simply because nobody ever bothered to teach them that it matters that they clear the fence without touching it.

Clearing the jump makes no sense to the dog. If he can scramble over it or knock it down, so much the better. To the dog, it's easier and it gets the job done faster.

Nobody ever said dogs were stupid. It's only natural for them to use the least effort to get the highest reward. Jumping without touching is a foreign concept to most dogs.

At one year old, Vino was athletic and eager to jump. His idea was to leave all his landing gear down and just crash through whatever was in his way. He didn't think it hurt too much, and I suspect he sort of enjoyed sending the rails flying (and even the standards sometimes).

But for agility, that simply would not do. I embarked on a six-month program to teach him one concept – that it mattered whether the bars stayed up. We worked with high reinforcement (for him, the two-hose game and tug-of-war).

He learned there was only way to get his reward – to jump cleanly. He still loves to jump, but now he leaves the rails in the cups more often than not.

The dog should learn this concept right from the start. He can learn to love to jump the right way – clearing the fence and earning his reward.

Keep the stakes high and the exercise fun. Let the dog learn how to be successful. All this can happen while the jump is just a low bar in the path of his recall.

Teaching Topography

Once the dog is old enough to have the physical capability, teach technique right from the start. This means the dog learns to jump up and over an obstacle by harnessing the power in his rear end, not relying on speed.

Start with the bar just below elbow height. Place the dog on a sit-stay on the other side of the jump. Use a jump you can see through for this, unless you have a friend to help. But the top bar should knock down easily – *very* easily.

Place the dog one stride back from the hurdle. At first, you won't know how far away that is. Mark the place where you leave him, so you can see whether to move him next time.

The goal is to position the dog one comfortable canter stride from his ideal take-off point – usually about the distance of one-half a canter stride from the base of the jump. We don't want him to launch himself over the jump from the sit position. We don't want him to trot. We don't want him to take two strides, or he can get up too much speed and not use his rear end. One comfortable stride is the ideal.

For those in horses, this only takes a few times to find the optimum set-up distance. Those new to the jumping sport have to develop their eye to be able to see when the dog takes one comfortable canter stride before jumping.

Enlist the help of a friend to watch in the beginning. Striding is much easier to see from the side than from the front. Using a video camera can help too.

The handler leaves the dog and steps over the jump. This is important because the dog tends to follow the path the handler takes. So wait until the dog understands the exercise before you walk around the jump. You'll have plenty of time for that later – when the jump is too high for you to get over anyway.

Three Equal Strides

The handler stands the same distance from the other side of the jump as the dog is. The ideal here is for the dog to make three equal canter strides – one to his take-off point, one over the jump, and then one more to the handler on the other side.

This teaches the dog rhythm and arc and how to gather himself for the jump – to harness the power in his rear end and jump out of his natural stride, without adding speed.

Stand back a little further the first few times, to give the dog extra room on landing. It's doubtful he'll jump perfectly the first time. Give him room to land without bumping into the handler. We never want to discourage effort.

Once you discover the ideal distance for your dog, measure it, stride it off or otherwise note it. This enables you to duplicate this distance when you move the jump to other places or practice at other jumps. Train your eye to see that distance when you position your dog. Test yourself by measuring it out.

Do your part if you want to teach your dog how to jump correctly. Just as a rider must help his horse get to the optimum take-off place for the jump, so the handler must learn to position his dog to help him get it right.

Foundation Training

This is the foundation exercise for jumping. All future learning stems from the dog grasping the concept and technique of this simple exercise. He also needs to develop the muscles and the timing that this exercise teaches.

When the dog jumps properly, without touching or knocking the bar, he gets high rewards – an excited "Yes!" and lots of positive emotional energy, praise and petting. Rejoice! Play the game or feed the food.

Reinforce all successful efforts – meaning the dog doesn't touch the jump. Only when you reinforce *all* correct performance here can the dog identify when improvement is needed to earn his reward. Jumping should be very exciting to the dog, so keep the rewards high.

If the dog knocks down the bar or touches the jump, just calmly turn away, but display no negative energy or disappointment. Show him what he could have had if he'd tried harder and performed properly. Go to the jump and set it up again. Take the dog with you.

By now, the positively trained dog understands he needs to try harder. He knows that if he doesn't get his reinforcement, something has gone wrong. He's used to thinking and reading your energy, so let him figure this out.

Calmly take him back to the start and let him do it again. Work this exercise from both sides of the jump. But if the dog fails to clear the jump and get his reward, take him back to the *same* side from which he started. Repeat the same exercise. Changing sides makes it a new exercise.

Let the dog learn. Let him concentrate. Let him think. Save your excited energy for a successful outcome. Stay calm for the rest of the routine to help him focus on the task at hand. Reward every successful jump. Only then can he distinguish between which behavior earns reinforcement and which doesn't.

This exercise is just to teach the dog what is expected and how to do it. Avoid getting distracted by teaching anything else. If the dog breaks the stay to come to you, no big deal. He's trying to do what you want. He knows what's next – and it's more fun than staying! Simply resolve to return to him more often and reinforce the stay. Make that part worth his while too.

However, part of the concept of jumping is that the dog does it on cue. Remember that behavior not on cue is useless. The dog doesn't get rewarded just for jumping, he gets rewarded for doing it when asked. He must learn to wait for the cue.

Word Association

As soon as the dog is jumping cleanly and consistently, start using only "Hup" and drop the "Come." This happens very quickly if you are making this exercise fun for the dog.

This is another one of those exceptions to the rule. Right from the start, "Hup" should mean to look for the jump and set himself up to jump it. Give the cue early enough so the dog can prepare himself to jump properly. Saying "Hup" as the dog is leaving the ground is way too late for him to make the right word association.

If the dog ever goes around the jump, lower it for a few times. Be sure you are still stepping over the jump, not going around it yourself. Remember that the dog tends to follow your path, so help him out in the beginning and show him where you want him to go.

If the dog comes around the jump more than a few times, especially when it is still at elbow height or below, have the dog checked out physically. Very few dogs refuse to jump such low obstacles unless they hurt somewhere, or are otherwise limited.

Be sure the dog is physically capable before continuing any sort of jump training. Always listen to what the dog is trying to tell you.

Shifting Context

Once the dog has mastered this basic exercise, shift context. Move the jump, or practice over a different jump. Change the bar to a board, or vice-versa.

Go different places. Give this foundation exercise plenty of time and attention so the dog gets it right every place and every time. That assures his future jumping success and builds his physical capability.

Then change what the handler does. Walk around the jump instead of over it. This tests whether the dog really understands the point of the exercise and the cue word.

When you have a friend to help you, turn your back to the dog and call him over. Have your helper tell you when the dog jumps so you can turn and greet him properly. Also have them tell you whether he jumped in appropriate stride and style.

These shifts in context assure that the dog understands this foundation exercise. When he does, it's time to move on. But don't hesitate to come back to this exercise whenever anything is not proceeding properly in future training.

Raising Criteria

With the jump still at elbow height, now place the dog back two strides from his ideal take-off point. This is not twice the distance away from the jump. Take into account the half-stride take-off distance to the jump. The new distance is about two-thirds further from the base of the jump.

Again, have a friend help you out if you're not used to seeing the dog's striding yet, or use a video camera. Now the dog should take two comfortable canter strides and jump out of stride. The goal in this exercise is for the dog to take five equal canter strides, clearing the jump with the middle one. The handler also increases his distance back from the jump to match the dog's.

The dog shouldn't increase his speed or try to leave out that extra stride. He should simply add one more comfortable stride, get to the same ideal take-off point, and jump efficiently and cleanly. Practice this new exercise until the dog gets it right consistently. Shift context in this exercise also, to make sure the dog understands completely.

Next, return to one-stride distance and begin to raise the jump, by only one or two inches at a time, until the dog is performing the exercise easily and consistently with the bar now at withers height, instead of elbow.

When the dog does this consistently and properly, keep the bar at withers height, but place the dog at the two-stride distance for several repetitions. If the foundation work was done properly, the dog should jump easily out of stride. Always reinforce when the dog leaves the bar up.

Let Them Learn

Now it's time to let the dog use what he has learned so far. With the jump still at withers height, set the dog back from the jump about six feet further than ever before to see if he can figure out his own striding.

Give him the chance to find his ideal take-off point and use his newly-acquired technique to jump cleanly and efficiently. Have a friend watch the first few times, or use the video camera. It is much easier to see what the dog does from the side view.

The handler stands slightly further back than the dog's two-stride distance. If the dog adds speed and miscalculates the jump, we don't want to punish him by making him run into the handler. Get out of his way and let him learn, but don't stand back too far. That would only encourage the dog to come faster and jump longer.

Leave the dog on a sit-stay. Having someone hold him changes the exercise entirely. The dog should approach the jump with his brain engaged, not hurl himself over it as fast as possible.

Give the dog a few chances at this exercise, from both sides of the jump. Let him figure it out. He should think it's great fun! If he clears the bar, but his style was not what you want, offer a medium reward.

Throughout this training, always reinforce great jumping with great rewards. That is the only way for the dog to know when something goes wrong – when the reward and emotional energy diminish.

If the dog continually wants to hurl himself over the jump at top speed (which very few do at this point), return to foundation training. If he knocks down the bar, no reward. Take the dog with you and put up the bar yourself. Then try again, from the same side.

By this time, most dogs approach the jump with concentration and focus, wanting to jump cleanly and properly to earn the highest reward. Proper technique has become muscle memory by now.

Let the dog do this exercise several times. It's fun for him and it cements learning.

The Test

Time for a little test. Keep the jump at withers height for all this work. When the dog really shows you Response, Responsibility and Reliability in the foundation exercises, place him as far as 10 or 20 feet back from the jump. You stand back that far too. Give the dog a chance to show off what he's learned.

If that goes well, have someone hold the dog on the other side of the jump, at least three canter strides away or further. Being held back makes the dog much crazier to come to you by inciting opposition reflex. He runs much faster, so he needs room to make a mistake at first. Adding this dimension challenges him to engage his brain, even when jumping at speed.

When he jumps well from having someone hold him, add another step. As you leave, attract him with his favorite toy. Get excited before he jumps. Wave the toy and jump up and down as he is released and while he is jumping. The toy here becomes the distraction as well as the motivation.

If he masters that task, next time turn and run away as he is released. Find out if he really understands the point of the exercise and takes Responsibility for leaving the bar up, no matter what you are doing.

Use the same simple reward system. If he knocks the bar, put away the reward. Take the dog with you to replace the bar. Then repeat the exercise – from the same side.

If he clears the jump, but leaps into the air with no thought for technique, use a moderate reward. Always appreciate effort.

When your dog jumps cleanly and carefully out of stride, give him all the reward you can muster. This is a big moment. He's overcome his natural inclination to hurl himself at the jump, and you've managed to teach him to use his brain, as well as his body, to jump. Good for you both!

Planning Approximations

The following approximations depend on the purpose of your training.

For companion: This dog has probably learned everything he needs to know to jump well and stay in condition. He's now a sane, safe, sensible jumper – ready to conquer every obstacle on your walks in the woods and enjoy jumping anything you ask him to, but be sure to keep the height reasonable.

If a dog is not in excellent physical condition and does not jump regularly, jumps should always be kept lower than the height of the dog's withers. If he uses the obstacle to get over when it's solid (like a fallen tree trunk), give him the credit he deserves for being so smart.

For obedience: These jumps usually aren't much higher than the dog's withers these days. Raise the jump slowly, up to the required height, and practice a few times. Then put the jump back to withers height, or lower, for any repetition training.

Teach the dog to carry a toy over the obstacle. Put the bar down to elbow height, or lower, and practice retrieves for a toy to teach him the new topography of carrying something in his mouth while jumping.

For Schutzhund: The challenge here is to teach the dog to jump 40 inches cleanly. Continue to place the dog two strides away as you raise the jump slowly, by one or two-inch increments. Once you raise any jump above withers height, *always* leave the dog at least two strides away. He needs a certain amount of speed to create enough impulsion to clear such a high jump.

To prevent the dog from going around the jump, set up some barriers for a few feet on either side of the jump. Going around makes a whole lot of sense to most dogs when the jump gets higher than 30 inches.

Use green mesh fencing, or panels from exercise pens, or similar, almost invisible material to prevent the unwanted behavior for a while. Be sure to raise rewards as the jump gets higher. Add tug-of-war or the two-hose game when the dog makes a great effort. Lower the jump when adding the retrieve and for any repetition training.

Teach the retrieve over the jump with a ball or hose first, and lower the jump even more. In case anything goes wrong in the jumping, you don't want the dog to associate it with the dumbbell. Put the two together only when jumping is perfect with a toy, and your flat retrieve is also perfect.

Once the dog knows how to jump properly, there's no need to rehearse the great effort continually. Keep the jump at withers height for repetitions and conditioning to avoid breaking the dog down physically or compromising his great attitude.

For agility: Cement the dog's learning. Teach him to jump any type of obstacle from any angle, but do this step by step. Leave the dog on a gentle angle and you stand at the same angle on the other side. Progress to where he masters a single jump from an acute angle, with you facing him at a serious angle on the other side.

Do the foundation exercises with a double (ascending and then square), a triple (always ascending), a plank jump, a solid wall, the tire and even a board across two lawn chairs. Then do them all at varying angles. Next, do them straight, but with someone holding the dog and you running away attracting him with a toy. Teach total Responsibility.

The Broad Jump

Do the same exercises with the broad jump, but teach the dog to jump up and over this jump properly. Most dogs tick the last board because they jump across the width, but without the height needed to make the necessary arc.

Set three light bars over the broad jump – one at each end and one in the middle. Set the first and last bars just above the ends of the broad jump boards and only an inch or two higher than the boards. But set the center bar several inches above the middle, depending on the size of your dog.

This is called a hog's back jump and it teaches the dog to arc correctly and get more height over the broad jump, as well as to stretch and be careful on the landing side. The broad jump requires different topography, so that's what this teaches the dog. Once he understands technique, replace the bars with thin, clear plexiglass rods to test his memory.

Advanced Jumping

Once the dog is confident and careful over all types of jumps, put them together. Start with a series of jumps – two at first and then more. Keep them a good distance apart in the beginning. Let the dog figure out his own striding and take-off points, as long as he leaves the rails up.

When he is proficient at this, have someone hold him to build speed and energy. Attract him with high motivation, like a favorite toy. Then let him figure out how best to negotiate the line of jumps – without knocking them down. Once he has mastered technique, the agility dog needs to learn how to jump properly at speed.

Of course the dog will flatten out and leave early when jumping at speed. That's what we want him to do. That's the fastest way around the course. But when he understands that it is important for him to leave the bars up, that becomes his Responsibility, no matter where you are or the angle he takes.

To get his job done properly, he learns to jump a little higher or tuck his legs a little tighter. And should he get into trouble, like arriving too close to a jump or being surprised by a jump off a tight turn, he knows how to use his body properly to create the impulsion needed to clear it.

Keep the rewards high for the agility dog. He should always love to jump. If he knocks a bar, no reward. Take him with you to replace the bar – thus calling his attention to the mistake. Then give him another chance. It's especially important for the agility dog to know that it matters if the bars come down.

The handler should always replace any knocked bars himself in all practice situations. This stops the game and calls the dog's attention to what went wrong. No nagging or punishment! Just change the energy so he tries harder next time.

By now, the dog should love to jump so much that he doesn't want the game to stop. Teach him the Consequence of his actions. Let Consequence drive Behavior. Let him learn to be Responsible.

Always consider temperament here. Most of the more sensitive dogs seem to want to clear the jumps naturally. Be careful not to use any negative emotional energy with a sensitive dog as this can be very discouraging for them.

When the dog is jumping through a series of jumps well, and using his brain to jump with proper technique, change the configuration. Have the jumps at various heights. Have the distances closer and further apart, but not so close together that the dog isn't successful.

A series of jumps with related distances, meaning the dog ideally takes one stride or two strides between them, is called a gymnastic. Some folks set up these gymnastics to include bounces.

A bounce is two jumps set so close together that the dog does not take a stride between the jumps – he takes off for the second jump right after he lands from the first. Beware of bounces – they are challenging. They take the greatest physical toll on the dog and can place serious demands on the flexibility of his spine.

Unless working with an experienced teacher who understands physiology, use them rarely. Consider bounces only for a dog who is well along in his jump training – one who is a true athlete and is in superb physical condition. Give the dog plenty of room at first and keep the jumps low.

Avoid doing two bounces in a row. It can break a dog down far faster than it can build him up. And there's nothing like it in any jumping competition these days anyway.

Teach the dog to jump on hills, slightly uphill and slightly downhill. Jump the dog downhill very rarely, and only on a very slight slope, to avoid too much stress on his front end assembly. Hills, even slight ones, greatly affect the dog's jumping technique and the impulsion he must generate and control, so he needs to learn how to handle them both.

Jumping for Agility

Once the dog shows Response, Responsibility and Reliability over all types of jumps and at different angles, and he is in great physical condition, vary the exercise. Start beside the dog and send him over the fences.

By now, he thoroughly understands that the word "Hup" means to look for the fence and set himself up to jump it cleanly. That's his Responsibility, no matter where you are. All that technique training is about to pay off.

When you see him bring his brain to adjust his stride, and concentrate his effort to leave the bars up, you can rejoice at the results of all that careful foundation training. To teach rhythm, build motivation, develop physical condition and prepare for courses, put the jumps in a big circle

Stand in the center and interrupt the flow at various places. Call the dog to you to play between jumps. Send him out over a jump for his toy. Reverse his direction. Teach him that you control access to the jumps and you control the rewards. All of this heaven comes through you!

Be sure to use your cue and tell him "Hup." This is not an exercise where the dog jumps what he wants, when he wants. He jumps when you tell him. He comes to you to play when you call him, or he chases the toy when you send him. Make yourself as much fun as the obstacles.

One very important concept for the agility dog to understand is that you control the game. Keep all this fun activity under stimulus control and you can look forward to success on the course.

As the dog responds consistently, change the distances between the jumps. Put them at varying heights. Then vary both the distances and the heights in the circle. Add the tire, a triple, a double and the broad jump.

Should the dog knock down a fence, guess what? Yep, the game stops immediately (not after three more jumps), while you and the dog go set up the bar.

By now, the jumping game itself is very rewarding for the dog. He won't like this interruption in the game. Bingo! No negatives. Just lower your emotional energy and take him with you to replace the bar.

Be a little disappointed. Dogs are masters at reading the energy. By now, the positively trained dog seeks out that affirming energy exchange. Ask him what happened. He knows.

Always consider the dog's temperament and sensitivity. Process what he shows you. He hasn't done anything wrong, he just made a mistake. Point it out and get back to the fun.

The final step is to intersperse contact obstacles on the circle between a series of jumps. This teaches the dog the concept and technique of using his speed for the jumps and then focusing and concentrating for accurate contacts. Use the simple flow of the circle to teach this critical part of agility – Responsibility and Reliability in obstacle performance, regardless of where you are or what comes next.

When the dog is proficient on the circle, he is ready to progress to the more complicated task of taking direction and making the turns required for sequences and, eventually, courses. The dog has a solid foundation upon which to build.

All you have to do is perfect your handling techniques. Your dog knows how to jump properly – and he loves it.

Always be cautious about jumping. No matter how much the dog loves to jump, it still takes a toll on his body.

When doing a lot of jumping, keep the bars low. Be sure the dog is in top condition and the weight of an athlete. Keep him fit with other physical exercise, not just jumping.

Avoid doing too much jumping two days in a row. Dogs can get sore muscles too! Practice tunnels and tables and weave poles instead to work different muscles.

Learn how to warm the dog up by gently stretching and bending each leg. Massage the major muscles. Have the dog run or play a little before he starts jumping.

Never jump a dog after eating, or when the footing is too hard or too slippery. Never jump a dog who is not sound, and be careful jumping in excessive heat.

If a dog ever refuses to jump, check out the physical possibilities first. Always listen to what the dog is telling you.

Once the dog knows how to jump properly, he needs to practice at full height only occasionally. Just throw in a few jumps at full height before a trial. He'll remember.

Watching a dog jump joyfully and correctly is a real treat. That's why the sport of agility is becoming so popular. It's fun for the dogs, the handlers and the spectators too!

A dog can enjoy jumping even more when he knows how to do it carefully and cleanly – not to mention when he expects super rewards for his extra effort. And an efficient jumper holds up physically for years longer.

JUMP FOR JOY !

26　The Send Away

" The tail is the gauge of the soul."
　　　　　　　　　　　– Manfred Heyne

The send away is required at the advanced levels of both competition obedience and for Schutzhund. This skill is not required for Novice obedience or for the initial B title (Traffic Safe Companion) in Schutzhund.

There is a reason why it is included only at the upper levels. Sending your dog away from you is a much more difficult exercise than come when called. Once again, the reason is that it makes no sense to the dog. Training is easy as long as the dog finds the request reasonable.

Exercises like searching empty blinds in Schutzhund, the weave poles and the pause table in agility, and the out-of-sight stays in obedience seem totally pointless to most dogs. So does running away from the handler in a straight line at full speed. It makes even less sense to the dog if the handler has spent months rewarding attention, heeling and recalls.

This is a basic training book, so we're not going to go into detail here about training the send away. We just want to advise you to start – and start early.

If you have any aspirations to compete in obedience trials or in Schutzhund, begin to train a send away soon after you start the recall. Plant the concept early in your puppy's brain – that there is a time when it is worth his while to go away from you, as well as a time to come when called. Show him that it makes sense right from the beginning.

337

Training the send away using a target is still the simplest and most efficient way. That method is explained and illustrated step-by-step in the *Schutzhund Obedience* book (Recommended Resources).

Teaching the dog to run to a visible target works especially well for competition obedience, since there is an actual ring gate to use. But the Positive Training Paradigm adds some new dimensions to this method.

Now we wean from the visible target sooner and we use it more intermittently. We want the dog to find something there as the Consequence, not the Antecedent, so that we follow the ABCs. And we shift context much earlier and a lot more frequently, training in different places as soon as the dog grasps the basic concept.

Send the young dog to anything he enjoys and knows the word for – to the car or to his crate. Then always go to him and reward him there. Use approximations to increase distance, until the dog goes away from you in a straight line to wherever you send him.

Second Reinforcer

Training the send away is an ideal place to use a second reinforcer sometimes. That means another person (other than the handler) comes in a gives the dog his reward, at least until the handler can get there.

It takes a little time for the dogs to understand that they get the reinforcement for the behavior, not for looking at (or going to) the reinforcer. But once they work this through and process this part of the puzzle, their understanding is solid and they perform the exercise with more precision and enthusiasm.

They never know quite when or how, from where or from whom, their reward is coming. But they get very clear about which behavior earns the reinforcement.

Using a second reinforcer works especially well for dogs who hesitate to go away from the handler because they are a little unsure. Now there are two cool people out there in training. It also works well for the young Schutzhund dog who is a little too true to his guarding nature and thus a little suspicious of strangers. When he thinks the judge might come and reward him, he views the person in a whole new light.

For those training competition obedience, avoid getting stuck working within the confining dimensions of a standard ring. As with recalls, longer send aways are lots more fun and much more motivational. Set up a huge ring if possible, or set up just one length of ring gates and have the dog go out to the center. Then increase the distance even further – until the dog is doing a double or triple length, or even a super long send away.

This shift in context not only solidifies the idea of running a straight line to the center, but it's fun. It builds speed and power and enthusiasm for the exercise, and it's great physical conditioning too.

The key to all the advanced exercises is to make them worthwhile to the dog. Teach concept and topography first. But most importantly, keep the dog trying. Keep it fun!

The advanced exercises get more challenging. They require the dog to perform longer behavior chains. The dogs have to think more. This is where purely positive training really pays off. That love of learning keeps shining through. The dogs rise to the challenge. They want to learn, and they're so pleased with themselves when they get it right, not to mention the fact that they earn such valuable rewards.

So hang in there with your dog. Go as far as you can, but get the send away started early. It doesn't have to be perfect, just instill the concept. The rest can come later.

KEEP THEM TRYING !

27   The Competitions

*"More often than not,
it is the handler who defeats the dog,
rather than the difficulty of the trial."*
     – L. Wilson Davis

Competitions can be great fun – if you have the right attitude and keep them in perspective. Trials are just a test of training.

If your dog is ready and you are confident, then the competition becomes a perfect opportunity for you and your wonderful dog to shine together. The two major reasons for trouble at trials are showing a dog too early and lack of proper preparation by the handler.

Competition can be a place where your teamwork triumphs. Run through a test before the trial – to be sure your dog can put it all together. Then start to work on yourself.

Prepare Yourself

Investigate the information available about sports psychology. Find out what the Olympic athletes know about mental preparation. Make a plan for trial day, just like Patty explains on her *Positively Ringwise* tape. (See Recommended Resources).

Another of my favorites is Lanny Bassham's *With Winning In Mind.* His Mental Management Program teaches how to deal with nerves and pressure. I listen to it on the way to every trial – if only to focus my mind on the positive.

If that doesn't work for you, then listen to music that puts you in the right mood – the victory themes from *Rocky* or *Chariots of Fire* – anything that makes you feel positive. Arrive feeling like a winner!

On trial day, you need to be there for your dog. Stay connected to him. He's depending on you – he can't do it alone. If you do your part, there's a good chance he'll do his.

There are lots of excuses – he's tired or bored, or he got distracted, or there's a female in season somewhere, or it's too hot, or the judge was wearing a funny hat. But if the dog didn't work well, whose fault is it?

No dog was put on this earth for the purpose of winning ribbons or trophies or titles for his owner.

No Wrong Dogs

No dog was born in the whelping box knowing how to heel or how to do weave poles. If the dog isn't doing something right, then it is because the trainer has failed to teach it properly, or has failed to make the task interesting enough for the dog to want to do it today.

There are No Wrong Dogs in the competition game.

Many dogs enjoy the teamwork of competition. They love the road trips and the excitement of new places. Some dogs live to work with their handlers and they delight in the rush of energy that flows through a brilliant performance.

But lighten up a little about trials. Remember that this is what you do for fun with your wonderful dog. Whatever happens, you take the same cherished companion home in the car with you.

Be sure training prepares the dog for what he will see in competition. He needs to know the Antecedents – your posture, eyes, hands, etc. – just the way he will see them on trial day.

Prepare Your Dog

Make a tape recording at a busy trial. Then play it – loudly – while you run through your routine. Finally, there's a constructive use for those boom boxes the kids insist on playing so loudly.

Set up the field the way it will look to the dog. Practice the preparation. Once in a while, show the dog exactly the same picture in training that he will see in a trial.

Do something that creates a little stress, like having a friend videotape your performance. Then work through that stress with your dog. Heel to Sousa marches. Get people to clap and shout, or use a recording. Generate excitement, and then practice being calm and focused.

When doing any sort of distraction training, always be fair. Set up for success. Start with new distractions far away. Wait for attention, then work on something simple first.

Stay connected to your dog. Always give him the chance to make the right decision. Reward him handsomely when he does. Make distractions more difficult only when he shows he can handle them.

If working in a group and your dog loses focus, or goes to another dog or person, or goes off to sniff around, end the game. Put him away. He lost the privilege of playing with you. Show him all the good stuff you have, then go feed another dog. Give him your dog's treats, while your dog watches. Better yet, play with another dog.

The dog only gets to play when he plays by the rules. Give him another chance in a minute or two. Usually, he can't wait to play again.

Advanced Training

When working on the complex advanced exercises, make a genuine effort to keep them different and fun. Do super-long recalls, retrieves and send aways.

Tom Dorrance advises to "Try to get the results in various approaches, so you don't wear out any one of them." When training scent articles, for example, toss two sticks into a pile of leaves – one heavily scented and marked.

Even if the dog gets the wrong one, you can't be too upset – you're only throwing sticks in the woods. Such shifts in context really stimulate the dog and cement learning.

Work on simple, fun stuff – like pairing reinforcers or Attention Sit for a game of tug. Be sure to work up and down the ladder of approximations, and to vary the reinforcement schedule.

Just because the dog can do the entire exercise, doesn't mean he has to rehearse that every time. Reinforce the start of the exercise, as well as the end, and don't neglect the middle. Be unpredictable. Interrupt the exercise sometimes and reinforce there. Get creative.

Avoid getting stuck in a trench – repeating the same training sequences over and over. Unless it works perfectly and your dog does it brilliantly – and loves doing it – change the scenario. Add a new wrinkle. Try something new and different.

Got A Problem?

"Got a problem? Put a cookie on it!" says Patty. This simple rule works well in the advanced exercises too. Be sure to set up for success the next time.

If you ever get to the point where you seriously contemplate giving your dog a correction, take the time to think about it. Look at the situation from your dog's point of view. Reread Chapter 9: The Corrections.

Consider your dog's temperament. Contemplate the career you've chosen for him. Resolve to work with your dog as a team. "Violence begins where knowledge ends." Bring your brain to training and think the problem through.

Put it off for now. You can always do it later. We've helped teach a number of dogs the motivational retrieve. Whenever they get stuck, we still joke that "We can always pinch their ear tomorrow!" We never do.

Think For Yourself

Try out some new thinking. Positive training gives you permission to think for yourself. Listen to your dog instead of to all the other people.

Remember, the people only have the opinions – the dog has all the facts. Look to your dog and he'll give you some great ideas on what works for him.

With purely positive training, nothing can go wrong. The dog keeps on trying and he always tells you what's working. In an atmosphere of the dog can do no wrong, there is no pressure for the trainer to have to do everything right.

So think it through. Ask for less – give more. Do something fun. Make it simple. Go back to basics and work on the little things, using high motivation. Avoid the Law of Diminishing Rewards. As the dog works harder – pay him more, not less.

Teach lots of Stupid (Smart) Pet Tricks – wave, touch, wipe your face, roll over, play dead, sit up and beg, etc. This keeps training interesting and fun for you and the dog.

Teach scent games. "Go Find It" means find anything with human scent on it, like a glove or the car keys. This can be a very useful game. Charra once found my car keys when I dropped them in a huge field while walking her in the dark on a road trip. What a dog!

Keep training interesting. Be daring and challenge your dog. Get the training out of the formal exercises to keep your dog using his brain and paying attention. Shift context whenever you can. Being unpredictable is definitely one of the hardest parts.

Be proactive. Put first things first. Think win/win and then set up for that success. Be enthusiastic and energetic. Learn to listen to your dog and enhance the relationship. Nurture your dog's spirit at every opportunity.

Give and Take

For success in competition, a handler needs patience, persistence, a sense of humor, humility, devotion, timing, steady nerves, a great relationship with his dog – and then a little bit of luck thrown in besides.

"The more you put in, the more you get back" is a perfect assessment of dog training. Always keep your heart open to what your dog tries to give back. In the end, love will get you further than luck.

It's true – some dogs work for the love of working and some work for the love of you. Through positive training, they all learn to love the work even more – because they get paid so well and it is a time of such joyous sharing. As the work gets more challenging and complex in the higher levels, the Trust Fund really starts to pay off.

If you ever make a mistake, apologize to your dog. It's okay with him. "To err is human, to forgive is canine." If he ever makes a mistake, separate the performance from the performer. He's still your marvelous dog.

Before the trial, focus your energy. Visualize perfection. Rehearse success. This is difficult for some people, but it can be a learned behavior.

You don't have to be born or raised a positive person. The truth about positive thinking is that, after hearing it and practicing long enough, you actually do start to *feel* positive!

Whenever you come out of the ring, no matter what happened, stay connected to your dog. Tune in to him. Celebrate or commiserate with him first, not your friends or your coach.

Your dog is the one who put in the performance for you and you can't do it without him. Prepare for the next trial by reinforcing your dog as soon as you leave the ring.

Always remember that when training breaks down, especially in the ring, all you have left is relationship. There will always be another dog trial, but there might not be another opportunity like this to improve your relationship.

Focus on the present. Stay in that Zen moment with your dog. Give him what he needs right now.

Enjoy The Process

As you get ready for competition, enjoy the process. Get excited about the plan. Look forward to the opportunity to showcase your training with your partner. Focus on the positive.

Good Luck with your dog. Keep in mind the definition of Luck – when the correct preparation meets the right opportunity! Focus on preparation and performance. Forget about the results for now.

On those first few trips away from home, make the daily routine as close to normal as possible for your dog, until he gets used to road trips and trials. Avoid changing anything, such as equipment or food or feeding schedule, right before the competition.

Get excited about showing your marvelous dog. You're about to reap the benefits of that special bond with your faithful and talented companion. Get in the mood and set your sights on success. Visualize that perfect performance.

STAY CONNECTED TO YOUR DOG !

28 The Final Word

We hope you enjoyed this preview of Purely Positive Training as much as we enjoy working with our dogs this way. It's been called a new religion and we admit to being converts. We know our dogs are glad because they've been the ones to show us how well it works.

We know what the skeptics say. We said some of the same things ourselves at first, but the dogs proved us wrong. Thank goodness for those who led the way and took the leap of faith to give the dogs that chance.

Patty believed. And a host of disciples kept the faith. For me, it was Ron Harris who first took the purist view and did the test. He pulled it off beyond our wildest dreams, with the help of his wonderful dog, of course.

Doing the Test

Ron took his young German Shepherd, Lars, all the way to Germany for his B and SchH. I titles. The dog was barely ready, but Ron vowed to go and fail, rather than compromise his purely positive training.

Ron refused to add any last-minute corrections to the program. Lars was a promising show dog (in conformation) with a pressing agenda, so it was not possible to let him have the training time we would have wanted.

On a hot Monday in July, Ron arrived in Germany. (Lars hates the heat.) By Wednesday, Ron wanted to come home. The weather was getting hotter and Lars was refusing to jump the hurdle on the trial field. He kept heading for the gate to leave. Ron was sure all training had broken down.

Then he happened to find out that there was an ultrasonic gopher repellent device on the trial field. You guessed it – right by the jump. Obviously, it was hurting Lars' ears. Regular club members knew to turn the device off before training, but they forgot to tell Ron about it.

Two days before the trial – what to do now? What else? Raise rewards and try to get the exercise back. With the gopher repeller turned off, Ron asked Lars for one retrieve over the jump and rewarded him with an intense game of tug on the burlap bite roll – a favorite with Lars. Then Ron crossed his fingers and hoped for the best.

Lars came through. He earned his B on Friday with a solid performance. The next day he made SchH. I with scores of 97-90-96, putting in a flawless retrieve over the high hurdle. When training breaks down, all that's left is relationship. Develop and nurture it, then you can depend on it.

Coming Through

Another young dog we help train went for a SchH. I title recently. She was in the middle of being in season – rarely ideal trial time for females anyway. The handler had stopped training the week before because of the dog's cycle.

On trial morning, the handler's van broke down. The poor dog had to ride around all day stuffed into a small crate tipped sideways on the back seat of a friend's car, with an indignant female Rottweiler in the front seat.

You guessed it. The dog not only came through, she put in the best obedience performance of her life – even better than in training! Once again, relationship triumphed.

Lars also put in a performance for SchH. II that was better than anything he had ever done in training, despite females in season having been worked on the trial field the day before for a breed survey. Now keep in mind that Lars is a breeding dog.

Two hours before the obedience portion, Ron just let Lars sniff around the entire area and then highly rewarded any attention he happened to offer. Lars kept his eyes on Ron throughout the long obedience routine and never, not once, dropped his nose to sniff.

These are certainly not the only stories of their kind. I could tell you so many more. To date, Vino has already come through for me in competition with a hole in his pad, as well as in wilting heat and pouring rain. Patty could tell you even more stories.

The Dog's Goals

It's easy to get caught up in our own goals and our own agenda. It's easy to forget what our dogs really mean to us. It's easy to forget the dogs' priorities.

They don't care if they're a CD, or a SchH. III, or an Agility Dog, or even a Champion. They don't care whether they win a ribbon or a trophy, or even earn a title. They only care that they are loved, that they get to do what they love and be with the people they love.

Remember that none of them arrive in the whelping box knowing anything about this training stuff. If the dog is distracted or inattentive, if he doesn't like the rain or the heat or the noise at a trial, then we have failed to make the game interesting or exciting enough for the dog.

It certainly isn't his fault, and he certainly doesn't deserve a correction. Resolve to make yourself more exciting. Nurture your dog's wonderful spirit. Resolve to make training more fun and rewarding for your dog.

Just a final word about spontaneous rehearsal. It's entertaining, we know, and it can't help but make us smile. It means you're doing your part well. Enjoy it – but be careful not to reinforce it.

Behavior not on cue is useless. Training is simply putting behaviors on cue. Without a cue (that all-important Antecedent), you end up with lots of cute behaviors – but no learning. This is a trap we all fall into at first, so we just want to warn you.

Our dogs are a precious gift that we should learn to appreciate. We must respect their individuality and nurture their spirit. We need to acknowledge the privilege our dogs grant us when they allow us to train them.

Be sure your training method
> – always enhances relationship,
> – always demonstrates your fairness as pack leader,
> – is always carried out with the utmost respect for your loving partner,
> – and always proves you worthy of your dog.

STRIVE TO BE WORTHY
OF YOUR WONDERFUL DOG !

ABOUT THE AUTHOR

Dogs and horses have been the themes of Sheila's life since she was old enough to decide her own path. Although she enjoys training and competing, Sheila always thinks of her dogs primarily as her companions. Over the past 25 years, she has trained dogs in a variety of disciplines and studied numerous related subjects.

A former newspaper editor with a degree in journalism, Sheila lives in southern Connecticut and is fortunate enough to be able to spend all her time now with her beloved dogs. She plays at agility trials, coaches a few teams in Schutzhund, writes articles for three national training magazines, evaluates puppies, teaches and lectures occasionally, and looks forward to the lessons that Vino and all the other dogs are still waiting to teach her.

PHOTO IDENTIFICATION

(All photos by the author unless otherwise noted.)

Front
Cover   Espe von der Kolonie SchH. III *(Schutzhund III)*,
        FH *(Fahrtenhund: Advanced Tracking Dog - German)*,
        CD (*Companion Dog*),
         Kklsse. Ia (*Koerklasse I – German Breed Survey*)

RECOMMENDED RESOURCES

All materials available through Direct Book Service
(800-776-2665), unless otherwise noted.

PUPPIES
The Positive Puppy Preview (audio). Sheila Booth.
> Podium Publications, Dept. P, P.O. Box 171, Ridgefield, CT 06877
> $20 + $5 Shipping & Handling.

Positively Ready (audio). Leslie Nelson. Puppy raising.
Sirius Puppy Training (video). Ian Dunbar.
Basic Dog Obedience/Puppy Guidance (video). Mary Owens.

POSITIVE TRAINING
SCHUTZHUND OBEDIENCE: Training in Drive.
> with Gottfried Dildei, by Sheila Booth. $24.95 + $5 S&H
> Podium Publications, Dept. P, P.O. Box 171, Ridgefield, CT 06877

Power of Positive Training (videos & audios).
> Ted Turner, Patty Ruzzo, Leslie Nelson.

Competitive Obedience for Winners. Brian McGovern.
The Culture Clash. Jean Donaldson.
Dogwise. John Fisher.
Don't Shoot the Dog. Karen Pryor.
Excelerated Learning. Pamela Reid.
The German Shepherd in Word and Picture.
> Capt. Max von Stephanitz.

The Inducive Retrieve. Sue Sternberg.
Management Magic. Leslie Nelson.
Patient Like the Chipmunks (video). Marian & Bob Bailey.

GENERAL
And the Animals Will Teach You. Margot Lasher.
Animals As Teachers and Healers. Susan Chernak McElroy.
Kinship With All Life. J. Allen Boone.
Souls of Animals. Gary Kowalski.

BEHAVIOR
Learning and Behavior. Paul Chance.
Think Dog. John Fisher.
On Talking Terms With Dogs: Calming Signals.
        Turid Rugaas.

HEALTH & NUTRITION
Complete Herbal Handbook for Dog & Cat.
        Juliette de Baircli Levy.
How to Have a Healthier Dog. Belfield & Zucker.
Give Your Dog a Bone. Dr. Ian Billinghurst.
Reigning Cats and Dogs. Pat McKay.
Four Paws, Five Directions. Cheryl Schwartz.
Dr. Pitcairn's Complete Guide to Natural Health.
        R.H. & S.H. Pitcairn.
Tellington T-Touch, An Overview.
        Tellington-Jones & Taylor.
Who Killed the Darling Buds of May? Catherine O'Driscoll.
        (888-697-9374)
*It's For the Animals – Guided Tour of Natural Care and
Resource Directory.* Helen L. McKinnon.
        Box 5378, Clinton, NJ 08809. (888-339-4382)
The Ultimate Diet: Natural Nutrition for Dogs and Cats.
        Kymythy Schultze.

COMPETITION
Positively Ringwise (audio). Patty Ruzzo.
With Winning In Mind (book & audio). Lanny Bassham.
That Winning Feeling (book & audio). Jane Savoie.
The Inner Athlete. Dan Millman.

HORSES
Dressage for the New Age. Dominique Barbier.
        Barbier Farms, 5943 Dry Creek Rd., Healdsburg, CA 95448
Souvenir. Dominique Barbier. Barbier Farms, (same as above).
The Man Who Listens to Horses. Monty Roberts.
        Random House, New York. 1996.
True Unity: Willing Communication Between Horse & Rider.
  Tom Dorrance.
        Give It A Go Enterprises, P.O. Box 28, Tuscarora, NV 89834

VETERINARY
American Holistic Veterinary Medical Association.
2214 Old Emmorton Rd., Bel Air, MD 21015 (410-569-0795)(FAX-7774)
American Veterinary Chiropractic Association.
623 Main St., Hillsdale, IL 61257 (309-658-2920) (FAX-2622)
Working K-9 Veterinary Consultation Services.
RR 3, Box 107, Guilford, VT 05301 (802-254-1015)